COMMERCIAL BANKS IN INDIA

Growth, Challenges and Strategies

COMMERCIAL BANKS IN INDIA

Growth, Challenges and Strategies

BENSON KUNJUKUNJU
Reader
Post-graduate and Research Department of Commerce
St. Thomas College, Kozhencherry, Kerala

New Century Publications
New Delhi, India

NEW CENTURY PUBLICATIONS
4800/24, Bharat Ram Road,
Ansari Road, Daryaganj,
New Delhi-110 002

Tel.: 23247798, 65396605
Telefax: 011-41017798
E-mail: indiatax@vsnl.com
www.newcenturypublications.com

Editorial office:
34, Gujranwala Town, Part-2,
Delhi - 110 009
Tel.: 27247805, 27464774

First Published - 2008

ISBN: 81-7708-150-0 (*10 digit*)
978-81-7708-150-3 (*13 digit*)

Published by New Century Publications and printed at Singhal Print Media, New Delhi -110 005

PRINTED IN INDIA

ABOUT THE BOOK

Banking sector in India has undergone remarkable changes since the nationalisation of 14 major commercial banks in 1969. The geographical and functional coverage of banks has surged at a rate that is unprecedented in the world. Similarly, services rendered by banks witnessed major changes after liberalisation of the financial sector carried out from the early 1990s. Banking system has now transformed itself into a vibrant financial service sector with many innovative and technology-driven services at their end.

Nationalisation of commercial banks in 1969 and 1980 was a mixed blessing. After nationalisation there was a shift of emphasis from industry to agriculture. The country witnessed rapid expansion in bank branches, even in rural areas. However, bank nationalisation created its own problems like excessive bureaucratisation, red-tapism and disruptive tactics of trade unions of bank employees.

Reforms in the commercial banking sector had two distinct phases. The first phase of reforms introduced subsequent to the release of the Report of the Committee on Financial System (Chairman: M. Narasimham), 1992 focussed mainly on enabling and strengthening measures. The second phase of reforms, introduced subsequent to the recommendations of the Committee on Banking Sector Reforms (Chairman: M. Narasimham), 1998 placed greater emphasis on structural measures and improvement in standards of disclosure and levels of transparency in order to align the Indian standards with international best practices.

Reforms have brought about considerable improvements as reflected in various parameters relating to capital adequacy, asset quality, profitability and operational efficiency. Unfortunately, commercial banks continue to face the problem of non-performing assets (NPAs). The present volume deals with various aspects related to the development of commercial banks in India, with particular focus on post-liberalisation (1991 onwards) developments.

ABOUT THE AUTHOR

Dr. Benson Kunjukunju is Reader, Post-graduate and Research Department of Commerce, St. Thomas College, Kozhencherry, Kerala. He has more than 25 years of teaching experience at both under-graduate and post-graduate levels. He secured his M.Com. M.Phil. Ph.D. degrees from the University of Kerala. He has already published one book dealing with institutional finance and rural development in India. He has also published a good number of articles in research journals and presented papers in national and international conferences/seminars.

PREFACE

A well-developed commercial banking system is a sine qua non for the economic development of a country. The volume of transactions made by commercial banks indicates the economic strides made by an economy. The size, niche and vintage of commercial banks in India vary from bank to bank.

It cannot be gainsaid that the banking sector in India has undergone remarkable changes during the last forty years. Since the nationalisation of 14 major commercial banks in 1969, the geographical and functional coverage of banks has surged at a rate that is unprecedented in the world. Nationalisation of banks brought about several diversifications, modifications and innovations in the structure and functioning of banks.

However, services rendered by banks witnessed major changes only after liberalisation, globalisation and financial sector reforms carried out from the early 1990s. Banking system has now transformed itself into a vibrant financial service sector with many innovative and technology-driven services at their end.

Soon after Independence in 1947, Government of India followed a policy of social control of important financial institutions. The nationalisation of the Reserve Bank of India (RBI) in 1948 marked the beginning of this policy. This was followed by the takeover of the then Imperial Bank of India in 1956 which was rechristened as State Bank of India. In another significant development, Government nationalised 14 major commercial banks in 1969. In 1980, 6 more commercial banks were nationalised and brought under public ownership.

Thus, prior to economic reforms initiated in early 1990s, banking business in India was a near-monopoly of the Government of India. The underlying philosophy of this approach was to encourage growth, via availability of adequate credit at reasonable/concessional rates of interest, in areas where commercial considerations did not allow for disbursal of credit.

As a result of state domination, India's financial system was characterised by barriers to entry, control over pricing of financial assets, high transaction costs and restrictions on movement of funds from one market segment to another. It was in this backdrop that wide-ranging financial sector reforms were introduced as an integral part of the economic reforms programme started in early 1990s.

Nationalisation of commercial banks in 1969 and 1980 was a mixed blessing. After nationalisation there was a shift of emphasis from industry to agriculture. The country witnessed rapid expansion in bank branches, even in rural areas. However, bank nationalisation created its own problems like excessive bureaucratisation, red-tapism and disruptive tactics of trade unions of bank employees.

Being a near-monopoly of the Government, the banking sector suffered from lack of competition, low capital base, low productivity and high intermediation cost. The role of technology was minimal and the quality of service was not given adequate importance. Banks also did not follow proper risk management systems and the prudential standards were weak. All these resulted in poor asset quality and low profitability.

Reforms in the commercial banking sector had two distinct phases. The first phase of reforms introduced subsequent to the release of the Report of the Committee on Financial System (Chairman: M. Narasimham), 1992 focussed mainly on enabling and strengthening measures. The second phase of reforms, introduced subsequent to the recommendations of the Committee on Banking Sector Reforms (Chairman: M. Narasimham), 1998 placed greater emphasis on structural measures and improvement in standards of disclosure and levels of transparency in order to align the Indian standards with international best practices. Reforms have brought about considerable improvements as reflected in various parameters relating to capital adequacy, asset quality, profitability and operational efficiency.

The key objective of reforms in the banking sector in India has been to enhance the stability and efficiency of banks. To achieve this objective, various reform measures were initiated that could be categorised broadly into three main groups: (a) enabling measures, (b) strengthening measures and (c) institutional measures.

Enabling measures were designed to create an environment where banks could respond optimally to market signals on the basis of commercial considerations. Salient among these included reduction in statutory pre-emptions so as to release greater funds for commercial lending, interest rate deregulation to enable price discovery, granting of operational autonomy to banks and liberalisation of the entry norms for financial intermediaries.

The strengthening measures aimed at reducing the vulnerability of banks in the face of fluctuations in the economic environment. These included, *inter alia*, capital adequacy, income recognition, asset classification and provisioning norms, exposure norms, improved levels of transparency, and disclosure standards.

Institutional measures focused on reforms in the legal framework pertaining to banks and creation of new institutions.

Unfortunately, commercial banks continue to face the problem of non-performing assets (NPAs), attributable, *inter alia*, to factors such as weak debt recovery mechanism, non-realisation of collateral and poor credit appraisal techniques. In spite of the significant improvements in the banking industry as a result of reforms, several challenges lie ahead, the most important being the need to bring down the NPA. The enactment of the Securitisation and Reconstruction of Financial Assets and Enforcement of Security Interest (SARFAESI) Act, 2002 has increased the momentum for the recovery of NPAs. However, banks need to intensify their efforts to recover their overdues and prevent generation of fresh NPAs.

The present volume deals with various aspects related to the development of commercial banks in India, with particular focus on post-liberalisation (1991 onwards) developments.

I express my sincere gratitude to Professor K.A. George, Principal, Christian College, Chengannur and Dr. S. Mohanan, Reader in Commerce, Mahatma Gandhi College, Thiruvananthapuram for their valuable guidance and encouragement during the course of writing this book. Thanks are also due to Mr. Sandeep Sury, Chief Executive, New Century Publications, New Delhi for his cooperation and understanding at every stage of the publication of this work.

Kozhencherry
Kerala

Benson Kunjukunju

CONTENTS

Preface vii-x

1. Indian Commercial Banks in Retrospect and Prospect **1-20**

1.1 Introduction

1.2 History of Commercial Banking in India

1.2.1 Presidency Banks

1.2.2 Growth of Joint Stock Banks

1.2.3 Swadeshi Movement: A Momentum for New Banks

1.2.4 Imperial Bank of India

1.2.5 Growth of Joint Stock Commercial Banks

1.2.6 Banking Regulations Act

1.2.7 Formation of the State Bank of India and its Subsidiaries

1.2.8 Shortcomings of Indian Commercial Banks after Independence

1.2.9 Social Control on Banks

1.2.10 Steps Towards Social Control

1.2.11 First Phase of Bank Nationalisation

1.3 Conclusion

2. Impact of Nationalisation of Commercial Banks **21-39**

2.1 Introduction

2.1.1 Achievements of Nationalisation

2.2 Lead Bank Scheme

2.3 Service Area Approach

2.4 Differential Interest Rate Scheme (DIR)

2.5 Priority Sector Advances

2.6 Changing Profile of Banking Services

3. Progress of Commercial Banks after Nationalisation **40-60**

3.1 Introduction

3.1.1 Scheduled Commercial Banks
3.1.2 Non- Scheduled Commercial Banks
3.2 Distribution of Branches of Commercial Banks
3.3 Growth of Deposits and Advances
3.4 Priority Sector Advances
3.5 Rural Credit Expansion
3.6 General Credit Card Scheme (GCC)
3.7 Regional Rural Banks
3.7.1 Introduction
3.7.2 Progress of Regional Rural Banks
3.7.3 Recapitalisation of RRBs
3.7.4 Regional Rural Banks at Crossroads
3.7.5 Report on the Working Group
3.7.6 Report on the Internal Working Group
3.7.7 Special Package Announced by RBI for Revitalizing RRBs
3.7.8 Restructuring of RRBs
3.7.9 Viability of RRBs

4. Liberalisation of Banking Services **61-88**
4.1 Introduction
4.2 Virtual Banking
4.2.1 Advantages of Virtual Banking
4.3 Emergence of Electronic Banking Products/Services
4.4 Automated Teller Machines (ATM)
4.4.1 Services Offered through ATMs
4.5 Debit Card
4.6 Point of Sale Terminals (POS)
4.7 Credit Card
4.7.1 Guidelines for Issuing of Credit Card
4.8 Smart Cards
4.9 Single Window Service
4.10 Door Step Banking
4.11 Bill Payments
4.12 Demat Accounts

4.13 Computerisation in Banks

5. On-line and Phone Banking **89-108**

5.1 Internet Banking: Introduction
5.2 Working Group on Internet Banking
5.2.1 Information only Systems
5.2.2 Electronic Information Transfer System
5.2.3 Fully Electronic Transactional System
5.3 Types of Risks Associated with Internet Banking
5.3.1 Operational Risk (Transactional risk)
5.3.2 Security Risk
5.3.3 Reputational Risk
5.3.4 Legal Risk
5.3.5 Money Laundering Risk
5.3.6 Cross Border Risks
5.3.7 Strategic Risk
5.3.8 Other Risks
5.4 Recommendations of the Working Group on Internet Banking
5.4.1 Security Organization
5.4.2 Access Control
5.4.3 Firewalls
5.4.4 Isolation of Dial up Services
5.4.5 Security Infrastructure
5.4.6 Isolation of Application Servers
5.4.7 Security Log (audit Trail)
5.4.8 Penetration Testing
5.4.9 Physical Access Controls
5.4.10 Back up and Recovery
5.4.11 Monitoring Against Threats
5.4.12 Education & Review
5.4.13 Log of Messages
5.4.14 Certified Products
5.4.15 Maintenance of Infrastructure
5.4.16 Approval for Internet Banking
5.4.17 Standing Committee

5.5 Advantages of Net Banking
5.6 Mobile Banking
5.6.1 Benefits of Mobile Banking
5.7 Telebanking
5.8 Phone Banking

6. Payment and Settlement Systems in India **109-133**
6.1 Clearing and Settlement Systems
6.2 Electronic Fund Transfer (EFT)
6.3 Special Electronic Fund Transfer (SEFT)
6.4 National Electronic Funds Transfer System (NEFT)
6.4.1 Operational Guidelines of NEFT.
6.4.2 Rights and Obligations of Customers
6.4.3 Rights and Obligations of the Bank
6.5 Electronic Clearing Services
6.6 Electronic Credit Clearing
6.7 Electronic Debit Clearing
6.8 MICR Cheque Clearing Facility
6.9 Magnetic Media Based Clearing System (MMBCS)
6.10 Cheque Truncation System (CTS)
6.11 Real Time Gross Settlement (RTGS)
6.12 Clearing Corporation of India Limited (CCIL)

7. Credit Information Bureau Services **134-150**
7.1 Credit Information Bureau
7.2 Credit Information Bureaus: International Scenario
7.3 Development of Credit Information Bureau in Asian Countries
7.4 Credit Information Services in India: A Historical Perspective
7.4.1 Collection and Dissemination of Information on Cases of Willful Default
7.5 Setting Up of Credit Information Bureau in India

7.6 Legal Obligation of Banks and FIs
7.7 Credit Information Bureau (India) Ltd., (CIBIL)

8. Mergers, Acquisitions and Bank Failures 151-169
8.1 Brief History of Bank Failures in India
8.1.1 Bank Failures during the Colonial Period
8.1.2 Failure of Joint Stock Banking with Limited Liability
8.1.3 Banks Failures during the Post Independence Period (1947-1991)
8.1.4 Bank Failures and Bank Mergers during the Post Financial Sector Reforms Period
8.2 Mergers in Banking Sector in India: 1992 to 1994
8.2.1 Bank Mergers: 1995 to 2000
8.2.2 Varma Committee Report on Bank Mergers
8.2.3 Bank Mergers: 2000 to 2005
8.2.4 Bank Mergers during the Year 2006
8.2.5 Bank Mergers during the Year 2007
8.2.6 Merger of Subsidiaries with Parent Bank
8.2.7 Recommendations of the Joint Parliamentary Committee and the Working Group
8.3 Strategy for Strengthening Weak Banks: International Experience

9. Commercial Banks in Insurance Business 170-195
9.1 Meaning of Insurance
9.2 Insurance Business in India: A Retrospect
9.2.1 Insurance Business in India: After Independence
9.3 Banking with Insurance Business: International Scenario
9.4 WTO and Financial Services
9.5 Concept of Universal Banking
9.6 Insurance Regulatory and Development Authority (IRDA) Act, 1999
9.7 Guidelines Issued by RBI for the Entry of

Commercial Banks in Insurance Sector
9.8 Guidelines for Entry of All-India Financial Institutions in Insurance Business
9.9 Modified Guidelines for Entry of Commercial Banks in Insurance Business
9.10 Commercial Banks in Insurance Business
9.11 Scope of Insurance Business in India
9.12 Benefits of Insurance Business to Commercial Banks
9.13 Indian Insurance Business at a Glance

10. Banking Ombudsman Scheme **196-220**
10.1 Introduction
10.2 Scope of the Scheme
10.3 Power and Duties of Banking Ombudsman
10.3.1 General Powers and Duties
10.3.2 Other Powers and Duties
10.4 Grounds of Complaints on Banking Services
10.4.1 Deficiency in Banking Services
10.4.2 Complaints Regarding Sanction, Disbursement and Disposal of Loans and Advances
10.4.3 Other Matters as may be specified by the Reserve Bank
10.5 Procedure for Filing Complaint
10.6 Procedure for Redressal of Grievances
10.6.1 Power to Call for Information
10.6.2 Settlement of Complaint by Agreement
10.6.3 Settlement by Award
10.6.4 Appeal before the Appellate Authority
10.6.5 Directions issued by the Review Authority
10.6.6 Rejection of the Complaint
10.7 Arbitration and Conciliation Procedure
10.7.1 Banking Ombudsman to Act as Arbitrator
10.7.2 Display of Details of Banking Ombudsman Scheme

10.8 Performance of the Banking Ombudsmen
10.8.1 Centre-wise Complaints Received
10.8.2 Grounds for Complaints
10.8.3 Break-up of complaints dealt with Bank Group-wise
10.8.4 Disposal of Complaints by Banking Ombudsman
10.8.5 Awards Issued
10.8.6 Other Information
10.9 Cost Details of Banking Ombudsman
10.9.1 Fixing of Service Charges
10.9.2 Customer Service Department

11. New Generation Banks **221-236**
11.1 Paradigm Shift in the Banking Industry
11.2 Guidelines for Entry of New Private Sector Banks
11.3 Commencement of New Private Sector Banks
11.4 Revised Guidelines for Private Sector Banks
11.5 Industrial Development Bank of India (IDBI)
11.6 Failure\Merger of New Generation Private Sector Banks
11.7 Financial Performance of New Generation Private Sector Banks
11.7.1 Non-Performing Assets
11.7.2 Capital Adequacy Ratio of New Private Sector Banks
11.7.3 Capital to Risk-Weighted Assets

12. Corporate Governance in Commercial Banks **237-256**
12.1 Genesis of the Concept of Corporate Governance
12.2 Conceptual Framework
12.3 Corporate Governance: Indian Scenario
12.4 SEBI Code on Corporate Governance

12.4.1 Mandatory Recommendations
12.4.2 Non-mandatory Recommendations
12.5 Significance of Corporate Governance in India
12.6 Corporate Governance in the Public Sector Banks
12.7 RBI's Initiatives on Corporate Governance in Banks
12.7.1 The Basel Committee for Banking Supervision (BCBS)
12.7.2 Advisory Group on Corporate Governance
12.7.3 Advisory Group on Banking Supervision
12.7.4 Consultative Group of Directors of Banks and Financial Institutions

13. Local Area Banks **257-270**
13.1 Meaning of Local Area Bank
13.1.1 Area of Operation and Branch Licensing
13.1.2 Share Capital
13.1.3 Advancing of Loans
13.1.4 Applicability of Statutes
13.1.5 Jurisdiction of the Banks
13.1.6 Appointment of CEO
13.1.7 Prudential Norms and Corporate Governance
13.1.8 Procedure of Licensing
13.2 Progress in Licensing of Local Area Banks
13.3 Commencement of Business by Local Area Banks
13.4 Failure\Merger of Local Area Banks
13.5 Working of Local Area Banks: Findings and Recommendations

13.5.1 Financial Performance of LABs

14. Indian Commercial Banks in Foreign Countries **271-284**

14.1 Brief History of Commercial Banks Abroad
14.2 Supervisory Initiatives Relating to Foreign Branches of Indian Banks
14.3 Overseas Operations of Indian Banks during 1998-2006
14.4 Branch Licensing Policy of Commercial Banks
14.4.1 New Branch Licensing Policy
14.4.2 Branch Authorisation Policy for Foreign Banks
14.5 Off-Shore Banking
14.5.1 Revised Norms of RBI for Off-shore Banking Units

15. Foreign Banks in India **285-291**

15.1 Norms for Opening of Foreign Banks
15.1.1 Revised Norms for Foreign Banks
15.2 Foreign Direct Investment (FDI) in Banking
15.3 Road Map for Presence of Foreign Banks in India
15.4 Foreign Banks Branch Presence in India

16. Commercial Banks: Challenges and Strategies **292-322**

16.1 Prudential Norms
16.1.1 Capital Adequacy
16.1.2 New Basel Capital Accord
16.1.3 Risks Encountered by Banks
16.1.4 Implementation of Basel II in India
16.1.5 Measures Adopted by RBI for Implementation of Basel II
16.1.6 Capital Adequacy Ratio
16.2 Non-performing Assets in Commercial Banks

16.2.1 Meaning of NPA
16.2.2 Classification of Advances
16.2.3 Reasons for NPA
16.2.4 Magnitude of NPAs
16.2.5 Regulatory Measures by RBI to Reduce NPAs
16.3 Banking Sector Reforms in India: An Overview
16.3.1 Contours of Banking Sector Reforms
16.3.2 Impact of Banking Sector Reforms

Index **323-332**

1

Indian Commercial Banks in Retrospect and Prospect

1.1 Introduction

A commercial bank is a dealer in money. Commercial banks are institutions, which deal with money and credit primarily for earning profit. These banks occupy a predominant place in the modern banking structure. They are financial intermediaries, which perform the dual functions of mobilization of deposits and deployment of surplus funds to the various sectors of the economy. A well-developed commercial banking system is a pre-condition for the economic development of the nation.

Commercial banks usually carry out most of the banking activities in every country. They play a vital role in giving a direction to the economy's development over time by financing the requirements of agriculture, business and industry. The operations of commercial banks record the monetary pulse of the economy. The volume of their transactions highlights the economic strides in the country. Thus, commercial development and progress of a country is largely dependent upon the services rendered by commercial banks. They play a crucial role in the economic development of a country and thus form the core of the money market operations in a developed country.

Commercial banks in India consist of 28 state owned banks, 28 private banks and 29 foreign banks totaling of 85 banks. Apart from these, there are 133 Regional Rural Banks also. Their size, niches and vintages vary from one another. Their ownership pattern also differs from state owned to private and foreign. The Government of India and the RBI owned State Bank of India. Jammu and Kashmir bank though not a private bank; it is treated as one by the authorities. Some financial institutions got successfully transformed from their original form into banks viz.

ICICI Bank and IDBI Bank. There are both new and old private sector banks. Kotak Mahindra Bank and Yes Bank are the newest banks, while a few are more than 100 years and more old. When compared to other developing economies commercial banks in India are in front in terms of their geographical coverage, operational capabilities, technological prowess and range of their products and services.

Modern commercial banking operations touch almost every sphere of economic activity. In the modern world, because commercial banks perform a variety of functions it is not possible to make an exhaustive list of their functions and services. Commercial banks in India though functionally diverse and geographically widespread, they played a crucial role in the socio-economic progress of the country in the post independence period.

The banking business in its oldest form originated in Italy where the early bankers were called moneychangers. They used to conduct their money changing business in streets seated on benches. The word bank originated from the Italian world 'banca'. Banca means bench. The origin of the modern banker can be traced back to the merchant bankers, moneylenders and London Goldsmiths. The merchants accepted deposits from their clients to carry on their trade; the moneylenders lend their surplus money to goldsmiths, who accepted the money and other valuables for safe custody. They possessed special facilities to keep under safe lock and key valuables of many kinds. A modern commercial banker performs these three functions namely accept deposits, lend money and safe custody of valuables of customers.

1.2 History of Commercial Banking in India

From very ancient times, banks constituted an indispensable part of the Indian economy. In India, the ancient Hindu scriptures refer to the money- lending activities during the Vedic period. During the Ramayana and Mahabharata eras, banking had become a full- fledged business activity and during the smrithi period, which followed the Vedic Epic periods the members of the vaish community, carried on the business of banking. Manu, the great law- giver refers to deposits, pledges, policy of loan and rates of interest in his books. The banker in the smrithi period performed most of those functions which banks perform in modern times, such as accepting of deposits, granting secured and unsecured loans, granting loans to Kings in times of grave crisis, acting as the treasurer and banker to the state and issuing and managing the currency of the country. Although the business of banking is as old as recorded history, banking institutions have changed very much in character and content since then.

The history of commercial banking in India had its origin in the seventeenth century with the establishment of trading centers by the East India Company. Unable to depend on indigenous bankers for trading and banking purposes, the East India Company encouraged the establishment of agency houses, which carried on trading and banking operations. Western style banking in India began with the launching of banking operations by Calcutta agency houses and trading firms for the benefit of their business. Both Messer's Alexander & Co. and Ferguson & Co. combined their banking with other kinds of business.

The history of commercial banking in India dates back to the establishment of 'Bank of Hindoostan', in 1770, which was a mere appendage of the former, and it was under the directions of the Europeans. However, this bank could not survive for long because of the failure of the parent firm in 1832. The Sholapur Bank Ltd. started by trading houses also went into liquidation in 1818 due to the unwise combination of banking business with trading operations by them. Faulty speculation and greedy profit motive by ignoring the principle of safety of banking operation was the reason for the failure of the agency houses that also led to the collapse of their banking department.

1.2.1 Presidency Banks: "The Bank of Calcutta" began its banking business in the year June 1806. The Government of India did not realize the need for banks till 1809 and in that year, a royal charter re-designated the "The Bank of Calcutta" as the "The Bank of Bengal". It was the first joint stock bank of British India sponsored by the Government of Bengal. It was established with a capital of Rs. 50 lakh, one-fifth of which was contributed by the Government, which shared the privilege of voting and direction. However, the power to issue currency notes was not given to the bank till 1823. In 1939, the bank was given the power to open branches and to deal in inland exchange.

Two other presidency banks namely "Bank of Bombay" and the "Bank of Madras" were formed in April 1840 and July 1843 with a capital outlay of Rs.52.25 and Rs.30 lakh respectively. The Government had subscribed Rs.3 lakh as capital in each of these banks. These three banks were called the Presidency banks, because they were partly financed by the East India Company.

The three presidency banks were governed by a Royal charter, which was revised periodically. The members of each of the board of directors, which managed the affairs of each bank, were mostly proprietary directors representing the large European managing agencies in India. The rest were government nominees, most were civil servants. Banking business was initially confined to discounting of bill of exchange or other negotiable instruments, keeping cash accounts and receiving deposits. Loans were restricted to one lakh rupees and the period of accommodation was limited to three months. They were given the right to issue notes in their own regions. The first legal tender currency was issued by these banks.

With the passing of the Paper Currency Act in 1860, the right of note issue of the Presidency Banks was abolished and the Government of India assumed the sole power of issuing paper currency with in British India from March 1, 1862. None of these three banks had any branches till 1862. Then they embarked on branch expansion at a rapid pace. By 1876, the Bank of Bengal had 18 branches, Bank of Madras and Bank of Bombay 15 branches each.

In 1876, The Presidency Bank Act was passed, and the Imperial Government decided to preserve these banks as stakeholders. And these banks came to be known as the 'Presidency Banks', and the bankers bank for all Indian joint stock banks.

1.2.2 Growth of Joint Stock Banks: In India, the Joint Stock Companies Act, 1850 was the first legislative enactment in the country, which enabled the corporate sector to enter into the banking business as per the provisions of this Act. Thus, the year 1860 marks a new era in the history of public sector banks in India, because it was in this year that the principle of limited liability of shareholders was first applied to joint stock banks. It was quite unfortunate for India that the crisis of 1862-65 came so soon after the introduction of this important banking legislation. As a result of the outbreak of the Civil War in USA India's cotton exports to Lancashire increased. This brought in immense wealth in the form of precious metals, which led to the flotation of several new banks but they were soon swept aside by disasters.

After presidency bank 'Allahabad Bank' was one of the oldest banks to be established in the year 1865 and for the next five years, no other bank was established. Among several others, the Bank of Bombay, which was established in 1840, went in to liquidation in 1868, but it was revived in the same year with the same name. In 1881, the first purely Indian bank i.e. "Oudh Commercial Bank" came into existence. Fall in the gold price during 1871-1893 also resulted in the slow growth of joint stock banking. Then the only important bank to start was The "Punjab National Bank", registered in 1895 with Lahore as its head office. The "Peoples Bank" was established in the year 1901 and the "City Union Bank Ltd" in 1904.

1.2.3 Swadeshi Movement: A Momentum for New Banks: Following the Swadeshi Movement of 1905, many Indian entrepreneurs launched banking institutions. Later many more banks sprung up like mushrooms. The number of Indian Joint Stock banks also increased remarkably during the period of 1906-21. Important banking ventures started during these period were; Bank of India Ltd. (1906), The Corporation Bank Ltd. (1906), The Indian Bank Ltd. (1907), The Bank of Baroda Ltd. (1908), The Canara Bank Ltd. (1910), The Central Bank of India Ltd., The South Indian Bank Ltd. (1911), The Karur Vysya Bank Ltd. (1916), The Catholic Bank Ltd. and The Union Bank of India Ltd.

(1920) and The Tamil Nadu Mercantile Bank Ltd. (1921).

1.2.4 Imperial Bank of India: The Bank of Bengal, the Bank of Bombay and the Bank of Madras referred as Presidency Banks got amalgamated in to the Imperial Bank of India, which came into existence on January 27, 1921 by the Imperial Bank of India Act of 1920. Although the Imperial Bank of India was created by the special Act (XLVII of 1920), the liability of its shareholders was limited as that of shareholders of all other banks registered under the Indian Companies Act. The only difference was that the word limited does not form part of its name, as it does in the case of banks constituted under the latter Act.

This Act, however, did not give the Bank power to issue notes and thus it was left without any control over currency of the country. However, it was allowed to hold government balances and to manage public debt and clearinghouses till the establishment of the Reserve Bank of India in 1935. The Reserve Bank of India was established as a body corporate under the Reserve Bank of India Act, which came into effect on April 1, 1935 with a paid up capital of Rs. 5 crore. The Reserve Bank of India was nationalized in 1948 soon after the country's independence. Though originally privately owned, after nationalization the RBI is fully owned by the Government of India. The Reserve Bank of India took over all the functions of the Imperial Bank of India, but the later was given the privilege of acting as agent of the former in places in which it had no branches.

1.2.5 Growth of Joint Stock Commercial Banks: During 1922-48 while the number of joint stock banks increased further and on there was a simultaneous failure of many banks. Andhra Bank Ltd. (1923), Karnataka Bank Ltd. (1924), Syndicate Bank Ltd. (1925), The Federal Bank Ltd. (1930), Viyaya Bank Ltd. (1931), Dhana Lakshmi Bank Ltd. (1935), Bank of Maharashtra Ltd. (1936), Indian Overseas Bank Ltd. (1937), Dena Bank Ltd. (1938), Lord Krishna Bank Ltd. (1940), Oriental Bank of Commerce Ltd. (1943) United Commercial Bank Ltd. (1943) etc. were established during this period.

The years 1917, 1932 and 1939 were years of banking crisis in India. During 1913-48, about 1100 banks failed. The important factors identified for bank failures were mismanagement, lack of experienced professional\managerial personnel, unhealthy competition among banks, irrational lending policies, paucity of funds, high interest rate on deposits, absence of a central regulating bank, lending major portion of funds to industrial sectors, speculative business and economic depression.

Following Second World War, there was a mushroom growth of banks with inadequate capital and the issue of both preference shares, deferred shares in addition to ordinary shares, and denied voting rights to preference shareholders, appointed managing directors for long periods with high salaries and perquisites. All these factors necessitated the enactment of a special legislation for banking.

The Second World War brought revolutionary changes in the Indian banking Industry. Due to the post-war and post-partition strains experienced by the economy, there was almost a continuous decline in the total number of commercial bank offices in the country. The number of bank branches dwindled from 4886 in 1946 to 4021 in 1953. This was mainly due to the closure of uneconomic branches followed by numerous bank failures and the movement towards amalgamation and consolidation of the banking structure in certain areas. There was exhaustive change in this situation after the country's independence due to several regulatory measures affected through the Banking Regulation Act. History of banking industry in India reveals that it evolved through a number of crisis and consequent bank failures.

1.2.6 Banking Regulations Act: After independence of the country in 1947, keeping in view the necessity of regulating rapidly growing business of banking institutions and their organizational problems, a separate Act known as 'The Banking Companies Act' was enacted. Following which a bill was introduced in the Parliament in March 1948 and was passed in February 1949. It came into force on March 16, 1949. The Act was then called the "Banking Companies Act, 1949", now known as the "Banking Regulations Act 1949". The provisions of this Act are in addition to the provisions of the Indian Companies Act of 1956, which are also applicable to banking companies. The Banking Regulations Act was amended many times keeping in view the new roles, which the banks were expected to play in accordance with the economic development of the country.

1.2.7 Formation of the State Bank of India and its Subsidiaries: After independence, there was a concerted demand for the nationalization of the Imperial Bank of India. However, the Government was not in favour of nationalization because of two reasons. First, the banks have branches outside India, which may create political problems and consequences of great magnitude. Secondly, it was thought that nationalization would devoid the banks of their useful commercial operations and functions. The 'Rural Banking Enquiry Committee' (1950) also recommended against nationalization.

The State Bank of India came into being as result of the implementation of the recommendation of the 'Committee of Directors' of the "All India Rural Credit Survey" appointed by the Reserve Bank of India in 1951. The committee recommended the setting up of the State Bank of India as one strong integrated state sponsored and state partnered commercial banking institution with an effective network of branches spread throughout the country. The SBI by further expansion of branches can be put in a position to take over cash from non- banking treasuries and to stimulate banking development by providing extended remittance facilities for co-operative and other banks and by following a policy consonant with the national policies adopted by the government and with out departing from the canons of sound banking business. In pursuance of this objective, the Imperial Bank of India was brought under public ownership from July 1, 1955 and was converted into the State Bank of India with the main objective of facilitating the extension of banking in rural and semi-urban areas.

Between October 1959 and May 1960, seven banks of the erstwhile princely states were also brought under the control and full or near-full ownership of the State Bank of India. These banks were founded under princely patronage and their details are given below:

Bhavanagar Durbar Bank was established in the year 1902 from which the 'State Bank of Saurashtra' owes its origin. Erstwhile Government of Mysore established 'State Bank of Mysore' in 1913. 'State Bank of Patiala' was founded by erstwhile Patiala State. 'State Bank of Hyderabad' was constituted as Hyderabad Bank in 1941 by the erstwhile State of Hyderabad. 'State Bank of Travancore' was originally established as Travancore Bank Ltd. in 1945 and was sponsored by the erstwhile Princely State of Travancore. 'State of Bikaner and Jaipur' were established by way of taking over of the business of Govind Bank Pvt. Ltd. in 1956.

In accordance with the provisions of the SBI Act of 1959, State Bank of India established its seven subsidiaries viz. (i) State Bank of Bikaner and Jaipur (ii) State Bank of Hyderabad (iii) State Bank of Indore (iv) State Bank of Mysore (v) State Bank of Patiala (vi) State Bank of Saurashtra (vii) State Bank of Travancore. The State Bank of India together with its subsidiaries is popularly known as the State Bank group. SBI is the largest commercial bank in India, in terms of branch network, resources and work force. Based on number of its branches it has the largest office net work of its kind in the whole world. State Bank of India had 100 per cent stake in State Bank of Hyderabad and State Bank of Patiala, 98 per cent in State Bank of Indore and 92 per cent in State Bank of Mysore. In the world setting, State Bank of India is the only Indian bank, which is placed 82nd position among the hundred big banks of the world having big assets.

1.2.8 Shortcomings of Indian Commercial Banks after Independence: Commercial banks can play an important role in directing the affairs of the economy in various ways. There were persistent complaints that banks in India were not discharging their functions in consonance with the objectives of our socialist democracy. The commercial banks in India during the 1960s merely acted as financial agencies and failed to give any lead to the nation's development. The economic history of many countries reveals that both economic development and growth of financial infrastructure go hand in hand.

One peculiarity of the Banking development in India is that majority of the banks were launched by business houses and were closely associated with such houses, for e.g. Central Bank of India was associated with the House of Tata's, United Commercial Bank with the House of Birlas, Indian Bank with the Rajas of Chettinad, and Punjab National Bank with Jains. They were formed with the objective of profit maximization and were guided by their business houses.

Their area of operation was confined to urban centers and port towns. Rural and interior areas were totally neglected by these institutions. In banking development while states like Assam, Jammu Kashmir, Utter Pradesh, Orissa, and Madhya Pradesh were totally neglected, states like Maharashtra, Gujarat and Tamil Nadu were adequately banked. The population per bank branch was 65,000 for the country as a whole but it was 1,88,000 for Assam, 1,41,000 for Meghalaya, 2,07,000 for Bihar, and 2,12,000 for Orissa. In 1967, it was observed that in 13 districts of India there were no commercial bank offices at all.

There were also regional disparities in the distribution of bank credit. The distribution of bank credit in 1967 indicates that the three states of Maharashtra (32.4 per cent), West Bengal (27.5 per cent) and Tamil Nadu (10.2 per cent) accounted for two- thirds of the total bank credit disbursed in the country.

Banks neglected for a long time the credit needs of several priority sectors of the economy such as, agriculture, small scale and cottage industries, retail trade and exports. The small farmers, industrialists, traders and the self-employed who were not in a position to offer any security were totally neglected in giving loans by banks. A substantial portion of bank credit was given to big and established business houses and both large and medium scale industries, which were in a position to offer securities. Bank credit was security oriented and they were not concerned about the purpose and end use of the loan. The share of credit received by medium and large-scale industries in 1967 accounted for 60 per cent of the total credit, while the share of credit for agriculture was only 2.2 per cent, which contributed more than three-fifths of the national income.

Banks were mostly in the hands of big industrial houses and a substantial portion of the credit was given to units under their control, which lead to the concentration of economic power. The members of the big business houses were associated with the banks as their directors. The boards of the Banks remained static without noticeable changes in personnel. Bank credit was also misused and diverted for hoarding and speculative activities.

1.2.9 Social Control on Banks: After Independence, India adopted a mixed pattern of economy. The two sectors, viz. private and public were allowed to function independently of each other. Public sector is owned and controlled by the government while the private sector is regulated through a system of licenses, permits, controls and legislative measures.

The banking system and banking business grew by leaps and bounds after independence, by way of the number of offices and volume of bank deposits and bank credits. The banking institutions are considered as the custodians of private savings and as powerful instruments for giving credit. In 1960, there were persistent complaints about the functioning of Indian commercial banks and the main complaint was about the banks not discharging their functions in consonance with the aims of our socialistic democracy. They were directing a substantial portion of their advances to large and medium scale industries and established big business houses and paving the way for concentration of economic power, monopoly and misdirection of resources. The members of the big business houses were associated with the banks as their directors and they were mainly interested in advancing loans to their firms on easy terms and conditions.

The Monopolies Enquiry Commission also acknowledged this fact. In its report the Commission observed, "We are bound to mention, however, that from the facts made available to us by the

Reserve Bank of India, it does appear to be true that there have been instances where considerable advances have been made by certain big banks on concessional terms, to concerns in which directors were interested." It was also noted that there should be an equitable and purposeful distribution of the bank credit amongst different sectors of the economy.

There were complaints that commercial banks were not advancing credit to those sectors requiring priority such as agriculture, small-scale industries and exports and to the hitherto neglected and weaker section of the community. It was also observed that most of the commercial bank offices were concentrated in urban areas where the branches proved to be economically viable. Fear of losses due to unremunerative working results made rural banking unattractive.

According to the Rural Credit Survey Committee, in 1951-52, the Indian Joint Stock banks provided hardly Rs. 5 crore as rural credit, accounting for only 0.09 per cent of the credit requirements of cultivators. At the end of 1961, 2494 banking offices were located in 222 towns having a population of 50,000 and above, and 2024 offices in 1060 places having a population of less than 50,000. The government examined the various alternatives including nationalization of banks to achieve the national objective of an egalitarian society.

Many political parties made a demand for the nationalization of commercial banks repeatedly and a vocal section of the ruling Congress party strongly supported nationalization. It was felt that nationalization was the only remedy to cure the maladies of banking in the private sector. At the Bhuvaneswar session of the congress party in 1964, a twelve- point programme of possible achievements, as a result of nationalization of banks was placed and this included measures to eradicate the entire range of economic and social evils and to achieve all aspirations of the people.

The government was not opposed to the demand for bank nationalization. However, the decision to nationalize the banks was not taken because of administrative difficulties and also the consequential effects on the economy of the country. Nationalization was disfavoured because it would severely strain and adversely affect the administrative and financial resources of the country and would weaken the structure of our mixed economy. As an alternative, the government from time to time tried to reform the commercial banking system through legislative and other measures. One such important measure was the social control of banks. As a matter of fact, the term 'social control' of banks was adopted for the first time by the then ruling Congress party in its 1967-election manifesto, stating that "it is necessary to bring the banking institutions under social control in order to ensure socio- economic growth and to fulfill our social purposes more effectively and to make credit available to the producers in all fields where it is needed".

A comprehensive scheme for social control of banks was enforced through a legislative measure on February 1, 1969 to ensure the need for economic growth and to fulfill our social objectives more effectively. The aim of social control was to bring about changes in the management and the credit policy of the commercial banks.

The objective of social control over banks was "to ensure without active take-over of banks into public ownership the achievements of those social ends that nationalization could conceivably secure. The major aim clearly was a more purposeful distribution of available credit in terms of accepted investment priorities and correspondingly more efficient mobilization of savings".

1.2.10 Steps towards Social Control: In December 1967, the Government initiated the scheme of social control over banks. The following steps were taken for this purpose:

A. Formation of a National Credit Council: The setting up of the National Credit Council was a first step in the direction of credit planning. The National Council was entrusted with the following functions.

- To assess the demand for bank credit from various sectors of the economy

- To determine priorities for disbursal of loans and advances and for investment in accordance with the availability of resources and requirements of priority sectors:
- To coordinate lending and investment policies between commercial banks and co-operative banks and other specialized agencies to ensure the optimum and efficient use of the overall resources.

B. Enactment of Banking Laws (Amendment) Act 1969: The actual implementation of the scheme for social control of banks started much earlier than the formal enforcement of the Banking Laws (Amendment) Act 1969. The Act came into force on February 1, 1969. A comprehensive scheme of social control of banks was enforced through legislative measures to realize the aim of economic growth and actualize our social goals more effectively. The aim of social control was to bring about changes in the management and credit policy of the commercial banks. It was proposed to close link between big business houses and big banks and to make that ineffective by the reconstitution of the boards of directors with the effect that at least 51 per cent of the directors were to possess special knowledge or practical experience in accountancy, agriculture and rural economy, banking, cooperation, finance, economics, law, small scale industry, and other areas relevant to the banking sector. To professionalize the top management, provisions were to be made for the appointment of a whole time chairman with special knowledge and practical experience in the working of commercial banks or in financial\economic or business administration.

C. Setting up of the Banking Commission: The government of India appointed a Banking Commission in February 1969 with Shri R.G. Saraiya as its chairman to conduct a comprehensive enquiry into the structure of banking and its financial needs, policies and practices of our banking system. Its terms of reference were the following. 1) to improve the geographical and functional coverage of commercial banks, 2) modernization of their operating methods, 3) cost and capital structure, 4) recruitment of personnel, 5) review of the existing legislation, procedures and 6) management policies.

1.2.11 First Phase of Bank Nationalisation: The scheme of social control initiated by the Government in December 1967 was found to be unsatisfactory and inadequate. There were complaints that the Indian commercial banks continued to direct their advances to large and medium scale industries and sectors demanding priority such as agriculture, small-scale industries and imports were not receiving the attention due to them from the banks.

Nationalization of banks began with the passing of the Reserve Bank (Transfer of Public Ownership) Act 1948 and it was a 'revolution' in the Indian banking system. This revolution did not merely signify a change of the ownership of these banks but it was the beginning of a co-coordinated endeavor to utilize an important segment of the financial mechanism for the country's economic development. It was stated that, in nationalizing the banks, Government was only putting into effect its programme for achieving the goal of a socialistic pattern of society and it was hoped that nationalization would effectively decentralize credits with the result that the priority sectors such as agriculture, small scale industries, exports, self employed entrepreneurs would be provided with liberal banking facilities and that banking units would be extended to rural areas. Nationalized banks are expected, to meet some of the demands of the public sector undertakings and to use the balance of the available resources for organized industries on the basis that new enterprises and those in backward areas will be given preference over the big business houses.

On July 19, 1969 fourteen major banks each having deposits of more than Rs. 50 crore and having between themselves aggregate deposits of Rs. 2,632 crore with 4,130 branches were nationalized and taken over by the Government. Over 85 per cent of the total deposits with the banking system passed into public control with the nationalization of these 14 banks. The total deposits with banks at the end of June 1969 were of the order of Rs. 4,600 crore and of this deposits amounting to Rs. 2,632 crore were accounted for by the 14 nationalized banks. The State Bank of India and its subsidiaries had deposits amounting to Rs. 1,300 crore.

Under section 3 of the Act as on July 19, 1969, 14 new banks with all the legal characteristics of a body corporate were established. Each of the new bank has a common seal and perpetual succession and subject to the provisions of the Act is empowered to acquire, hold and dispose of the property, to contact, and to sue and can be sued in its own name. The undertaking of each of the 14 major banking companies' stands vested in and transferred to each of the 14 corresponding new banks from July 19, 1969. Each of the 14 new banks bear the same name as the corresponding old banks except that the words "The" and "Limited" of the corresponding old banks are deleted. Further United Commercial Bank has been renamed as "UCO Bank" by the Banking Laws (Amendment) Act 1985 so as to avoid confusion in the international operations of the Bank in view of the existence of a bank with the same name set up in Bangladesh. The list of banks nationalised and the amount of compensation paid is given in Table 1.1.

In the first nationalization Act (22 of 1969), certain provisions were made and principles laid down to determine the quantum of compensation. Schedule II of the Act provided that the compensation would be an amount equal to the sum total of the value of the assets of the bank less the sum total of its liabilities. The methods of calculating the sum total were provided in Part I and Part II of the schedule. While declaring the Act void the Supreme Court held that the methods were irrelevant and illusory; certain important classes of assets were omitted; the method of valuing the lands and buildings was not relevant to the determination of compensation and was illusory; the principles for determining the value of liabilities were also illusory; important components such as goodwill and the value of unexpired period of lease were excluded; even the mode of payment violated the constitutional guarantee as the scheme was to pay the compensation in the form of bonds maturing after many years and carrying certain rate of interest liabilities.

Table 1.1: Names of Banks Nationalised and the Amount of Compensation Paid (Rs. lakh)

S. No.	Name of the Banks	Amount of Compensation
1.	Central Bank of India Ltd.	1,750
2.	Bank of India Ltd.	1,470
3.	Punjab National Bank Ltd.	1,020
4.	Bank of Baroda Ltd.	840
5.	United Commercial Bank Ltd.	830
6.	Canara Bank Ltd.	360
7.	United Bank of India Ltd.	420
8.	Dena Bank Ltd.	360
9.	Syndicate Bank Ltd.	360
10.	Union Bank of India Ltd.	310
11.	Allahabad Bank Ltd.	310
12.	Indian Bank Ltd.	230
13.	Bank of Maharashtra Ltd.	230
14.	Indian Overseas Bank Ltd.	250

The mode of payment is at the option of the banking company, by cash or in Government securities, or partly by cash or partly in securities. Cash is payable by 3 equal installments carrying interest at 4 per cent per annum from July 19. 1970. Government securities will be transferable, promissory notes or securities of the central Government repayable at par and maturing at the end of: (i) 10 years from July 19. 1970 carrying interest at 4.5 per cent per annum and\or (ii) 30 yeas from July 19. 1970 at 5 per cent per annum.

A. Need for Nationalisation of Banks: The long title of the Ordinance promulgated on July 19. 1969 explained that the fourteen banks taken over by the Government "in order to serve better the needs of development of the economy in conformity with the national policy and objectives."

The broad objectives of the Government decision to nationalize 14 banks in 1969 were summed up by the then Prime Minister Mrs. Indira Gandhi in Parliament on July 21, 1969, as follows: " While the nation is committed to establish a socialistic pattern of society, the Government felt that the public ownership and control of the commanding heights of the national economy and of its strategic sectors were essential and an important aspect of the new social order which we are trying to build. As the financial institutions are amongst most important levers of the achievement of its social objectives, the nationalization of banks was felt as a significant step in the process of public ownership over the principal institutions for the mobilization of people's savings and canalizing them towards productive purposes. The Government felt that the public ownership of the major banks will help in the most effective mobilization and development of national resources so that our objective can be realized with a great degree of assurance".

At the time of nationalization of banks, Smt. Indira Gandhi in her broadcast to the nation (on July 19, 1969) announced the broad objectives of nationalization and the special task assigned to the nationalized banks.

B. Objectives of Nationalisation of Banks: Following are some of the main objectives of bank nationalization.

- To ensure provision of adequate credit to the neglected sectors such as agriculture, cottage and small-scale industries, retail trade, exports, artisans and self-employed persons.
- To prevent the diversion of bank finance to anti-social, less productive, low- priorities sectors and to big industrialists and businessmen.
- Giving a professional bent to bank management
- Reduction of regional imbalances in banking facilities by opening of branches in rural\remote and unbanked areas
- Development of banking habits among people
- Equitable distribution of economic power by removal of control of banks by a few big industrialists and business houses

- Provision of adequate training as well as reasonable terms of service for bank staff

C. Arguments for Nationalisation of 14 Major Banks: Eminent persons argued that the restrictions imposed by social control measures were capable of being flouted in spirit though observed in form. For instance, the restrains on advances to directors and their interested concerns could be mutually adjusted amongst bankers in such a way as to defeat the very purpose of such restraints. It was stated that it would take a long time for the banks to throw away their traditional outlook; indirect control, howsoever stringent the laws for that may be, will not achieve the purpose. Compared to indirect control, direct control would be more effective to meet the pressing needs of the time. The country could not afford the trial and error method and "an element of dynamism and new vigor into the process of our development was necessary".

One further argument was that the major banks were operating mostly with other people's money. "Against a total deposit of Rs. 2,750 crore at the end of December, 1968, the paid up capital was only Rs. 28.5 crore or just a little over one per cent. It was stated that in nationalizing the 14 banks, the Government was merely putting into effect its own long decided programme for achieving the socialist pattern of society.

D. Arguments against Nationalisation: Several eminent persons opposed the measure. They argued that 168 days i.e. from February 1, 1969, the day of imposition of social control to July 19. 1969 the day of nationalization- was too short a period to judge the results of 'social control' and there was no reason to conclude that it had failed. There were on the contrary ample indications that the banks welcomed the spirit of co-operation and willingness. For instance, from June 1968 to March 1969 credit given by 20 major banks to agriculture increased from Rs. 30 crore to Rs. 97 crore and to small industries from Rs. 167 crore to Rs. 222 crore. The floating of the Agricultural Finance Corporation by the scheduled banks was also a very significant step.

The opponents further argued that there was no such pressing need for nationalization as was made out by the Government. The timing of the step was determined by political tussles and it was the result of inter-party struggles for power. They argued that a switch over to the public sector is not the only remedy for the evils present in the private sector; the process merely results in substitution of one set of evils with another. The internal control of the banks by Government will lead to more harmful evils; public sector institutions are generally notorious for their lack of dynamism and competitiveness.

The opponents also argued that the record of performance of public sector undertakings has not been a rosy one. Public control leaves the door wide open for corruption and favouritism. Their performance is always far from commendable. They often incur heavy losses. The common man maintain a justifiable belief that public sector undertakings do not respect an individual and delays and lethargy in work and service are the bane of such undertakings. In a personalized service like banking, these evils are likely to be more damaging for institutions and individuals alike.

1.3 Conclusion

Since the nationalization of fourteen major banks, the geographical and functional coverage of commercial banks have increased at a rate that is unprecedented in the world. The Indian banking system passed through a revolution in the sixties, which unleashed a chain reaction of rapid changes. "Commercial banking was converted in to mass banking from class banking". From 'orthodox methods and conventional constraints' it moved in to an era of speedy social changes. It was transformed from a profit seeking institution into one of service giving to the poor and needy sections. The banking service acquired new meanings, orientations, directions and dimensions. The nationalization process thus proclaimed and ushered the beginning of social, mass and innovative banking.

2

Impact of Nationalisation of Commercial Banks

2.1 Introduction

The banking sector in India has undergone spectacular changes during the last thirty-five years. Gone are the days when commercial banks were only "purveyors of credit' and now they act as catalytic agents in the nations economic progress. After nationalization, the public sector banks have given up their traditional approach of maximizing profits for the shareholders, to a development role in the interest of the country. There has been a remarkable expansion of bank branches after nationalization of commercial banks. Till July 19, 1969, most of banking business was carried on by the joint stock banking companies, although there existed some private banking institutions, and indigenous bankers and banks formed under special Acts.

After eleven years of the first phase of banks' nationalization, an ordinance was promulgated on April 15, 1980, by the President of India for the acquisition and transfer of undertakings of six more private banking companies. In the second phase of nationalization, private banks having time and demand liabilities of not less than Rs. 200 crore each were nationalized. This further extended the area of public control over the country's banking system. Compared to the first phase of nationalization only banks having deposits exceeding Rs. 50 crore each alone were nationalized. The objective of the second nationalization was to enhance the capacity of the banking system to meet more effectively the needs of the developing economy and to promote the welfare of the people in conformity with the national policy.

The undertakings of six private banks were transferred to six corresponding banks under the Banking Companies Act of 1980. The list of banks nationalised and the amount of compensation paid is given in Table 2.1.

Table 2.1: Names of Banks Nationalised and the Amount of Compensation Paid (Rs. crore)

S. No.	Name of the Bank	Amount of Compensation
1.	Andhra Bank Ltd.	6.10
2.	New Bank of India Ltd.	5.10
3.	Vijaya Bank Ltd.	2.40
4.	Punjab and Sind Ltd.	2.10
5.	Corporation Bank Ltd;	1.80
6.	Oriental Bank of Commerce Ltd.	1.00

The total amount of compensation paid in respect of the transfer of undertakings of the above six banks was Rs. 18.50 cores. The compensation was paid in the form of cash and government securities. Each of the corresponding new banks bears the same name of the old bank except that the words "The" and "Limited" were deleted.

Thus from April 15, 1980, the number of public sector banks increased to 28, including the State Bank of India and its 7 subsidiaries and excluding Regional Rural Banks. With the nationalization of six more banks in 1980, ninety-one per cent of the entire banking system was brought under the public sector. The total deposits of six newly nationalized banks at the end of June 1980 were Rs. 2,773 crore and those of twenty nationalized banks were Rs. 22,854 crore. The total deposits of all scheduled commercial banks during this period stood at Rs. 33,377 crore. The New Bank of India got merged with the Punjab National Bank in 1993, and this reduced the number of nationalized banks to 19.

2.1.1 Achievements of Nationalisation: The progress made by the banking industry since nationalization has been very significant and impressive. There was a rapid expansion of branches of commercial banks not only in the metropolitan and urban areas but also in the rural and semi-urban areas that were hitherto neglected by the commercial banks. Mobilization of substantial deposits and spreading the habit of banking has been the other significant achievements of the nationalized banks.

Changes have taken place in the field of credit by advancing it to the hitherto neglected sectors of the economy like agriculture, small-scale industries, micro enterprises, economically and socially weaker sections, small borrowers and such priority sectors. To realize the objectives of nationalization, public sector banks now give special attention to the growth potential and developmental needs of the areas where the branches are situated. They keep in view the needs of the underdeveloped areas and backward sections of the population. The nationalized banks also play a vital role in the implementation of various anti- poverty programmes of Governments.

2.2 Lead Bank Scheme

After the introduction of social control over commercial banks in 1967, there were complaints regarding regional imbalances in economic development. This problem was discussed by the National Credit Council (NCC), which was constituted as one to ensure social control over commercial banks. The council also studied the needs of various sectors of the economy and to allocate credit to promote economic growth, especially in the backward and rural areas of the country. This Council constituted study groups to study this problem and to make appropriate recommendations. The study group on 'Organizational Framework for the Implementation of Social Objectives' under the chairmanship of Mr. D.D. Gadgil recommended for an "Area Approach" to be followed by commercial banks. They also recommended that the public sector banks should be given specific districts wherein they should be asked to bring about integrated development of banking facilities in their specified area with a view to meet all their essential credit needs.

In the light of the recommendations of the Study Group, The

Reserve Bank of India constituted a committee under the chairmanship of Mr. F.K.F Nariman in August 1969. The committee recommended a scheme to involve commercial banks, co-operative institutions, government and semi-government agencies in the process of their economic development. Based on the Study Group's recommendation, the Reserve Bank of India initiated the Lead Bank Scheme in December 1969.

Under the lead bank scheme all the then 338 districts (with the exception of the metropolitan areas of Bombay, Calcutta, Madras and union territories of Chandigarh, Delhi and Goa) in the country were allocated to the State Bank of India and its seven subsidiaries, 14 nationalized banks and 2 private sector banks. Later one more private sector bank joined the scheme. The allotment was made in such a way that each bank played its lead role in more than one state and each state had more than one lead bank. The districts were allocated on the basis of the size of the bank, the adequacy of its resources for handling the volume of work, contiguity of districts, the regional orientation of the bank etc.

The lead bank which is allocated a specific district is to play the role of the 'Consortium Leader' of all the banking and financial institutions functioning in the district. The bank, which is to act as a leader in the specified district, is supposed to get the cooperation of all other commercial and co-operative banks and other financial institutions in the district. It is the duty of the lead bank to coordinate the various banking institutions and financial activities as far as the financial requirements of the district are concerned. The lead bank is expected to promote all round development of the allotted district. However, the lead bank is not expected to have a monopoly of banking business in the allotted district. They are also expected to maintain liaison with district authorities and quasi-government agencies engaged in development activities.

The first task of a lead bank in its allotted district is to conduct a thorough survey for identifying the areas of credit gap and the growth centres in the district for opening branches of commercial banks so as to meet the legitimate credit needs of the district. A lead bank in a district was assigned with the following tasks.

- Survey the resources and potential for banking development in its district,
- Survey the number of industrial and commercial units and other establishments and farms which do not have bank accounts or which depended primarily on moneylenders,
- Examine the facilities for marketing of agricultural produce and industrial production, storage and warehousing space, and the linking of credit with marketing in the district,
- Survey the facilities for stocking of fertilizers and other agricultural inputs and for repair and servicing of the equipment,
- Recruit and train staff for offering advice to small borrowers and farmers and for follow-up and inspection of the end – use of loans,
- Assist other primary lending agencies, and
- Maintain contacts and liaison particularly with Government and quasi-Government agencies.

It is supposed to be a continual study or survey work aiming at potential deposit mobilization, locating areas where credit would be needed, and thereby leading to economic growth of the district. As a follow-up action, the lead banks constituted Consultative Committees at district levels to serve as a forum for discussion among the banks and other financial institutions, exchanging information about lending to the priority sectors in the district, identifying bankable schemes and evolving methods of financing them in a coordinated manner, and allotting banks to unbanked centres identified during the survey.

By June 1974, the lead banks carried out surveys in all the 338 districts and bank branches were opened in the identified unbanked centres. The year 1974 marked the completion of the first phase of operation of the Lead Bank scheme. The RBI constituted two study groups in August 1975 to review the working of the Lead Bank Scheme in Maharashtra and Gujarat since its inception, and to formulate appropriate guidelines for its effective working. The report revealed that the first phase of the Lead Bank Scheme for identifying the potential centres for banking operations and the opening of bank branches therein had been a success, the progress of the second phase, viz. the formulation and implementation of area development programme, was however slow.

As recommended by the Study Groups, a High Power Committee was appointed by the Reserve Bank of India in March 1976 to monitor the overall progress of the Lead Bank Scheme, study specific problems in its implementation, and issue policy guidelines for its effective functioning. On the basis of a study undertaken by RBI, the scope or functions of the Lead Banks were expanded in 1976. Each Lead Bank is to formulate district credit plan covering all the possible bankable projects in the district and allocate credit plan targets among various banks functioning in the district and also among other financial institutions like cooperative credit societies and Regional Rural Banks.

By the end of June 1978, Lead Banks prepared district credit plans in respect of 380 districts of which 363 plans were launched. But these district credit plans prepared by the Lead Banks were criticized on various grounds viz.

- Agriculture and allied activities did not receive due emphasis and attention
- The district credit plans are not properly aligned with the various developmental schemes prepared for the district; and
- The district plans failed to take due note of the role of cooperative societies which are an important source of credit for the district.

The RBI issued new guidelines to the Lead Bank for preparing district credit plans for the year 1980-82. As per the new guidelines, the share of small and marginal farmer's in the credit provided for the agricultural sector in the district should reach the target of 50 per cent by the end of 1982-83, that banking sector's lending to priority sector should not be less than one-third of their total lending. Subsequently the target for lending to priority sector was raised to 40 per cent of total credit provided by all the banks and financial institutions in the district and that 40 per cent was to be reached by 1985.

In March 1985, the Government of India set up a working group to review some aspects of the Lead Bank Scheme and to suggest measures to make the scheme more effective and result oriented. The district credit plan is to be formulated by the Lead Bank on block wise basis because the national policy was to make the block the basic geographical unit for formulation of economic plans. At the end of June 1987, the Lead Bank Scheme covered 438 districts in the country.

The guidelines for the preparation of the fourth round of District Credit Plans (DCPs) covering the three-year period from January, 1988 to December, 1990 as approved by the High Power Committee on Lead Bank Scheme were communicated to all Lead Banks in March, 1987. According to the guidelines issued by the Reserve Bank of India, on the basis of District Credit Plans, the Lead Banks are to prepare and implement the Annual Action Plans (AAPs), in all the districts of the country. District level review committee meetings are also to be convened by lead banks at half yearly intervals to review the progress in implementation of district credit plans.

The focus of Lead Bank Scheme (LBS) was to enhance the proportion of bank finance to priority sectors. The objective of the scheme was to coordinate and control the activities of banks and other developmental agencies to facilitate the flow of credit to the priority sector.

The lead bank scheme, which was initially introduced in December 1969, covered 338 districts, later it was extended to 438 districts by the end of June 1987. By March 1994, the Lead Bank Scheme covered all 493 districts in the country.

During the year 1997-98, the number of districts covered under the Lead Bank Scheme in the country got increased to 536 districts on March 31, 1998. There were 21 new districts because of the reorganization and division of some of the existing districts.

Public sector banks were entrusted with the lead responsibility of these districts.

The Lead Bank Scheme covered 567 districts as on March 31, 1999 as against 536 districts as on March 31, 1998. During the year 1998-99, thirty-one new districts were formed because of reorganization and bifurcation of districts, and all of them were put under public sector banks.

The LBS has covered 575 districts as on March 31, 2000 as against 567 districts as on March 31, 1999. During the year 1999-2000, 8 new districts were formed as a result of reorganization and division of districts and the lead responsibility in respect of these districts was assigned to Public sector banks. In November 2000, division of the existing states of Bihar, Uttar Pradesh and Madhya Pradesh in that order created three new States viz., Jharkhand, Uttaranchal and Chhattisgarh. Consequent upon the creation of the above new states, the SLBC convenership of all the six states (new as well as existing) has been assigned to some of the public sector banks by the Central Government in consultation with the Reserve Bank. At end of March 31, 2001, Lead Bank Scheme spanned 576 districts in the country.

At the end-March 2004, the Lead Bank Scheme covered 587 districts including the six new districts formed due to reorganization/bifurcation of the existing districts. The scheme was modified to include term loans for agriculture and allied activities and a reasonable component to meet the consumption needs, besides the existing facility of providing crop loans.

2.3 Service Area Approach

Although commercial banks have achieved large and rising levels of rural credit dispensation, several deficiencies in the existing system of planning and dispensation of such credit persisted. The Service Area Approach (SAA) was the outcome of a high-level seminar organized by the Reserve Bank of India in January 1988. The commercial banks face a number of problems because they are assigned with the responsibility to meet the credit needs of hitherto neglected sectors, sections and areas.

Lending by rural bank branches became somewhat hazardous because its dispersal in a large number of villages spread over a wide area made close supervision of the end-use of funds difficult and impractical. Coordination between various lending institutions was difficult to achieve and double financing was not eliminated completely. Besides, field orientation of bank managers and their public contacts at the village level were insufficient. Therefore, it was felt that it would be desirable to evolve a new strategy of rural lending considering that an intensive network of rural branches of commercial banks and RRBs were already developed. After widespread consultations and discussions, a rural lending strategy was developed and implemented.

In 1988 the Reserve Bank of India issued guidelines with regard to service area concept suggested by the then Finance Minister. Accordingly, each of the rural and semi-urban branches is allotted 15 to 25 villages for the preparation of village plans based on detailed surveys of allotted villages. After the completion of the surveys, the branch managers were to prepare annual credit plans for each of the villages in the service area.

The SAA was introduced in April 1989 with a view to bring about an orderly and planned development of rural and semi-urban areas of the country. Under the SAA, all rural and semi-urban branches of banks were allocated specific villages, generally in geographically contiguous areas, the overall development and the credit needs of which were to be taken care of by the respective branches.

The principal aim of SAA was to ensure that every remote village in the country would have access to banking facilities. The SAA was also intended to solve problems associated with the identification of genuine borrowers and supervision of the end-use of credit. It was to improve the level of coordination between banks and other financial\development institutions. The service area approach had the following important features.

- Identification and allocation of service area for each bank branches.

- Survey of villages in the service area for assessing the potential for lending activities and identification of beneficiaries for assistance.
- Preparation of credit plan on an annual basis for the service area by each branch.
- Coordination between credit institutions on the one hand and field level development agencies on the other on an on-going basis for the effective implementation of the credit plans.
- System of continuous monitoring of progress in the implementation of the plans.

The ultimate objective of the SAA was to improve the quality of lending. It was to rationalize rural lending, reduce cost of supervision formulated and adhered on priority basis both by reducing the number of villages in which the bank branch operate and also by avoiding duplication in lending in the villages by branches of more than one bank. The branch managers are required to carry out a survey of each village in their service areas on a prescribed format with the help of state government officials at the village and bank credit plans for a year in the light of information thus gathered and in consultation with the villagers concerned.

The idea of SAA was to improve field orientation of branch managers, enhance their public contacts and enable them to identify viable enterprises for lending. At the same time, they were expected to pinpoint rural infrastructure deficiencies and lack of availability of the physical inputs needed for making rural credit more productive. These deficiencies are discussed at a block level committee, which finalizes and approves the credit plans. The branch managers were also required to ascertain the lending plans of co-operative institutions in their service areas in order to draw a comprehensive picture of total credit activities therein.

Consequent upon the announcement made in the Mid-term Review of Annual Policy Statement for the year 2004-05, and based on recommendations made by the Advisory Committee on Flow of Credit to Agriculture and Related Activities from the

Banking System, the Service Area Approach (SAA) scheme was reviewed on December 8, 2004. RBI decided to dispense with the restrictive provisions of the scheme, while retaining the positive features of the SAA such as credit planning and monitoring of the credit. These relaxations were introduced with a view to enable rural borrowers to have easy access to institutional credit from any bank of their choice at a competitive price and to provide banks, public and private, with a level playing field.

Table 2.2 shows the allocation of villages to commercial banks under the service area approach. It is evident from the table that the SAA is a vast programme which covered 6,18,216 villages by 42,158 branches of public and private sector and Regional Rural Banks. 3,66,382 villages in the country were allotted to 26,016 branches of various public sector banks under the service area approach. RRBs and private sector banks were allotted 2,36,592 and 15,242 villages respectively under this approach.

Table 2.2: Allocation of Villages under Service Area Approach

Institutions	No. of Branches	Number of Villages Allocated	Average village per branch
Public Sector Banks	26,016	3,66,382	14
Private Sector Banks	2,489	15,242	6
Regional Rural Banks	13,053	2,36,592	17
Total	42,158	6,18,216	14

The average number of villages allotted per bank branch was worked out as 17 in case of RRBs, 14 in public sector and 6 in the case of private sector banks.

2.4 Differential Interest Rate Scheme (DIR)

The Differential Interest Rate (DIR) scheme was introduced in December 1972. In order to ensure the availability of credit to the weaker sections of society, the Government instituted a scheme whereby a percentage of the aggregate advances of banks must be given to this group at concessional rates.

DIR scheme was introduced following the recommendations of a Committee chaired by Dr. R.K. Hazari. The committee submitted its report in December 1970. This committee was constituted by the initiative of Shri Y.B. Chavan, the Former Finance Minister of India. In the meeting of the chairmen of banks, he highlighted the need to provide credit at low rate of interest for productive purposes for the low-income groups having no access to any bank. Participation in the scheme was mandatory on an agency basis for all public sector banks, non-nationalized banks having lead responsibilities and the sponsoring banks of the RRBs. Initially the scheme was made applicable to only 163 industrially backward districts in the country and in 1977; the scheme was extended to all the industrially backward districts. From 1978, the Government directed all the private sector commercial banks to implement the scheme along with the public sector banks. The DIR scheme now covers all the districts across the country.

The DIR scheme covers those people with small holdings, self-employed persons, handicapped persons and those engaged in tailoring, garment making, running way side tea stalls, repairing shoes and making baskets and for purchase of milk animals, poultry farming etc. The scheme also covers institutions for physically handicapped persons, orphans and women.

The outstanding advances of the PSBs under the DIR scheme stood at Rs. 432.82 crore at the end of March 2000, which accounted for 0.18 per cent of the total outstanding advances of these banks. The advances to SC/STs under DRI by the PSBs amounted to Rs. 257.6 crore forming 59.5 per cent of total DIR advances at the end of March 2000 as against Rs. 324.29 crore forming 63.8 per cent at end-March 1999. The outstanding advances of PSBs under the DIR Scheme at the end of March 2004 amounted to Rs. 315 crore under 3.7 lakh borrowers accounts. This forms only 0.1 per cent of the total advances outstanding at the end of 2003-04, which is less than the target of 1.0 per cent.

Banks have to lend one per cent of their net credit under the DIR scheme. However, at the end of March 2007, most of the banks both public and private sector lended only half per cent of their net bank credit under this scheme. As a mark of social commitment towards weaker sections and to achieve the stipulated level of one per cent of lending, the Union Government in its budget 2006-07, proposed to increase the limit of loan under the DIR scheme. Accordingly, with effect from 1 April 2007, the amount of loan under this scheme got enhanced from Rs. 6,500 to Rs. 15,000 and that of the housing loan from Rs. 5,000 to Rs, 20,000 per beneficiary at a rate of four per cent interest.

2.5 Priority Sector Advances

The main objective of introducing social control over the banks and subsequent nationalization of the major commercial banks in the country was to ensure that credit was routed to various sectors of the economy in accordance with the priorities of national plans. In pursuance of this policy, the hitherto neglected sectors namely agriculture and agro-based activities, small industries and small transport operations, retail trade, small business etc were designated as 'priority sectors' for lending operations. This categorization was to ensure increased flow of credit to these sectors in accordance with the guidelines framed by the RBI. Advances by public sector banks to the priority sectors has certain advantages such as concessional rates of interest, concessional rates in regard to margin requirements, relaxation in respect of procedural formalities etc.

As per the latest RBI guidelines to the banks, the following types of advances come under the category of priority sector lending. This comprises agriculture (both direct and indirect), small scale industries, small operations of road and water transport, small business, retail trade, professional and self-employed persons, state sponsored organizations for Scheduled Castes/Scheduled Tribes, education loans, housing loans (both direct and indirect), consumption loans, micro-credit, loans to software, food and agro-processing sectors.

In order to calibrate bank credit to the changing needs of the society, the scope and definition of priority sector was widened by including more and more new items and by enhancing credit limit of the constituent sub-sectors. Accordingly, RBI issued the following revised guidelines in the financial year 2004-05:

1. The ceiling on credit limit under the priority sector to farmers against hypothecation of agricultural produce (including warehouse receipts) increased from Rs. 5 lakh to Rs. 10 lakh.
2. The limit on advances under the priority sector for dealers in agricultural machinery, including drip/sprinkler irrigation systems was increased from Rs. 20 lakh to Rs.30 lakh and for distribution of inputs for allied activities from Rs.25 lakh to Rs.40 lakh.
3. Under priority sector, banks were allowed to extend direct finance of up to Rs.15 lakh to the housing sector irrespective of their location.
4. Investments by banks in the mortgage-backed securities have been classified as direct lending to housing within the priority sector lending subject to certain conditions.
5. Loans advanced to distressed urban poor to prepay their debt to non-institutional lenders, against appropriate collateral or group security, have been classified as advances to weaker sections within the priority sector.
6. Investment limit in plant and machinery for seven items belonging to sports goods, which figure in the list of items reserved for manufacture in the small-scale industries (SSI) sector, was enhanced from Rs. 1 crore to Rs. 5 crore for the purpose of classification under priority sector advances.
7. Banks were also advised to make efforts to increase their disbursements to small and marginal farmers to 40 per cent of their direct advances under Special Agricultural Credit Plans (SACP) by March 2007. All private sector banks were also

asked to formulate SACP targets from 2005-06 with an annual growth rate of at least 20-25 per cent of credit disbursements to agriculture.

8. Investment by banks in securitized assets representing direct lending to the SSI sector have been classified as their direct lending to the SSI sector under priority sector lending, subject to certain conditions.
9. It was decided that investments made by banks on or after April 1, 2005 in the special bonds issued by certain specified institutions would not be eligible for classification under priority sector lending and such investments which have already been made by banks up to March 31, 2005 would cease to be eligible in a phased manner for classification under priority sector lending.
10. It was decided that investments made by banks on or after July 1, 2005 in venture capital would not be eligible for classification under priority sector lending, while such investments already made up to June 30, 2005 would not be eligible for classification under priority sector lending with effect from April 1, 2006.

The domestic public and private sector scheduled commercial banks has stipulated a target of 40 per cent of net bank credit for lending to the priority sectors. Within this, sub-targets of 18 per cent and 10 per cent of net bank credit were have been stipulated for lending to agriculture and weaker sections, respectively. Domestic scheduled commercial banks having a shortfall in lending to the priority sector/agriculture are required to contribute to the Rural Infrastructure Development Fund (RIDF) established by the National Bank for Agriculture and Rural Development (NABARD).

A target of 32 per cent of net bank credit was stipulated for lending to the priority sector by foreign banks. Of this, the aggregate credit to small-scale industries should not be less than 10 per cent and to the export sector not less than 12 per cent of the net bank credit. In the case of foreign banks operating in India, those who fail to achieve the priority sector-lending target or sub-targets were directed to deposit an amount equivalent to the shortfall with Small Industries Development Bank of India (SIDBI).

In order to line up bank credit to the changing needs of the society and enhance the flow of credit to the priority sector, the following policy initiatives were taken by the RBI during the year 2005-06:

Detailed guidelines were issued to banks for stepping up credit to Small and Medium Enterprises (SMEs).

1. A One-time Settlement Scheme for recovery of NPAs below Rs. 10 crore under SME accounts were communicated to public sector banks for implementation.
2. Banks were advised to ensure restructuring of debt of all eligible SMEs at terms which were, at least as favourable as the Corporate Debt Restructuring mechanism in the banking sector.
3. In order to offer small borrowers an opportunity to settle their NPA accounts with banks and to become eligible for fresh finance. In December 2005, banks were advised to provide a simplified mechanism for one-time settlement of loans where the principal amount is equal to or less than Rs. 25,000 and which have become doubtful or lost assets as on September 30, 2005. In the case of loans granted under Government sponsored schemes, banks were advised to frame separate guidelines following a State specific approach to be evolved by the State Level Bankers Committee (SLBC).
4. In December 2005 banks were allowed to introduce a General Credit Card (GCC) Scheme for issuing general credit cards to their constituents in rural and semi-urban areas, based on the assessment of income and cash flow of the household, and without any insistence on security and the purpose or end-use of the credit. Banks could utilize the services of local post offices, schools, primary health centres, local government functionaries, farmers associations or clubs, well-established community-based agencies and civil society organizations for identifying borrowers for issuing of cards. To encourage the

implementation of the scheme, fifty per cent of the credit outstanding under loans for general purposes under GCC scheme was made eligible for classification as indirect finance to agriculture within the priority sector.

5. Banks were advised that loans to power distribution corporations/companies, emerging out of bifurcation/ restructuring of State Electricity Boards (SEBs), for reimbursement of the expenditure already incurred by them for providing low tension connection from step-down point to individual farmers for energizing their wells, may also be classified as indirect finance to agriculture.

2.6 Changing Profile of Banking Services

Prior to nationalization, Indian banks used to concentrate mainly on their traditional functions like accepting of deposits and lending of money. Receiving deposits and lending of funds were the traditional functions and the core of banking activity. After the nationalization, Indian banks began providing customer friendly services and functions to their customers.

Realizing the importance of savings in India's developing economy, several deposit schemes were evolved. To attract savings from all sorts of people banks began to offer innovative deposit schemes with wide range of options to suit the requirements of customers. Deposits were accepted under various types of accounts namely, current, savings bank, fixed deposit, recurring deposit and home-safe accounts.

The second important function of a bank is to advance loans to their customers. Banks offer different kinds of borrowing facilities to their customers. Various types of credit facilities are term loans, cash credit and overdraft, money at call and short notice, and discounting of negotiable instruments. They also provided packing credit, export credit, housing, educational, consumer and vehicle loan, loan for self-employment, agricultural loans etc. Loans are also granted against approved securities such as gold, silver, government securities, shares, stocks, national saving certificates, marketable goods etc.

Besides those main functions, banks have expanded their activities to cater to the varied needs of their customers. Banks perform certain agency functions for their customers namely:

- Collection of cheques, bills, interest, dividend, rent, subscription etc.
- Purchase and sale of various types of securities such as shares, stocks, bonds and debentures.
- To act as executors, trustee and attorney for the customers will.
- To remit funds on behalf of the clients by cheque, draft, mail transfers or telegraphic transfers etc.
- To act as correspondent, agent or representative of their clients.
- To make payments on behalf of their customers in accordance with the execution of standing instructions.
- Acting as agents for any government, local authority or any other customer etc.

In addition to agency functions, banks also provide many general utility services such as:

- Providing locker facility to their customers for keeping their valuables.
- Issuing of bank draft, gift cheques, and traveller 's cheques.
- Issuing of letter of credit for foreign trade.
- Underwriting securities issued by government, corporations, public and private bodies.
- Acting as referee with respect to the financial standing, business reputation and respectability of the customers.
- Dealing in foreign currencies.
- Managing issue of shares or debentures etc.

Banking sector services undergone major changes only after the liberalization, globalization and economic reforms. The economic reforms in 1991 unleash fierce competition among banks. Banking system has now turned into a dynamic financial service sector with many innovative and technology driven services. Deregulation has opened up new opportunities for banks to diversify into investment banking, insurance, mortgage financing, depository services, securitization etc. With the introduction of the new technology in banking sector, customers are fast moving away from the traditional branch banking system to the convenient and comfortable electronic banking services or virtual banking. The deregulation and technological advancements have altered the face of banks from one of mere intermediary to one of provider of quick and efficient and customer friendly services. The banks are now competing with one another to offer value-added services to their customers. Several banks have been positioning themselves as a 'one stop shop' for all financial services with a comprehensive range of products.

3

Progress of Commercial Banks after Nationalisation

3.1 Introduction

Commercial banks are the oldest banking institutions in the organized sector of Indian Money Market. With a wide network of branches spread across the country, commercial banks have a major role in the banking operations as a whole. They provide the largest slice of funds for trade, commerce, agriculture, industry and other sectors of the economy. As a group commercial banks form the predominant part of organized banking system in India. The Indian commercial banking system consists of:

- Scheduled Commercial Banks, and
- Non- Scheduled Commercial Banks

3.1.1 Scheduled Commercial Banks: A Scheduled bank is one, which is registered under the provisions of the Second Schedule of the Reserve Bank of India Act. Scheduled banks come within the ambit of the various credit control measures of the Reserve Bank of India. They are required to maintain certain minimum balance in their accounts with the Reserve Bank of India. Scheduled banks are entitled to borrowing and rediscounting facilities from the RBI. The following conditions must be fulfilled by a bank for inclusion in the second schedule:

- The bank concerned must be carrying on banking business in India.
- The bank must have paid-up capital and reserve of an aggregate value of not less than Rs. 5 lakh.
- It must convince the Reserve Bank of India that its affairs are not being conducted in a manner detrimental to the interests of the depositors.

Scheduled Commercial Banks consists of public, private sector and foreign banks and Regional Rural Banks. Public sector bank consists of 19 nationalized banks, State Bank of India, its 7 subsidiaries, and the newly started IDBI Bank.

3.1.2 Non- Scheduled Commercial Banks: Banks, which are not included in Second Schedule of the Reserve Bank of India, are known as non- scheduled commercial banks. Non-scheduled commercial banks are not entitled to all those facilities that the scheduled banks avail from the Reserve Bank of India. It is obligatory on the part of these banks to carry a portion of deposits with the Reserve Bank of India or in vault with the bank itself and prepare their annual accounts and balance sheet in accordance with requirements stipulated by the Banking Companies Act.

The development of the Indian Commercial Banking system from 1969 to 2006 is given in Table 3.1.

Table 3.1 portrays the progress of commercial banking system in India. Since the nationalization of banks in 1969, there had been tremendous growth in the number of commercial banks. The number of commercial banks increased from 89 in 1969 to 305 in March 1999. As result of reorganization and merger of weak banks with strong banks, the number of commercial banks dwindled to 290 at the end of March 2004. Due to reorganization and amalgamation of RRBs, the number of commercial banks further reduced to 222 at the end of March 2006. As on March 2006, commercial banking system consist 28 public sector banks, 133 Regional Rural Banks and 4 non- scheduled commercial banks. Private sector banks including foreign banks in the commercial banking system reduced from 78 in March 1999 to 57 at the end of March 2006.

Number of Regional Rural Banks as on June 30, 2006 was further reduced to 109, after amalgamation of 36 RRBs into 12 RRBs between April 1 and June 30, 2006.

The progress of commercial banks in branch expansion is exhibited in Table 3.2.

Table 3.2 shows that the commercial banks in India have achieved tremendous progress in branch expansion during the last four decades. The number of bank offices in India increased from 8262 at the end of June 1969 to 69,306 at the

Table 3.1: Growth of the Indian Commercial Banking System (1969-2006)

Branches	June 1969	June 1974	June 1979	June 1984	June 1989	March 1994	March 1999	March 2004	March 2006
Public Sector Banks	22	22	22	28	28	27	27	27	28
Private Sector Banks	51	43	53	53	50	49	78	62	57
Regional Rural Banks	-	-	56	162	196	196	196	196	133
Non-Scheduled Banks	16	9	5	4	4	4	4	5	4
Total	89	74	136	247	278	276	305	290	222

Table 3.2: Progress of Commercial Bank Branches in India (1969-2006)

Item	June 1969	June 1974	June 1979	June 1984	June 1989	March 1994	March 1999	March 2004	March 2006
Number of Commercial Bank Branches	8262	16936	30202	45332	57698	61803	64939	67118	69306
Population per Office (000)	64	35	21	16	14	15	15	16	16
Credit Deposit Ratio (per cent)	77.5	73.1	66.6	67.5	60.3	51.6	51.7	55.9	70.1

end of June 2006, registering a compound growth rate of 5.91 per cent per annum. This progress indicates a more than 8.4 fold increase in number of branches during 37-year period.

The pace of branch expansion has been high during the 10-year period since nationalization, which showed a compound growth rate of 13.8 per cent. During this 10-year period, the average rate of growth of new offices was 2,195 a year.

Table 3.2 further reveals that the pace of branch expansion of commercial banks was relatively slow after 1989, which showed a compound growth rate of 10.21 per cent, and the average rate of growth of new branches per year was 2472 a year. The compound growth rate for branch expansion during a period of 30 years was further reduced to 7.1 per cent and average rate of new offices per year was reduced to 1889.

The average population coverage by a bank office in India was 64,000 persons in June 1969. It dwindled from 64,000 to 35,000 during 1969-1974 and to 21,000 by the end of June 1979. It slid down to 14,000 by the end of June 1989 and further increased to 16,000 in 2004.

The Credit Deposit Ratio of scheduled commercial banks was 77.5 per cent in June 1969. Table 3.2 indicates that the credit deposit ratio was declining gradually over the years. The C-D Ratio at the all India level got declined from 77.5 per cent in 1969 to 51.7 per cent in 1999. It is obvious from the table that the target of 60 per cent credit deposit ratio has not yet been achieved by banks in most years. At the end of March 2006, the C-D ratio improved and stood at an all-time high level of 70.1 per cent.

Further analysis on CD Ratio reveals that among bank-groups, foreign banks had the highest C-D ratio (85.8 per cent) at the end of March 2006, followed by new private sector banks (77.2 per cent), old private sector banks (63.9 per cent) and public sector banks (54.9 per cent) in that order.

3.2 Distribution of Branches of Commercial Banks

In March 2006, 19 nationalized banks represented 49.1 per

cent (34012) of the total branches in the country. The branches of RRBs accounted 20.9 per cent (14486) of the total network. State Bank of India and its seven subsidiaries had third position with 13,831 branches representing 19.9 per cent of the total branches. Branches of old (1950) and new private sector (4566) banks represented 6.6 and 2.8 per cent respectively of the total branches in the country. Foreign banks (262) and Non Scheduled Banks (26) in total represent only .5 per cent of the total branches. The newly started public sector IDBI Bank had 173 branches.

The branch expansion programme of commercial banks and the growth of rural branches and its percentage share to the total bank branches are presented in Table 3.3.

Since the nationalization of banks, there has been a rapid stride in branch expansion particularly at the rural level. The number of rural branches (Table 3.3) went up from 1,832 to 30,776 during June 1969 to June 2006, accounting for 44.3 per cent of the total number of branches compared to hardly 22.2 per cent in 1969, indicating a 16.8 fold increase. The share of rural branches to total branches went up to an all time high of 57.2 per cent in March 1994, but its share got reduced to 50.6 per cent in March 1999 and to 44.3 per cent in June 2004. The share of rural branches to total branches has been declining from 1994 onwards. As against this, in semi-urban centres (population 10,000 to 1,00,000) and also in metropolitan\port towns there was a decline in the percentages, in the first case from 40.2 per cent to 22.1 per cent and in the latter from 20.1 to 16.2 per cent during the period of 1969-2006. In urban centres the percentage of change is not so worth mentioning. However, in absolute numbers there was more than an 8-fold increase of branches in urban centres, 6.8-fold increase in metropolitan cities and 4.6 fold in semi-urban areas over a period of 37 years from June 1969 to June 2006.

The rural bank branches in India recorded a compound growth rate of 8.14 per cent. Where as the corresponding growth rate in branches in urban, semi-urban, and metropolitan centres were only 6.05, 4.2 and 5.3 per cent respectively.

Table 3.3: Population Group-wise Distribution of Commercial Bank Offices in India (1969-2006)

Year	Rural Branches	Semi-Urban Branches	Urban Branches	Metropolitan Branches	Total Branches
June 1969	1832 (22.2)	3322 (40.2)	1447 (17.5)	1661 (20.1)	8262 (100)
June 1974	6155 (36.5)	5089 (30.0)	2899 (17.1)	2783 (16.4)	16936 (100)
June 1979	13333 (44.1)	7845 (26.0)	4717 (15.6)	4307 (14.3)	30202 (100)
June 1984	25372 (56.0)	9262 (20.4)	5769 (12.7)	4929 (10.9)	45332 (100)
June 1989	33014 (57.2)	11166 (19.4)	7524 (13.0)	5995 (10.4)	57699 (100)
March 1994	35329 (57.2)	11890 (19.2)	8745 (14.1)	5839 (9.5)	61803 (100)
March 1999	32857 (50.6)	14168 (21.8)	9898 (15.3)	8016 (12.3)	64939 (100)
June 2004	32212 (48.0)	15035 (22.4)	10937 (16.3)	8934 (13.3)	67,118 (100.0)
June 2006	30776 (44.3)	15,370 (22.1)	12,008 (17.3)	11,263 (16.2)	69,417 (100.0)

3.3 Growth of Deposits and Advances

Table 3.4 gives an idea of the progress recorded by commercial banks in mobilization of deposits and outstanding credit since 1969 to 2006.

Table 3.4: Growth of Deposits and Outstanding Advances in Commercial Banks (1969-2006)

(Rs. crore)

Year	No. of bank branches	Deposits	Advances
June 1969	8,262	4,646	3,599
June 1974	16,936	10,756	7,858
June 1979	30,202	28,671	19,116
June 1984	45,332	64,620	43,613
March 1989	57,698	1,47,854	89,080
March 1994	61,803	3,23,632	1,66,844
March 1999	64,939	7,22,203	3,68,837
March 2004	67,118	15,04,416	8,40,785
March 2006	69,417	21,64,477	15,16,557

The growth of bank deposits since nationalization of major commercial banks in July 1969 has been amazing. Deposits of commercial banks aggregating to Rs. 21,64,477 crore at the end of March 2006 represented a spectacular increase over that of Rs. 4,646 crore as on June 30, 1969. This shows a compound growth rate of 18.6 per cent. The bank deposit from 1969 to 2006 recorded a 466-fold increase.

The total outstanding credit of commercial banks in the country increased substantially and steadily from Rs. 3,599 crore in June 1969 to Rs. 15,16,557 crore in March 2006 registering a 421 fold increase with a compound growth rate of 18.3 per cent per annum. The compound growth rate on deposits (18.6 per cent) and advances (18.3 per cent) of commercial banks for a period of thirty-seven years were almost same percentage.

3.4 Priority Sector Advances

The main objective of introducing social control over the banks and subsequent nationalization of the major commercial banks in the country was to ensure that credit flows to various sectors of the economy in accordance with the national plan priorities. In pursuance of this policy, agriculture and agro-based activities, small industries and small transport operations, retail trade, micro business, professionals and self-employed and educational loans were designated as 'priority sectors' for their lending operations. This categorization was to ensure increased flow of credit to these sectors in accordance with the guidelines framed by the RBI. Advances of public sector banks to the priority sectors enjoy certain advantages such as concessional rates of interest, concessional rates in to margin requirements and relaxation in respect of procedural formalities.

The priority sector advances by public sector banks increased significantly from Rs. 441 crore in 1969 to Rs. 4,01,865 crore in March 2006 a 911 fold increase showing a compound growth rate of 20.2 per cent per annum. Its share to total advances also jumped from 14.96 per cent to 40.3 per cent by 2006, thus exceeding the 40 per cent target.

The priority sector advances as a percentage share of total advances are reportedly on the decline of late. For instance, in 1994 the priority sector advances fell short of target by more than 2.2 per cent. By March 1999, the advances of the public sector banks to the priority sectors were nearer to the overall target of 40 per cent and were short of target by only 0.8 per cent.

Total public sector bank credit to agriculture direct and indirect increased from Rs. 162.29 crore in June 1969 to Rs. 1, 54,900 crore in March 2006. The Table further reveals that within priority sector lending, the advances to small-scale industries constituted 8.1 per cent of the total credit at the end of March 2006. The number of priority sector accounts also increased from 2.6 lakh in June 1969 to 348 lakh in March

2006 thus registering a 134-fold increase and a compound growth of 14.13 per cent per annum.

3.5 Rural Credit Expansion

The commercial banks in India for a long period confined their operations to urban centres, receiving deposits from the urban public and financing trade and industry in urban areas. An important argument in support of bank nationalization was that commercial banks kept themselves away from the need of financing agriculture and remained largely indifferent to the credit needs of farmers for agricultural operations and land reclamation. An overview of the growth in total credit and rural credit disbursements of commercial banks in India is given in Table 3.5.

Table 3.5: Rural Credit Expansion of Commercial Banks in India (1969-2006)

(Rs. crore)

Year	All India		
	Total Credit	Rural Credit	%age share of Rural Credit to Total
June 1969	3,609	55	1.5
June 1974	8,065	427	5.3
June 1979	19,822	1,661	8.4
June 1984	45,468	6,740	14.8
June 1989	89,361	14,553	16.2
March 1993	1,62,467	22,906	14.1
March 1999	3,82,425	53,909	14.1
March 2004	8,80,312	5,020	9.7
March 2005	11,52,467	1,09,975	9.5

The total credit outstanding in the country has gone up from Rs. 3,609 crore in June 1969 to Rs. 11, 52,467 crore in March 2005 registering a 319-fold increase and a compound growth rate of 17.36 per cent.

The credit disbursement in the rural areas also remarkably increased from Rs. 55 crore to Rs. 1, 09,975 crore registering a compound growth rate of 23.5 per cent. The proportion of rural credit increased from 1.5 per cent to 16.2 per cent by June 1989 but it declined to 14.1 per cent in March 1999. The proportion of rural credit further dwindled to 9.5 per cent at the end of March 2005.

At March 2005, outstanding credit at metropolitan centres represented 62.7 per cent of the total credit. Urban and semi-urban centres accounted 16.4 and 11.4 per cent respectively of the total outstanding credit in the country.

3.6 General Credit Card Scheme (GCC)

In order to provide hassle- free credit to bank customers in rural areas with out the insistence of security, RBI issued guidelines on December 27, 2005 regarding the issue of General Credit Card (GCC) scheme. In rural areas the extent of ATMs and point of sale are limited. Hence, all commercial banks RRBs including are allowed to issue General Credit Card Scheme to their rural and semi urban customers. Banks issue such cards based on an assessment of their customers with regard to their income and cash transactions of the household.

General Credit Card Scheme is in the nature of an overdraft or cash credit with no end use stipulations. The credit facility given under this scheme will be in the nature of revolving credit. The GCC holder will be entitled to draw cash from the specified branch of a bank up to the limit sanctioned by. GCC need not necessarily be in the form of a credit or debit card but is issued in the form of a passbook. Banks have the flexibility for fixing the limit. However, the total credit limit under GCC for an individual should not exceed Rs. 25,000. The interest rate on the facility may be charged, as considered appropriate and reasonable by the bank. The eligibility limit may however be periodically reviewed and revised\cancelled depending on the transaction record of the account holder. Women may get preference under the GCC scheme. Fifty per cent of the credit up to Rs. 25,000 outstanding under GCC will be eligible for being considered as indirect agricultural finance.

3.7 Regional Rural Banks

3.7.1 Introduction: In the multi-agency approach, RRBs have an important role in the rural credit structure, along with co-operatives and commercial banks. Regional Rural Banks were set up under the Regional Rural Banks Act, 1976. RRBs are meant to operate as State sponsored, region based and rural oriented commercial banks.

The decision to establish RRBs in India was taken by the then Prime Minister smt. Indira Gandhi in 1975, with the primary objective of developing the rural economy for meeting the financial needs of the weaker sections of rural community. A Working Group was appointed by the Government under the Chairmanship of Sri M Narashimham, to study the possibility of establishment of an alternative agency to provide institutional credit to landless labourers, rural artisans, small and marginal farmers.

Based on the report, the Government of India promulgated the RRBs Ordinance dated September 26, 1975. On October 2, 1975 five RRBs were established in four states. In the year 1976, Regional Rural Banks Act was passed by giving legal form and status to the emergency ordinance. The Central Government is empowered, on the request of any bank called 'Sponsor Bank' to establish in a State or Union territory one or more RRBs. These banks are operating under the regulatory supervision of NABARD, which has the responsibility of laying down the policies, to supervise their operations, provide refinance facilities, to monitor their performance and to attend their problems.

The basic objective of this type of rural financial institutions was to feel and get familiarized with local needs, and to remain a professionally managed alternative channel for credit dispensation to small and marginal farmers. Agricultural labourers, socially and economically weaker sections of population were its target group and their purpose was to develop agriculture, trade, commerce, small scale and cottage industry and other productive activities. These banks were also meant to provide assistance for the marketing of agricultural and other products through marketing organizations and help in the holistic development of the villages. RRBs were expected to mobilize resources from rural areas and play a catalytic role in developing agriculture and rural economy by deploying such mobilized resources to rural sectors for the needy who are not covered by scheduled commercial banks in spite of their large network of branches. Keeping this objective in view, the capital of RRBs was contributed by the Central Government, concerned State Government and Sponsor Bank in the proportion of 50:15:35.

During the first decade of their operations and up to 1987, RRBs concentrated on expanding credit services which marked by the high credit deposit ratio of more than 100 per cent. Thereafter, the CD Ratio dwindled, showing a reorientation in their activities. However, the credit-deposit ratio improved to 55.7 per cent in 2005-06 from 41.3 per cent in 2000-01.

3.7.2 Progress of Regional Rural Banks: Table 3.6 gives a general picture of the growth and geographical coverage of RRBs since 1975.

Table 3.6 discloses that the RRBs have come a long way since the establishment of the first five of them in October 1975. As on March 2005, there were 196 RRBs in 26 states covering 523 districts in the country. Due to reorganization and amalgamation of RRBs, the number of RRBs reduced from 196 in March 2005 to 133 in March 2006.

The number of branches of RRBs increased from 17 to 14,488 during the period of December 1975 to June 2006. The RRB branches alone constitute 20.87 per cent of the total bank branches in the country and 79.5 per cent of them are in the rural areas. Semi-urban and urban\metropolitan branches represent only 16.7 and 3.8 per cent respectively of the total branches. The share of the RRBs in the total number of all rural branches is 37.4 per cent.

Table 3.6: Progress of Regional Rural Banks in India (1975-2006)

Performance Indicators	Dec. 1975	Dec. 1980	Dec. 1985	Dec. 1990	March 1995	March 1999	March 2005	March 2006
Number of RRBs	6	85	188	196	196	196	196	133
Number of States Covered	5	17	21	22	23	23	26	26
Number of Districts Covered	12	144	333	380	425	451	523	525
Total number of Branches	17	3279	12606	14511	14509	14475	14484	14488
Total Credit Advanced (Outstanding Rs. crore)	0.10	243	1408	3548	6291	11016	31803	38520

While considering the growth of advances also (Table 3.7), it can be seen that the volume of outstanding credit rose rapidly from a paltry amount of Rs. 10 lakh in December 1975 to Rs. 38,520 crore in March 2006.

3.7.3 Recapitalisation of RRBs: Government took several measures for reconstruction\ recapitalization of the RRBs. Following the first phase of recapitalization i.e. in 1995-96 and 1996-97, the performance of RRBs improved. However, by the introduction of prudential norms of asset classification, income recognition and provisioning for the RRBs did not produced the expected results.

The yearly budgetary allocation for recapitalization of RRBs is shown in Table 3.7.

Table 3.7: Recapitalisation of Regional Rural Banks (1994-1999)

Year	Amount (Rs. crore)
1994-95	300
1995-96	447
1996-97	400
1997-98	400
1998-99	152

To strengthen the capital base of RRBs, the Government of India through budgetary allocations infused capital for the RRBs. The process of recapitalization initiated in 1994-95 continued up to the year 1999-2000.

In the fourth Phase of 1997-98, 90 RRBs were given capital support to the extent of Rs. 400 crore. This consists of 15 RRBs, which were getting capital support for the first time, and 75 RRBs that received assistance in the earlier phases, got further amount allotted to strengthen their capital. A total sum of Rs. 2,188 crore has been infused as additional capital support to 187 out of 196 RRBs through six phases of recapitalization of the loss-making RRBs till January 2000. Out of 187 RRBs, 158 RRBs were fully recapitalized and 29 RRBs only partially. Further, while seven RRBs are yet to be taken up for recapitalization, two profit making RRBs do not need any capital support. During the year 2000-01, the Government of India did not take up recapitalization exercise and no budgetary allocation was made for the year 2001-02.

3.7.4 Regional Rural Banks at Crossroads: Regional Rural Banks established under the RRB Act 1976 have rendered yeomen service for the economic upliftment of the rural people, especially those living below the poverty line. The rural and semi-urban branches of RRBs constitute 96 per cent of their branch network. As on March 31, 2006, the deposits and outstanding advances of RRBs were Rs. 71,329 crore and Rs. 38,520 crore respectively. RRBs have done well in the mobilization of rural deposits. The loans of RRBs under priority sectors accounted for 79.3 per cent of the total. The involvement of RRBs in providing credit support to small and retail trade and other non-farm rural activities are better than that of co-operatives and commercial banks.

Even though RRBs succeeded in achieving their basic objectives, they are suffering from a number of maladies. In the wake of the introduction of financial sector reforms in 1991-92, the commercial viability of RRBs emerged as the most crucial factor in deciding about their desired role in the emerging economic scenario. However, the performance of most of the RRBs remains far from satisfactory. The financial health of RRBs got weakened mainly due to its limited business flexibility with limited scope for expansion/diversification combined with smaller size of loans with higher exposure to risk-prone advances and professional inefficiency in financial deployment.

3.7.5 Report on the Working Group: NABARD taken several initiatives to revitalize RRBs. Government of India had set up a Working Group under the Chairmanship of Mr. M.V.S. Chalapathi Rao, Managing Director, NABARD in 2001 to examine various aspects of functioning of RRBs and to make recommendations for RRBs to become an effective institution for the development of the rural economy. The Group submitted its report during August 2002, suggested amendments to several provisions of RRB Act besides making a number of recommendations to improve the viability and performance of RRBs.

3.7.6 Report on the Internal Working Group: Following the recommendations of the Working Group, an Internal Working Group on RRBs was set up by the Reserve Bank. The Group examined various options available within the existing legal framework for strengthening of RRBs. They suggested far-reaching measures including mergers and acquisitions of RRBs, change in sponsorship through involvement of private banks, appointment of chairman from the related sectors, minimum capital requirement and a host of new avenues of business to augment their fee-based incomes. The group proposed a change in sponsorship by which new banks both private as well as public to be involved with RRBs. With a view to improve the competitiveness, work culture, management and efficiency of RRBs a change in sponsorship may be considered. The committee also suggested to maintain the CRAR of RRBs at 5 per cent and with the passage of time they are expected to align themselves with Basel-I norms. To increase the non-interest income of RRBs they may be permitted to act as agents for the distribution of products of mutual funds and insurance companies.

The process of amalgamation of RRBs gained further momentum only when the Finance Minister, Mr. P Chidambaram gave a nod for such a process in nine states. Accordingly, if a sponsor bank had more than one RRB in a State, all the RRBs in that State under a sponsor bank should be consolidated in to one RRB. He also stressed the need to provide adequate capital support to RRBs, which will enable them to have a net capital adequacy ratio of 5 per cent. The share of sponsoring institutions in the capital structure of RRBs should be increased to make them a majority stakeholder. In the long run RRBs can be converted in to vibrant and professional subsidiaries and area-specific Special Business Units (SBUs). Even co-operative banks can be merged with these SBUs subsequently.

An Advisory Committee appointed by the Government under the Chairmanship of Shri V.S. Vyas "to improve the flow of credit to agriculture sector and other related activities" also recommended for the restructuring of RRBs. The Committee submitted its report in June 2004.

3.7.7 Special Package Announced by RBI for Revitalizing RRBs: To revitalize and to improve the financial strength of RRBs, Reserve Bank of India announced a special package in December 2005. Following are the important proposals of the package:

- Sponsor banks were advised to provide lines of credit to RRBs at reasonable rates of interest to strengthen their resource base.
- RRBs were given access to inter-RRB term money/borrowings and to the repo/CBLO markets.
- RRBs were permitted to set up off-site ATMs, issue debit/credit cards and to handle pension/Government business as authorized sub-agents of banks to conduct Government business.
- Reserve Bank indicated that taking into account their financial position, requests from RRBs could be considered for opening of currency chests.
- Reserve Bank to review the existing norms for conduct of various types of foreign exchange transactions by RRBs with a view to allow them to undertake non-trade related current account transactions to release foreign exchange for certain specified purposes such as overseas education, business travel, medical treatment and private visits. The role of RRBs and their financial performance evolves in response to policy initiatives as well as changing business environment.

To strengthen RRBs and improve their performance, the Reserve Bank allowed RRBs to lend to non-target groups, deregulation of deposit and lending rates, and permitted investment of their surplus funds in profitable avenues. These measures were, supported with well-defined business plan preparation from the branches, time bound implementation for attaining profitability, human resource development programmes, and organizational development initiatives as an integrated tool for turnaround.

3.7.8 Restructuring of RRBs: Following the recommendations of the Internal Group, Reserve Bank examined various alternatives available within the existing legal framework for strengthening of RRBs. The Group, in its Report submitted in June 2005, observed large variations in the number of districts covered and the branch network of RRBs.

The Internal Working Group in its report stated that 47 RRBs covered only one district each, 111 RRBs covered 2 to3 districts, 29 RRBs 4 to5 districts and 9 operated in 6 to 9 districts. Similarly, 72 RRBs had up to 50 branches, 87 RRBs 51 to100 branches, 21 RRBs 101 to150 branches and 16 had more than 150 branches. As many as six sponsor banks had only one RRB sponsored by them. While 11 sponsor banks had 2 to 4 sponsored RRBs, 3 sponsor banks had up to 10 RRBs and 8 sponsor banks had more than 10 RRBs sponsored by them scattered in different States. Of these, only 2 sponsor banks had more than 20 RRBs.

In order to improve the operational viability of RRBs and take advantage of their economies of scale by reducing transaction cost and taking into account, the route of merger/amalgamation of RRBs was suggested. The restructuring was to be a two-phased one as suggested by the committee:

- Merger of RRBs of the same sponsor bank of the same State.
- Merger of RRBs sponsored by different banks of the same State. Merger of RRBs with the sponsor bank was not provided for in the RRB Act of 1976. Further, such mergers will be against the purpose of setting up of RRBs as local entities meant to provide credit to weaker sections primarily.

Amalgamation of RRBs would enable them to become bigger in size with a larger area of operation. It would also help them to function in a competitive environment more effectively by taking advantage of the economies of large scale and reduction in transaction cost. The process of pruning the number of RRBs would also make it more convenient for the sponsor banks to manage their affairs. The Group submitted its report in June 2005, observed large variations in the number of districts covered and the branch network of RRBs.

As per the recommendations of the Committee, the Government of India in consultation with NABARD and the concerned State Government and sponsor banks initiated State-level amalgamation of RRBs. The process of sponsor bank-wise amalgamation of RRBs at the State level started on September 12, 2005 with a notification indicating the formation of 9 amalgamated entities. Till October 31, 2006, 137 RRBs were amalgamated to form 43 new RRBs, sponsored by 18 commercial banks spread over 15 States thus bringing down the total number of RRBs in the country to 102 from that of 196. The amalgamation process of phase-I is in the process of being completed.

3.7.9 Viability of RRBs: The RRBs as a group were incurred a loss of Rs. 426 crore in the year 1995-96. RRBs made a profit of Rs. 73 crore for the first time during 1997-98 and improved the same to further Rs. 601 crore and Rs. 608 crore during the years 2000-01 and 2001-02 respectively. The viability based categorization of RRBs as on March 31, 2002, showed that out of 196 RRBs, 86 RRBs wiped off their accumulated losses and in a way attained a sustainable viability whereas 89 other RRBs have achieved a turn around and attained a current viability status leaving only 29 RRBs, which continued to incur losses. The viability-based review of RRBs showed that the loss making RRBs are concentrated in three states viz. Madhya Pradesh, Bihar and Orissa and in four sponsors viz. UCO Bank, State Bank of India, Bank of India, and Bank of Baroda. Low productivity, high transaction costs, lower CD ratio, negative margins, low recovery rates and high NPAs are identified as the important causes for non-viability of these RRBs.

Net profits of RRBs further increased to Rs. 769 crore during 2003-04. The net profits declined thereafter to Rs.748 crore during 2004-05 and to Rs. 510 crore in 2005-06. Net profits of

RRBs were dwindled mainly because of reduction in net margin and payment of arrears. The overall financial strength of RRBs improved significantly over the last few years. The ratio of gross and net NPAs declined sharply during the year to 7.3 per cent and 4.0 per cent, respectively, enabled by improved recovery to the extent of 80 per cent. The productivity of RRBs, both in terms of per branch and per employee, increased significantly during last 10 years. In view of amalgamation of RRBs, the number of both profit making and loss-making RRBs dwindled to 111 and 22, respectively, at March 2006 from 166 and 30 respectively, at the end of March 2005.

NABARD is providing full guidance and support to calibrate the , process of amalgamation. Revised guidelines on organisational set-up, appointment of Chairmen and fixation of seniority of staff were issued by NABARD to sponsor banks for implementation in their respective RRBs in the post-amalgamation period.

4

Liberalisation of Banking Services

4.1 Introduction

Financial sector reforms are indispensable to equip overall structure of economy capable of reallocating resources to more productive uses. Financial sector plays a major role in the mobilization and allocation of resources of a country. In financial sector, nearly eighty per cent of the sources of funds are from the banking sector. Hence banking sector reforms have become an important ingredient for financial sector reforms in India. Banking sector needs to be strengthened for the overall vitality and stability of the financial system. Hence, first and second-generation financial sector reforms are centered on the banking system in the country.

Changes have taken place in Indian economy from the time of then Finance Minister of India, Dr. Man Mohan Singh who unveiled the New Economic Policy through his maiden Budget for the year 1991 of the Government of India. The much-debated New Economic Policy was the outcome of acute financial crisis faced by the country in mid 1991 caused primarily by the political uncertainty, which got aggravated with the Gulf War. During this period, the country was passed through an unprecedented economic crisis following the strain on balance of payment, galloping inflation, depleting condition of foreign exchange reserves and many other macroeconomic imbalances. The new economic policy was based on a combination of measures aimed at economic stabilization and structural reforms to overcome the shortcomings of a socialistic pattern of economy pursed by India for the past 40 years. The overall package was aimed at enhancing the productivity and efficiency of the economy as a whole and to make it competitive internationally.

The new economic policy is structured on the pillars of

deregulation, liberalization, privatization and globalization. When a country switches over to a liberalized regime from a strictly controlled and regulated one the economy as a whole becomes open, accessible and competitive. This implies that the government will gradually withdraw from direct economic management and entrepreneurship activities, which are to remain guided by market forces and factors.

The banking sector in India remained a regulated one and rigid since the nationalization of banks in 1969. Up to 1990, the concept of an independent regulatory authority had no relevance. With the liberalization of the Indian Economy, the Indian banking system also followed it suit and slowly entered into a market driven competitive system.

The economic policy of structural adjustment got a big boost in India in June 1991. Close on the heels of announcement of the National Economic Policy, the Government appointed a high level committee on financial sector reforms under the chairmanship of Narasimham which was to examine exhaustively all aspects relating to the structure, organization functions and procedures of the system.' The committee submitted its first report in November 1991 and its second one in 1998. Second generation reforms meant to strengthen the banking sector in India and to make it globally competitive began in1998. Government of India accepted most of the major recommendations of the Narasimham committee and many of its recommendations were implemented by the Reserve Bank of India.

The Narasimham Committee (I&II) made several recommendations to improve the productivity, efficiency and profitability of the banking and financial systems. In September 1990, RBI set up another committee on customer services, under the chairmanship of Sri. M. N. Goiporia, Chairman, State Bank of India to examine the problems related to customer services in India and suggested measures to improve the situation. The Rangarajan Committee on Computerization in banks and Saraf Committee (1994) on technology issues made several recommendations; RBI implemented many of them.

The Narsimham committee suggested that there should be functional autonomy, flexibility in operations and loosening of banking regulations. The committee envisaged major changes in banking sector by way of reduction in cash reserve ratio and statutory liquidity ratio requirements, deregulation of interest on deposits and advances. Its other recommendations were recapitalization of weak public sector banks, merger of banks to prune their numbers, adequate financial infrastructure in terms of supervision, audit, and sophisticated technology for improving customer service, operational efficiency and voluntary retirement scheme.

The Narsimham committee also proposed introduction of prudential norms such as income recognition, asset classification, provisioning and capital adequacy norms, and transparency in operations and improvement in productivity, efficiency and profitability of banking operations. The committee recommended entry of foreign banks, new private sector banks and local area banks. The committee further advocated the introduction of universal banking, setting up of special recovery tribunals, introduction of banking ombudsmen scheme etc.

The liberalization and economic reforms in 1991 unleashed stiffer competition among banks. The financial sector became intensely competitive with several new competitors like private banks, foreign banks, non-banking financial companies, merchant bankers mutual fund and insurance companies.

The new generation private sector banks rapidly expanded their operations by opening branches mainly in the metros and cities by providing state of the art services and facilities to their customers. New generation and foreign banks operate in a highly sophisticated environment by offering up-to-date products and services with enhanced personnel efficiency attracting many new clients.

Several banks have been positioning themselves as a "one-stop shop" for all financial services with a comprehensive range of products like deposits, loans, credit cards, debit cards, depository services, investment advice, utility bill payments and various other transactional services. Apart from these there, banks also entered into the business of selling third-party products like mutual funds and insurance products to their retail customers.

4.2 Virtual Banking

The growing universalisation and internationalization of banking operations, driven by a combination of factors, such as, the continuing deregulation, heightened competition and technological advancements, have altered the face of banks from one of mere intermediator to one of provider of quick, efficient and consumer friendly services.

The practice of banking was subjected to a significant transformation in the nineties. Banks and other financial entities in India entered the world of information technology and computer networking only very recently. The introduction of liberalization measures in the banking sector and the emergence of new private sector and foreign banks equipped with latest technology, led to increased competition in the banking sector. With the introduction of the new technology in banking sector, customers are fast moving away from the traditional branch-banking system to the convenience and comfort of remote electronic banking services or virtual banking. With E-Banking, the brick and mortar structure of the traditional banking gets converted into a click and portal model thereby giving real shape and form to the concept of virtual banking. In virtual banking, brick and mortar structure or physical bank branch is no more required for rendering banking services

Virtual banking denotes the rendering of banking and related services through extensive use of information technology without direct physical recourse to the bank by the customer. The services are delivered to the customers by relying solely on information technology. The origin of virtual banking in the developed countries can be traced back to the seventies when the Automated Teller Machines (ATMs) got installed for the first time. The most important types of virtual banking services are Automated Teller Machines (ATMs), Shared ATM networks, Electronic Funds

Transfer, Phone-banking, Smart Cards, Stored-Value Cards, Debit card, Credit card, Internet and Intranet banking.

4.2.1 Advantages of Virtual Banking: The financial benefits of virtual banking services are manifold.

- Virtual banking has the advantage of having a lower cost of handling a transaction via the virtual resource compared to the cost of handling the transaction via the branch.
- The increased reflex to customer requirements under virtual banking vis-à-vis branch banking can enhance customer satisfaction and thus to higher profits for the bank.
- It helps to retain the existing customers and to attract many newer customers.
- Virtual banking reduces the staff cost in operating branch networks which leads to cost efficiency.
- Virtual banking allows better quality of services and an enlarged range of services coming to the customer speedily and accurately and at his\her convenience.
- Virtual banking provides round-the-clock, anywhere, speedy and more reliable service to its customers than branch banking.

Virtual banking had very good head start in most Indian banks both at the urban and rural areas.

4.3 Emergence of Electronic Banking Products/Services

Improved customer service has become very important for public and private sector banks to survive and to grow in the emerging deregulated financial market. Consequently, banks are under increasing pressure to 'offer today what customers would expect tomorrow'. The banks now compete with one another to offer value-added services to customers to expand their customer bases.

Up to date products and services which Indian banks offer to their customers are; 1) ATMs, 2) Credit Card 3) Internet Banking 4) Mobile Banking 5) Phone Banking 6) Telebanking 7) Utility bill payment and other regular periodical payment facilities 8) Insurance Products 9) Single Window Service 10) Investment and Financial advisory Services 11) Electronic funds transfer options to cover third party customer accounts within the same bank, funds transfer across banks 12) Electronic clearing service integration with e-commerce transactions like booking of tickets for rail and air travel etc.

4.4 Automated Teller Machines (ATM)

Till the beginning of 90s, banks had only one delivery channel which was the branch. Technology has opened up several options of delivery channels. By the end of 1990, private and public sector banks in India came up with their own ATM net works under the initiative of the Indian Banks Association in Mumbai. The Bank of India was the first nationalized bank to render ATM facilities to its customers in Mumbai.

ATM has become the most popular and convenient delivery channel used by people in the rural and in urban areas. ATM is the most accepted and popular user-friendly technology for even the rural customers. An automated teller machine is one, which a customer can use with a card having PIN to withdraw cash, information and other services. ATM is a modern device introduced by the banks to enable the customers to have access to money day in day out with out visiting the bank branches in person.

ATMs have already become popular in India and they enable the customers to withdraw their money 24 hours a day, 7 days a week and round the year. The system is known as 'Any Time Money' or 'Any Where Money', because it allows the customers to withdraw money from the bank from any of its ATMs round the clock even on Sundays and National holidays. Through this facility, customers of the bank are not restricted to remain a customer of the branch where the account is maintained.

The services of ATMs are made available by the banks both at the bank premises (On-site ATMs) and also at convenient locations (Off-site ATMs) viz. at public places like petrol bunks, markets, railway stations, bus stands, airports etc. Depending upon the volume of business, banks install required number of

ATMs for their customers at convenient places in the same town.

Another significant milestone in this mode of delivery channel was the introduction of the Shared Payment Network System (SPNS) of ATMs by the Indian Banks' Association in Mumbai. Under this system, banks having no ATM facility in a locality provide ATM services to their customers in that locality through a tie up with other banks with ATM to share their ATM. The ATM sharing in India across banks started with SWADHAN. The network became operational from February 1997 to provide round the clock electronic banking services to the customers of twenty-eight member banks. For instance, State Bank of India has arrangement with Andhra Bank, Corporation Bank, Dena Bank, HDFC Bank, Indian Bank, Indusind Bank, Punjab National Bank, UCO Bank, ICICI Bank, UTI Bank etc. to share their ATMs. ATM sharing systems through proper connectivity and switching technology provides a real opportunity for banks to serve their customers on a nationwide basis. International ATM sharing facility has also become a reality in both North America and Europe.

Banks generally supply ATM card to their customers free of cost. However, some banks levy a nominal fee on customers annually for using Automated Teller Machines. Certain banks also impose fees on customers for using ATMs under the shared network scheme. Now most banks direct their customers to withdraw cash up to a certain limit through ATM, rather than through the bank counter. The upper limit of withdrawal per day from ATM varies from bank to bank.

ATMs are beneficial to the banks in many respects. ATM can help the banks to reduce the number of people thronging at bank's counters. With regard to cash vending, ATMs are faster and accurate than manual operations. Use of ATMs brings down the load of voucher preparation, and its upkeep by the banks. ATMs can also provide a number of value added services to their customers.

ATM also enables the banks to redeploy their existing staff for other services and thereby making savings in salary. ATM has brought about a great change for the better in the quality of banking service. It will also enable the banks to widen their customer base by obliterating the geographical constraints. ATM helps banks to retain their customer loyalty because convenience acts as tremendous psychological boost to customers at all time.

4.4.1 Services Offered through ATMs: Following are the important services offered by the banks through their ATMs.

Cash and cheque deposit, transfer of funds between accounts, printing of mini statement, paying of insurance premium, balance enquiry, Product information, change of Personal Identification Number (PIN), ordering of cheque book, receipt of cash, recharge of prepaid mobile card, option for mobile banking etc.

Progresses in installing of ATMs by Commercial Banks in India is depicted in Table 4.1.

Table 4.1 discloses that 21,147 ATMs were installed by commercial banks by the end of March 2006. Nationalized banks accounted for the largest share of installed ATMs, followed by the new private sector banks, SBI group, old private sector banks and foreign banks.

Number of ATMs as a per cent to the total number of branches, the table further reveals that foreign banks (339.8 per cent) and new private sector banks (313.4 per cent) have the largest number of ATMs when compared to their branch net work in the country. The corresponding percentages for SBI Group and Nationalized banks were 39.4 and 20.9 per cent. Foreign banks with a branch presence of 259 have 880 ATMs in the country. New private sector banks have 6,112 ATMs but their corresponding branch presence is only 1950.

Off-site ATMs as percentage to total ATMs was the highest in the case of foreign banks, followed by SBI group, new private sector banks, nationalized banks and old private sector banks. Of the total ATMs of foreign banks 73.6 per cent are off-site ATMs, followed by SBI group 67.4 per cent and new private sector banks 63.1per cent. In total 52.1 per cent of ATMs in the country were off-site ATMs.

Table 4.1: Commercial Bank Branches and Number of ATMs as in March 2006

Name of the Bank	Number of Bank Branches	On-Site ATMs	Off-Site ATMs	Total ATMs	Total ATMs as % of branches
Nationalized Banks	34,185	4,812 (67.2)	2,353 (32.8)	7,165	20.9
SBI Group	13,831	1,775 (32.6)	3,668 (67.4)	5,443	39.4
Old Private Sector banks	4,566	1,054 (68.1)	493 (31.9)	1,547	33.9
New Private Sector banks	1,950	2,255 (36.9)	3,857 (63.1)	6,112	313.4
Foreign banks	259	232 (26.4)	648 (73.6)	880	339.8
Total	54,791	10,128 (47.9)	11,019 (52.1)	21,147	38.6

Figures in parentheses indicate per cent of total ATMs.

Indian banks are now planning to install Rural Automated Teller Machines (Rural ATMs), in order to encourage its use in a rural environment by rural customers. Low cost ATMs are being developed under the aegis of IIT, Chennai. When lack of literacy became a problem, finger print identification and IRIS recognition can be the useful tools for access control. Supplementing written text with verbal instructions in the local language can also be used as access tools. Rural ATMs can be operated without owning an ATM card. Small farmers can now use their Kissan Credit Cards to access ATMs. The deployment of rural ATMs will help in lowering the cost of transaction and carrying out banking transactions from non-branch locations. The under mentioned services can be carried out through rural ATMs. Viz. cash deposits and withdrawals, payment of utility bills, payment of insurance premium, collection of loan EMIs, account information, mini statement, balance inquiry, product information etc.

At the end of the year 2006, City Bank had launched

biometric ATMs with multi language voice navigation features for the use of City Bank Pragati customers, which is its no-frills savings account facility for micro-finance customers, Offered directly and in partnership with MFIs. Currently, it has two biometric ATMs for 700 Pragati customers.

4.5 Debit Card

Consumers and merchant establishments all over the world changed their attitude from one of transacting in hard cash and to one in its place of electronic cash. Debit card is a prepaid card with some stored value, which optimizes conveniences for the customers. A customer possessing a Debit Card need not carry cash. It is like carrying cash from the bank account, without the inconvenience or risk of carrying liquid cash. In other words, Debit card allows ‘anywhere any time accesses’ to the customers with their savings or current account.

To receive a Debit Card an individual need only to open an account, either current or savings with the issuing bank. However, debit card facility does not extent to cash credit and other loan accounts. The banks should issue cards to its customers only having good financial standing, with satisfactory records of accomplishment for at least six months. A Personal Identification Number (PIN) will be issued to the customers for using the Debit Card. Debit card can be used at all outlets that accepts such cards for payment viz. department stores, petrol pumps, jewelry shops, restaurants, textile shops, hospitals, airlines, railways etc.

Debit Card works in the same way as a credit card for purchase transactions at merchant outlets, the only difference is that the transaction amount is directly debited to the bank account of the customer. After finishing the purchases, submit the card to the business outlet. Then cardholder has to enter the personal identification number on the shop’s PIN pad. The merchant on an Electronic Data Capture Terminal for authorization will swipe the Debit card. When the card is swiped through the electronic terminal, it dials the acquiring bank system, which validates the PIN and finds out from the issuing bank whether to accept or not the transaction. The terminal will seek an approval regarding the availability of balance in the account from the card-issuing bank. After a successful authorization or an approval from the bank, the terminal will print a charge slip. The transaction generated by the point of sale will be conclusive and binding on the cardholder. The customers account will subsequently be debited for the transacted amount. The bank has the authority to debit the designated account of the cardholder for all withdrawals effected by the card holder by using the card. Like Credit Cards, signature verification is a must for all Debit Card transactions.

Hence, presence of the cardholder in person with the card at the time of every purchase is unavoidable and cardholder has to check the amount on the charge slip and sign on the same. The business establishment will return a copy of the charge slip and the card after verifying the holder's signature.

Presence of the cardholder in person along with the card at the time of every purchase is very essential therefore debit card cannot be used for mail order, telephone order or internet transactions. Debit Card seldom permits a customer to spend over and above his cash balance in the bank. In India, most of commercial banks compete with one another to offer this facility to their customers.

4.6 Point of Sale Terminals (POS)

The Point of Sale (POS) terminal is a machine that facilitates merchant transactions through Swipe of a card in an online environment. Merchant business establishments operate point of sale in their premises in order to accept plastic cards. The POS terminals facilitate electronic funds transfer. The points of sale devices are connected as backend to interface with the main servers where the immediate authentication of the transaction is made. POS system identifying the cardholder and check whether the customers account has sufficient funds to cover the purchase. The POS machine has a display screen, keypad and a printer with the facility to transact both online and offline. Any of the available communication medium can be used for networking. The terminals can be integrated with magnetic stripe or smart card interface for authentication of the customers.

The customized POS terminals can support both debit and credit cards and can also be made to support different kinds of plastic including magnetic and smart chip based cards to make the merchant transaction possible without making use of cash.

4.7 Credit Card

In India Commercial banks, introduced the credit card facility in the early eighties. Credit card is a convenient medium of exchange. It is a cute card made of plastic. It has a method of identification of users by means of either signature identification or a stamp size photo of the cardholder. It authorizes the holder to charge goods or services to his account for which he is billed. Credit card is otherwise called 'plastic money'. The most important difference between a Credit card and a Debit card is that while credit card is a 'post paid' one the latter is a 'pre paid'.

Credit cards are designed to reduce the use of either cash or cheque for transactions. It enables a customer to purchase goods or services with in prescribed limits from certain authorized retail and service establishments with out making immediate cash payments. The customer thus possessing a credit card need not carry any cash and is empowered to spend wherever and whenever he wants goods or services with his credit card with in the limits prescribed by his banks. It reduces the physical movement of cash and enables bankers to transfer money electronically.

The customers can avail the credit card facility only in those establishments, which accepted them. After purchase of goods or services, the customer will hand over the card to the supplier\seller who swipe the card in an electronic terminal, which read the cardholders name, card number etc. On accepting the card by the machine, the supplier records the amount of the transaction in the machine. The imprinter of the machine print a sales voucher showing the card holders name, card number, card type, name of the business establishment, transaction ID, invoice number, amount of transaction etc. The holder signs the voucher and the signature is cross checked by the supplier with that of the specimen signature on the card.

The signed voucher is then sent to the bank, which pays it after deducting its service charges. Once in a month the bank sends a statement of all the credit purchases in the previous month to the credit card holder and the latter has to remit the amount either by cash or cheque. Credit card statement will be dispatched on a particular date in every month free of cost in the mailing address of the cardholder or online. The monthly bill amount can be remitted to the bank either totally or in installments under the revolving credit facility scheme. If revolving credit facilities are granted by the bank for the payment of the bill amount, the bank charges interest for the outstanding balance. The business establishments will receive the money from the institution operating the plan either in the same day or in the next day.

Credit cards are generally issued by banks only to those prompt customers having either savings or current account. The banks should issue cards to its customers only having good financial standing, with satisfactory records of accomplishment. The credit limit or purchasing power is fixed by the bank issuing the card. On the basis of credit limits bank issues different types of credit cards to its customers. The credit limits of card vary from bank to bank. The bank assumes the risk and responsibility of collecting the dues from the customers and they permit cardholders a 'cash advance facility' from its branches. The upper limit of the cash advance facility will be fixed by the bank.

Banks, which issue cards, tie up with the international organizations like Master, Visa, Maestro, Cirrus, American Express, Diners, Discover etc. that issue credit cards. Card issuing banks give a service charge to the card issuing international organizations. While certain banks issue credit card free of cost to their customers, some other banks charge a small amount from the customers as annual service charge. Loyalty bonus is also given by banks to their customers for encouraging bulk purchases using credit card by them. Usually the card issuing institution supply a guide or booklet with the card containing detailed terms and conditions, risks on the account when the card is lost or misused and other relevant information with regard to the usage of the card.

Credit cards began to be used in USA as early as 1920's and their use began to increase after 1950. Diners Club introduced their credit card in 1950 and the American Express Company in 1958 and Bank of America in 1959.

In India, the Central Bank of India was the first bank to introduce the credit card known as 'Central Card' in the middle of 1981. Credit card facility became immensely popular among customers in India by 1990. With the introduction of credit card system, the concept of every- where and any time banking became a reality. Convenience and easy acceptability of credit cards and technological advancements have paved the way for continuous rise in credit card-based of payments and transactions.

4.7.1 Guidelines for Issuing of Credit Card: The Reserve Bank of India has initiated several steps to encourage the use of credit card transactions in an efficient and a safe manner. The Reserve Bank of India took the initiative to ensure that the rules, regulations, standards and practices of the card issuing banks, accord with the best international practices. In order to ensure best international practices in credit card operations, the Reserve Bank of India in October 26, 2004, constituted a Working Group under the chairmanship of Shri R. Gandhi to study the 'Regulatory Mechanism for Cards'.

Based on the recommendations of this Working Group and the feedback received from card issuing banks, non banking finance companies and the public, guidelines on credit card operations of banks were issued by the RBI in November 2005. The most important features of the guidelines are given below:

1. Each bank /NBFC must follow a standard policy for credit card operations incorporating Fair Practices Code for credit card released by the IBA in March 2005.
2. Before issuing a credit card, the issuing institution must independently assess the applicant based on self-declaration or credit information supplied by the customer. Based on the

information received the institution must assess the credit risk and fix the credit limit for the credit card holder.

3. The card issuing institution would be solely responsible for the fulfillment of the conditions of Know Your Customer (KYC) requirements.
4. Add-on cards (i.e. those that are subsidiary to the principal card) will be issued to the principal cardholder, only on the condition that the liability will be that of the principal cardholder.
5. While applying for the credit card, the terms and conditions such as credit limit, cash withdrawal limit, joining fees for primary card holder and for add-on card holder, annual membership fees for primary and add-on card holder, billing statements-periodicity and mode of sending, Cash advance fee, Service charges levied for certain transactions, interest free (grace) period, prevailing rate of interest should be communicated to the card holder in clear and simple language. They should also furnish to the card holder charges in case of default, methods of computation of overdue, overdue interest charges, finance charges for both revolving credit and cash advances, renewal and termination procedures. Contact particulars of 24 hour call centres of card issuer, particulars of officers to be contacted, grievance redressal, Procedure to be followed in case of loss, theft and misuse of card- mode of intimation to card issuer and all other valid information which the customer requires to operate the card effectively should be furnished to them.
6. Card issuer should ensure that there is no delay in dispatching monthly bills. Sufficient time for payment of bill i.e. at least 10 days should be given to the customer before the interest starts getting charged. The issuer should charge interest only after the last date mentioned for payment.
7. The card issuer should not levy any charge that was not clearly indicated to the credit card holder at the time of issue of the card. They must obtain the prior consent of the cardholder for levying fresh charges. They need not obtain

such consent of the cardholder in case of service taxes, which are levied by the Government or any other statutory authority from time to time.

8. Changes in charges other than interest rate should be effected in to only with prior notice of at least one month.
9. If a customer has any dispute on any bill, the card issuer should provide explanation and, if necessary, documentary evidence to the customer within a maximum period of sixty days in a spirit of amicable redressal of grievances.
10. To avoid frequent complaints of delayed billing, the credit card issuing institution should consider providing bills and statements of accounts on-line.
11. Credit card issuer should be extremely careful in the appointment of service providers while outsourcing, ensuring that they seldom compromise on quality of customer service.
12. The terms and conditions for payment of credit card dues, including the minimum payment due, should be so stipulated to ensure that there is no negative amortization.
13. Card issuer will be responsible for all acts of omission and commission of their direct sales marketing and recovery agents with regard to customer's rights like their personal privacy, preservation of customer records, maintaining confidentiality of customer information and fair practices in debt collection.
14. In case, an unsolicited card is issued and activated without the consent of the recipient and the latter is billed for the same, the card issuing bank/NBFC shall not only reverse the charges forthwith, but shall also pay a penalty without any murmur to the recipient amounting to twice the value of the charges reversed.
15. Card issuing institution should not reveal the information regarding customers received at the time of opening the account or issuing the credit card to any other person or organization without obtaining their specific consent.
16. Before reporting the default position of a card holder to CIBIL or any other credit information company authorised by

the Reserve Bank, the credit card issuer must serve advance notice to the card holder of its intention of reporting. While reporting they should stick on to a procedure duly approved by their boards.

17. In the matter of recovery of dues, card issuer should ensure that they and their agents, adhere to the instructions on Fair Practice Code for lenders as recommended by the Reserve Bank as also the IBAs Code for collection of dues and repossession of security.
18. Card issuer or their agents should not resort to threats or harassment of any kind, either verbal or physical, against any person in their debt collection efforts.
19. Card issuer should constitute a grievance redressal machinery for credit cards and give wide publicity to it through electronic and print media.
20. If the customer does not get a satisfactory reply for their complaints from the card issuer within a maximum period of thirty days from the date of his lodging the complaint, he will have the option to approach the office of the concerned Banking Ombudsman for redressal of his grievance.
21. The Standing Committee on Customer Service in each credit card issuing institution may review, on a monthly basis, the credit card operations, including reports of defaulters to the CIBIL and credit card related complaints. It may take measures to improve the services and ensure the orderly growth of the credit card operations.
22. Card issuers should quote Annualized Percentage Rates (APR) on card products (separately for retail purchase and cash advance, if they are different). The method of calculation of APR should be given with one or two examples for better comprehension. The APR charged and the annual fee should be shown with equal prominence. The late payment charges including the method of calculation of such charges and the number of days should be prominently indicated. The manner in which the outstanding unpaid amount will be included for calculation of interest should also be specifically shown with

prominence in all monthly statements. Even when the minimum amount indicated to keep the card valid has been paid, it should be indicated boldly that the interest will be charged on the amount due after the due date of payment.

23. The card issuing institution should obtain prior consent of the card holder for upgrading credit cards, enhancing credit limits and for any other changes in the terms and conditions.
24. The card issuing institution should maintain a Do Not Call Registry (DNCR) containing the phone numbers (both cell phones and land phones) of customers as well as non-customers (non-constituents); who have informed the institution that they do not wish to receive unsolicited calls/SMS for marketing of its credit card products.
25. The intimation for including an individual's telephone number in the Do Not Call Registry (DNCR) should be facilitated through a website maintained by the bank/NBFC or on the basis of a letter received from such a person addressed to the bank/NBFC.
26. With a view to ensure the quality of customer service relating to the credit card operations on an on-going basis, each card issuing institution must review on a monthly basis the credit card operations including reports of defaulters to the CIBIL, credit card related complaints, measures taken to improve the services, steps taken for the growth in the credit card operations etc. in their Standing Committee on Customer Service.

Progress in credit card based payments for a period of three years from 2003-04 is depicted in Table 4.2.

The mode of credit card based payments increased enormously both in terms of volume and value from the year 2004-05. In the year 2005-06 also credit card based payments recorded a substantial increase. It accounted 1560.66 lakh transactions for Rs. 33886.47 crore that are higher than the pervious year by 20.55 per cent in volume and 31.92 per cent in amount.

Table 4.2: Growth in Credit Card-based Payments (2003-06)

Year	Counts (in lakh)	Amount (Rs. crore)
2003-04	1001.79	17662.82
2004-05	1294.72 (29.24)	25686.36 (45.42)
2005-06	1560.66 (20.55)	33886.47 (31.92)

Figures in brackets indicate percentage of change over the previous year.

4.8 Smart Cards

Progress is being made towards developing standards for newer payment instruments like SMART cards. A pilot project on SMART Card technology in India titled 'SMART Rupees System (SMARS)' was initiated by the Indian Institute of Technology, Mumbai to find out the viability and use of SMART cards as retail payment instruments within the country. It came out with a set of recommendations on SMART cards standards. With a view to examine these recommendations and to determine the standards for the Indian banking industry, the Reserve Bank in September 1999 set up a 'Working Group' to study and recommend 'SMART card based Payment System Standards'. The Working Group submitted its Report to the Reserve Bank in January 2000 and they were accepted by the Reserve Bank.

Smart cards looks like a plastic card and contain a small microprocessor or computer chip on the face of the card. Smart card is actually a debit card loaded with a sum of money. It can be used for both small payments and prepaid telephone card. Such a card facilitates small purchases with exact change viz. a cup of coffee or tea, a newspaper, bus, railway fare etc. On finalizing, the purchases submit the smart card to the merchant outlet. The merchant establishments need a special device to transfer the money from the smart card. The moment the card is inserted into the machine, money gets transferred from the smart card to the merchant. There is no need of waiting for an authorization or signing a receipt to settle with the bank as in debit card\credit card.

Like Debit Card, to receive a Smart Card an individual need only to open an account, either current or savings with the issuing bank. The banks should issue smart cards to its customers having good financial standing, with satisfactory records of accomplishment for at least six months. The outstanding balances or unspent balances stored on the smart cards should be subject to the computation for the purpose of maintenance of reserve requirements. In the case of smart cards having stored value, no interest should be paid on balances transferred to the smart cards.

4.9 Single Window Service

Single window service in banks is a novel technique adopted by commercial banks to attract and retain the customers. Before the introduction of single window service system, there were separate counters for each service of a bank. The customer, who required more than one banking service at a time, had to approach different counters. The customers used to wait and stand in a queue before each counter when he needed more than one service in a day.

Under single window service system, the banks provide all required banking services through a single counter. These services are cash and cheque deposits, withdrawal of money, issuing of demand drafts, transfer of funds, issue of cheque book etc. Under this scheme, a customer need not approach different counters for these banking services.

Many commercial banks in India have already introduced single window service to their customers. However, most of the banks in India still provide only limited banking services under single window system to their customers. These services mainly pertain to deposit and withdrawal of money. The services provided through single window system are thus inadequate in every respect when compared to those available in foreign banks.

4.10 Door Step Banking

Technology has made a tremendous impact on banking. The

major challenge faced by the banks in the present fierce competitive environment is not only the retention of their present customers, who are snatched by other banks, but also to broader their customer base by the use of technology solutions. The banks will be under pressure to increase their profitability and explore avenues for new business by providing new and innovative products, enhancement of efficiency and reduction in costs. Banks now focus on increasing their non- interest income by laying renewed stress for marketing various fee-based products like retail lending, infrastructure finance etc.

A vast majority of our population still lacks access to formal banking channels. Banks try to deliver financial services and products with the help of alternative channels. These channels are more reliable and cheaper for the existing customers. It also helps to attract customers from unbanked areas.

In order to increase the customer base and to improve their income, banks now offer various products and services at the doorstep of their customers. Doorstep banking means banking services and products made available to a customer at his\her place of residence or work. Banks thus become proximity to the customer's place of residence or work.

Under traditional banking, a customer needs to visit the branch in person for each and every service. Under doorstep banking, banks render their services\products either directly or through agents appointed by them. Under this system, there is no need for the customer to visit the branch for getting services or products from the bank. Through doorstep banking, banks play a vital role in meeting the personal, social, professional and financial requirements of customers in a very effective manner.

RBI recently issued modified guidelines for doorstep banking. In order to ensure transparency regarding the rights and obligations of customers, uniformity in approach and to clearly delineate the risks involved, it was decided to lay down general principles and broad parameters to be followed by banks while offering doorstep services to their customers. The engagement of intermediaries as business facilitators\agents involves significant reputational, legal and operational risks, hence banks advised to give due consideration to such risks. RBI also advised banks to offer 'doorstep' banking services to their customers only with the prior approval of their boards and in accordance with the guidelines issued by the RBI. They are also advised to review the operation of doorstep banking by its board on a half yearly basis, during the first year of its operation and subsequently on an annual basis.

4.11 Bill Payments

Over the last few years, the banking sector witnessed a proliferation in the use of IT based delivery channels and internet banking activity. Some of the new facilities provided are funds transfer options, utility bill payments and other regular periodical payment facilities and integration with e-commerce transactions such as bookings for rail and air tickets. With electronic banking, customers now in a position to deal with banks and get many of their requests serviced through desktop computers, telephones and Automated Teller Machines of banks.

Payment of utility bill and other regular periodical payment facilities is a novel technique adopted by banks since 1994 to attract new customers and to retain their existing customers. Under this system, the bank facilitates the speedy and instant payment of utility bills of customers of electricity, water, telephone, mobile phone, insurance premium, tuition and hostel fees of wards etc. For availing this facility, a customer is required to register with the bank branch or its ATM for the payment of utility bills and insurance premium.

4.12 Demat Accounts

Banks undertake to purchase and sell shares and debentures of joint stock companies on behalf of its customers. Only members of the stock exchange can do the function of purchase and sale of securities. The amendment in the stock exchange regulations Act permits the banks to become members in the stock exchange.

Internet banking provides banks with an opportunity to enter the world of e- broking, made possible by the SEBIs approval of internet trading in stocks. Internet banking account, electronically records holdings of dematerialized shares. An e-investment account for equity trading enables trading in shares on the internet. In internet banking payments and share transfers are handled automatically and seamlessly without separate paper work.

In January 1998 Securities and Exchange Board of India initiated Demat Accounts system to regulate and improve stock investing. This is done through Depository Participants (DP) with National Securities Depositories Ltd., (NSDL) as the co-coordinator. The investor opens an account called Demat Accounts with the depository participants. These depositories transact business through electronic media. They get shares in electronic form. Then they send the actual sales to the investor. The banker should strictly follow the customer's instructions, use skill, and care in execution of sale and purchase of order. When the customer gives an order for purchase of securities, the banker should ensure that sufficient funds are available in the account of the customer. The investor has to pay charges for opening and maintaining of demat account. There are certain advantages and benefits in this system, which are the following. There is less paper work, no loss of share certificates, any bad deliveries and lower transaction costs. It facilitates the banks in enlarging the non-interest income and their overall profitability.

A few banks provide the customer the facility through internet to enquire into his demats account holding details, transaction details and status of instructions given by him. These web sites still do not allow online transactions for their customers. SBI has launched an online trading facility eZ@ sbi. Account, in partnership with Motilal Oswal Securities in the year 2006.

4.13 Computerisation in Banks

Modernization of banking operations by introducing new technological devices and computerization received special emphasis in order to promote competitiveness and efficiency of banks. The development and use of communication networks have helped the banking industry to ensure improved banking services to customers.

Technological changes have entered Indian banks well before the nationalization of major banks in 1969. But the banks introduced the mechanization\automation only in selected operations and in a very slowly manner. Computers were nowhere in picture at that time. The most important developments through computerization came following the recommendations of the Rangarajan Committee. The Rangarajan Committee was appointed in July 1983 to review the scope of mechanization in banks and to draw up a roadmap for mechanization especially computerization. The committee made an in depth study of the problems and after a thorough study spanning more than a year, the recommendations came at the end of 1984. The Rangarajan Committee recommended mechanization in a phased manner at all levels viz. Branch, Zonal, and Regional office level. After the recommendations of the Rangarajan Committee, a high-level committee headed by Executive Director Mr. Ratnagar, was constituted to implement the programme of computerization.

Based on the recommendations of the Rangarajan Committee an agreement was signed in October 1993 between Indian Banks Association (IBA) and Union of Bank Employees regarding computerization in banks. In the bipartite settlement, the IBA specifically laid down that there should not be any retrenchment consequent to computerization. Further, jobs for which mechanization was to be introduced should be specified.

As per the above agreement, 4,523 branches of public sector banks were eligible for partial or full computerization as on 30 June 1996. Public sector banks also installed 9659 Advanced Ledger Posting Machines in 3099 branches, 377 mini computers at regional\zonal office levels and mainframe computers in 15 banks.

Even after the settlement of 1996, there was no smooth, sailing for the management in the field of introduction of technological changes especially computerization. It remained a cause of disagreement between the unions and the management.

The high power Committee headed by Executive Director of RBI Shri. W.S. Saraf and representatives from banks, Government nominees, research, academic and educational institutions to study and evaluate technological problems recommended immediate computerization in banks.

Even though public sector banks were late entrants in respect of computerization of branches, of late it has been given great importance by these banks. Further as per directions of the Central Vigilance Commission (CVC) public sector banks were required to conduct seventy per cent of their business in branches through computerization before January 1, 2001. Figures at the end of March 2001 indicate that 23 banks have achieved the target, while two banks have computerization levels ranging between 60 and 70 per cent and two others were at a level below 60 per cent. In contrast, the new generation private and some old private sector banks have already achieved high levels of automation. Since all public sector banks have already crossed the 70 per cent level of computerization of their business in 2003, the Central Vigilance Commission advised the banks to achieve 100 per cent computerization.

It is now recognized that computerization of operations of Branches, Controlling Offices and the Head Offices is the only way by which senior managements in banks can drawn information on the size of operations of branches located at different places on a daily basis. To achieve this objective banks are now implementing Core Banking Solutions (CBS), which is gaining popularity in recent times. The Core Banking Solutions (CBS) provides a host of benefits such as anywhere banking and access quick funds movement at minimal costs and that too in an efficient manner. While new private sector banks, foreign banks and a few old private sector banks have already put in place core banking solutions, public sector banks are adopting increasingly similar systems.

Under the core banking system, banks provide web-server and the requisite software, which is connected to the main server. The entire system software, data for the entire bank etc. are stored in a centralized server with its host standby server being placed at a different location and connected through high speed and efficient network. Branches are provided online nodes to receive requests from customers and to provide them services across the counter. The nodes provided at remote branches are connected through effective satellite links with enough redundancy to provide reliability as well as adequate bandwidth. Once the required hardware and software are set in, the customers can access the web-server for their basic banking operations using any standard browser at any location.

Progress in computerization of branches of public sector banks was given in Table 4.3.

Table 4.3 portrays the level of computerization of the branches of public sector banks during the last two years ending 31, March 2006. The table reveals that public sector banks have achieved tremendous progress in computerizing their branches and are moving rapidly to achieve 100 per cent computerization.

Table 4.3: Computerisation in Public Sector Banks

S. No.	Computerisation in Public Sector Banks	As on March 31, 2005 (Per cent)	As on March 31, 2006 (Per cent)
1.	Branches already Fully Computerised #	60.0	48.5
2.	Branches Under Core Banking Solutions	11.0	28.9
3.	Fully Computerised Branches (1+2)	71.0	77.5
4.	Partially Computerised Branches	21.8	18.2

#: Other than branches under Core Banking Solutions.

As on March 31, 2006, public sector banks crossed the level of 77.5 per cent computerization of their business, where as the corresponding percentage on March 2005 were only 71. The number of branches providing Core Banking Solutions has also increased significantly from 11.0 per cent as on March 31, 2005 to 28.9 per cent as on March 31, 2006. The number of branches partially which got computerized decreased from 21.8 per cent to 18.2 per cent during the last two-year period.

Table 4.4 discloses the extent of computerization in public sector banks as on March 31, 2006.

Table reveals that at the end of March 2006 out of 27 public sector banks, branches of 10 public sector banks were 100 per cent computerised and in five banks more than 90 per cent of their branches were computerized. Table further reveals that 22 Public Sector Banks had more than 50 per cent computerised branches and only five banks had less than 50 per cent computerised branches.

Table 4.4: Extent of Computerisation in Public Sector Banks (as on March 31, 2006)

Extent of Computerisation (in percentages)	Number of Banks*
Nil	-
Up to 10 per cent	1
More than 10 and up to 20 per cent	-
More than 20 and up to 30 per cent	2
More than 30 and up to 40 per cent	2
More than 40 and up to 50 per cent	-
More than 50 and up to 60 per cent	3
More than 60 and up to 70 per cent	2
More than 70 and up to 80 per cent	2
More than 80 and up to 90 per cent	-
More than 90 and less than 100 per cent	5
Fully Computerised	10
Total	27

*excludes IDBI Ltd.

The percentage of fully computerized branches to total branches at the end of March 2006 were as low as in the case of Punjab and Sind Bank (9.6 per cent) followed by United Bank of India (26.6 per cent), UCO Bank (27.5 per cent), Union Bank of India (33.3 per cent) and Syndicate Bank (35.0 per cent).

In Nationalized, Banks 68.5 per cent of the branches are fully computerized and 25.4 per cent partially computerized. Fully computerized public sector banks are Andhra Bank, Bank of Baroda, Corporation Bank and State Bank of India and its six subsidiaries. Computerization is nearing completion in Vijaya Bank (99.9 per cent), Dena Bank (99.4 per cent), Punjab National Bank (97.6 per cent) and Bank of India (96.6 per cent).

At the end of March 2006, the branches of SBI and its Seven Subsidiaries got fully computerized with the exception of State Bank of Indore where the rate of computerization is only 98.4 per cent. However, in State Bank of Indore all the computerized branches (98.4 per cent) are connected to CBS. Whereas in State Bank of India and State Bank of Mysore with 100 per cent computerization provide Core Banking Solutions only at 29.8 per cent and 23.9 per cent of its branches.

Between September 1999 and March 2006, public sector banks incurred an expenditure of Rs. 10,676 crore on computerization and development of communication networks.

5

On-line and Phone Banking

5.1 Internet Banking: Introduction

Banks have traditionally been in the forefront in making use of technology to update their products, services and efficiency. They began using electronic and telecommunication networks for delivering a wide range of value added products and services for a long time. With the popularity of personal computers, easy and better access to internet and world wide web (www) it is being used increasingly by banks as a channel for receiving instructions and delivering their products and services to their customers.

Internet banking also called on-line banking is nothing more than traditional banking services delivered through an electronic communication device viz. the internet. It demolishes the traditional geographical barriers and thus reaches out to customers across the world. It is an efficient and cost effective delivery mechanism for banking services. Through internet banking, banks are in a position to offer extensive range of products and services of varied content and sophistication.

Economic integration within and across countries, deregulation, advances in telecommunications, and the growth of the internet and wireless communication technologies are changing dramatically the structure and content of financial services. Internet banking is a product of e-commerce in the field of banking and financial services. Internet banking enables customers to open accounts, pay bills, know account balances, forward loan applications, calculate interest, view and print copies of cheques and deposits, transfer funds, stop payments, recording of stop-payment instructions, reorder cheque books and statements and receive banking industry news, send and receive messages to and from the bank through e-mail and other forms of traditional banking services. Different banks have different levels of such services offered, starting from level-1 where only information is disseminated through Internet to level-3 where online transactions are put through.

A number of banks have set up banking portals, which enables their customers to access facilities like eliciting information, querying on their accounts etc. Banks now view with one another to introduce newer and larger products and services to their customers. Broadly, the levels of banking services offered through internet can be categorized in to three types:

First Level: Basic Level Service: Under this system of internet banking, the website of the banks bulge with information about many products and services offered to customers and members of the public in general. It also receives and replies to customers' queries through e-mail.

Second Level: Simple Transactional Websites: The second level Simple Transactional Websites, allow customers to submit their instructions, applications for different services, queries on their account balances etc. They do not permit any fund-based transactions on their accounts,

Third Level: Fully Transactional Websites: Internet banking services are offered by Fully Transactional Websites which allow the customers to operate on their accounts for transfer of funds, payment of different bills, subscribing to other products of the bank and to transact purchase and sale of securities, etc. These forms of Internet banking services are offered by traditional banks, as an additional method of serving the customer or by new banks which deliver banking services primarily through internet or other electronic delivery channels as value added services.

5.2 Working Group on Internet Banking

In order to promote safety and reliability of e-banking activities, the Reserve Bank of India constituted a Working Group to examine the different issues relating to internet banking. The Group was headed by Shri S.R. Mittal, Chief General Manager in Charge of the Department of Information Technology, RBI and comprised experts from the fields of banking regulation and supervision, commercial banking, law and technology.

The Working Group examined in detail various issues of internet banking and gave its recommendations favouring an appropriate internet banking system. It examined different aspects of internet banking viz. legal, regulatory, security, technology, supervisory and operational with particular reference to the following:

- Risks to the organization and the banking system by way of Internet banking.
- Identifying gaps in supervisory and legal framework with reference to the existing banking and financial regulations, IT regulations, tax laws, depositors and consumer protection, criminal laws, money laundering and other cross border issues and suggesting improvements for their adoption and application.
- Recommending minimum technology and security standards, in conformity with international standards and addressing issues like system vulnerability, digital signature, information system audit etc.
- Clearing and settlement arrangement for electronic banking and electronic money transfer; linkages between i-banking and e-commerce.
- Any other matter, which the Working Group may think as relevant to Internet banking.

In its report, the Working Group has classified the internet banking products into three types, based on the levels of access granted, which are as follows:

5.2.1 Information only Systems: General purpose information like interest rates, branch locations, ATM locations, product features, loan and deposit calculations etc., are provided on the bank's website, with facilities for downloading various types of application forms. The communication is normally carried on through e-mail. There is no interaction between the bank's application systems and the customer. No identification or authentication of customers is done. In this case, the possibility of any hacking or an unauthorised person getting access to the protection system of the bank through the internet will be minimized.

5.2.2 Electronic Information Transfer System: These systems provide customer-specific information in the form of account balances, transaction details, statement of accounts, etc. The information is mainly in the 'read only' format. Identification and authentication of the customer is through a password. The information is drawn from the bank's application systems either in batch mode or off-line. In this case also, the application system is not be directly accessed through the internet.

5.2.3 Fully Electronic Transactional System: These systems have transactional capabilities of a bi-directional nature. The customers for on-line update can forward transactions. They require a high degree of security and control. In such an environment, web server and the application systems are linked over secure infrastructure, which comprise the basic requirements in terms of technology covering computerization, networking and security; inter-bank payment gateway and legal infrastructure for introduction of internet banking with a fully Electronic Transactional System in India.

5.3 Types of Risks Associated with Internet Banking

Even though internet banking is a highly cost effective channel for delivery of banking services, it is not free from risks. Apart from reduction in cost of transactions, internet banking also brought about a new set of risks, that too in new forms. Regulators and supervisors all over the world are aware of different types of risks in internet banking. An important and distinctive feature of internet banking is that here technology plays a significant part as a source and tool for control of risks. Because of faster and speedier information technology, there is no finality either in the types of risks or measures to control them. Very often, they evolve continuously. Some of the risks in internet banking are the following:

5.3.1 Operational Risk (Transactional risk): Operational risk is the most common form of risk associated with internet banking. It takes the form of inaccurate processing of transactions, non-enforceability of contracts, compromises in data system integrity, privacy and confidentiality, unauthorized access/ intrusion in to bank's systems and transactions.

This type of risks arise out of weaknesses in design, inadequacies in technology, implementation and monitoring of banks' information system, human factors like negligence by customers and employees, fraudulent activity of employees etc.

5.3.2 Security Risk: Security risk which happens because of unauthorized access to a bank's critical information stores like accounting system, risk management system, portfolio management system, etc. A breach of security will result in direct financial loss to the bank.

This type of risks arises because of unauthorized access by both outsiders and insiders to the system. They include unauthorised access to the system through back doors, brute force and hijacking, sniffing or spoofing, to retrieve and use confidential customer information and by inserting virus that can disrupt services and affect integrity of information. Employees expose banks to security risk from internal sources like fraud. Spreading inaccurate information about bank products, a virus-disturbing bank's system and thereby causing system and data integrity problems. Employees being familiar with different systems and their weaknesses become potential security threats in a loosely controlled environment. They manage to acquire the authentication data in order to access the customer accounts causing losses to the bank viz. add customer assets, subtract customer liabilities, or interrupt operation etc. It may result in loss of data, theft of or tampering with customer information, disabling of a significant portion of bank's internal computer system by denial of services.

Thus, access control is of paramount importance. Controlling access to banks' system has become more complex in the internet environment which is a public domain and attempts for unauthorized access can emanate from any source and from anywhere in the world with or without criminal intent.

Data privacy and confidentiality issues are relevant even when data is not being transferred over the net. Data residing in web servers or even banks' internal systems are susceptible to corruption if not properly isolated through firewalls from Internet.

5.3.3 Reputational Risk: Reputational risk arises due to loss of reputation or confidence of customers of the bank with respect to banks services and products marketed through internet. Reputational risk is considerably high in electronic banking than in traditional brick and mortar banking. Such situation may lead to customer discontinuing their use of product or service of the bank. Main reasons for this risk is the product not working to the satisfaction and expectations of the customers, significant system deficiencies, significant security breach (both due to internal and external attack), inadequate information furnished to customers about product use and problem resolution procedures, significant snags in communication networks that obstruct customers' access to their funds or account information particularly when there are no alternative means to access accounts.

5.3.4 Legal Risk: Legal risk also arises in electronic banking by way of violation of, or non-conformance with laws, rules, regulations, or prescribed practices, or when the legal rights and obligations of parties to a transaction are not well documented. Internet banking is relatively a new area where, the rights and obligations in some cases are uncertain and applicability of such laws and rules is uncertain or ambiguous, thus causing legal risk. Other reasons for legal risks are uncertainty about the validity of some agreements formed via electronic media and law regarding customer disclosures and privacy protection. A customer, who is inadequately informed about his rights and obligations, may not take proper precautions in using Internet banking products or services, leading to disputed transactions and unwanted litigations against the bank or other regulatory agencies.

5.3.5 Money Laundering Risk: As Internet banking transactions are conducted remotely banks often, find it difficult to follow traditional methods for detecting and thereby preventing undesirable criminal activities. Application of money laundering rules may also be inappropriate for some forms of electronic payments. Thus, a bank gets exposed to the money laundering risk. This may result in the legal sanctions against banks for non-compliance with "know your customer" laws.

5.3.6 Cross Border Risks: Internet banking by its very nature is technology based and oriented. It is designed to extend the geographic reach of banks and their customers. Such market expansion can transcend national borders involving risks of various kinds.

It includes legal and regulatory risks like uncertainty about legal requirements in some countries and jurisdiction ambiguities with regard to the responsibilities of their national authorities. Such considerations expose banks to legal risks associated with non-compliance of different national laws and regulations, including consumer protection laws, record-keeping and reporting requirements, privacy rules and money laundering laws.

5.3.7 Strategic Risk: This risk happens when a new product or service is introduced by a bank. The degree of this risk depends upon how well the institution has addressed the various issues related to development of a business plan, availability of required resources to support this plan, credibility of the vendor (if outsourced) and level of the technology used in relation to prevalent technology etc.

5.3.8 Other Risks: Traditional banking risks like credit, liquidity, interest rate and market risk are also inherent in Internet banking. These risks get intensified because of the very nature of Internet banking and because of the use of electronic channels for transactions and absence of geographical limits. However, their practical consequences are of a different magnitude for banks and their supervisors when compared to operational, reputational and legal risks. This is particularly true in the case of banks, which engage in a variety banking activities when compared to banks, or bank subsidiaries that specialize in internet banking.

A. Credit Risk: Credit risk occurs when a party does not settle an obligation for full value, either when it is due or later.

Banks may not be able to correctly appraise the credit worthiness of the customer at the time of extending credit through remote banking procedures, which heighten the credit risk. At present, banks generally deal with familiar customer base. Facility of electronic bill payment in Internet banking causes credit risk when a third party intermediary fails to carry out its obligations with regard to payment. Proper evaluation of the creditworthiness of a customer and audit of lending process are indispensable. Yet another facility of Internet banking is electronic money. Various types of risks are associated with it when a bank purchases e-money from an issuer in order to resell it to a customer; it exposes itself to credit risk when the issuer defaults on him\her obligation to redeem electronic money.

B. Liquidity Risk: Liquidity Risk arises out of a bank's inability to meet its obligations when they are due and without incurring unacceptable losses. But the bank will ultimately meet its obligations. For a bank engaged in electronic money transfer activities it is important that it ensure that funds are adequate to cover redemption and settlement demands at any particular time. Failure to do so will expose the bank to liquidity risk and lead to legal action and risking the banking regulations.

C. Interest Rate Risk: Similarly banks dealing with electronic money face interest rate risk because of adverse movements in interest rates causing decrease in the value of assets relative to outstanding electronic money liabilities. Banks also face market risk because of losses in on-and-off balance sheet positions arising out of movements in market prices including foreign exchange rates. Banks accepting payment in foreign currency for electronic money are offered subject to this type of risk.

D. Risk of unfair competition: Internet banking is likely to intensify the competition among various banks. The open nature of internet may induce a few banks to use unfair practices to outsmart their rivals. Any leaks in network connection or operating system etc., may allow them to interfere in a rival bank's system.

Thus, it can be found that along with the benefits, internet banking carries with it various risks for individual banks in particular and the banking system in general. The rapid pace of technological innovation is likely to change the nature and scope of risks, which banks face. There must be a balance between risks and benefits. Supervisory and regulatory authorities are required to develop methods of identification of and new risks, assessing, managing and controlling exposure to risks. However, authorities have to bear in mind that the development and use of Internet banking are still in its infancy or in their early stages, and policies that hamper useful innovation and experimentation should be avoided. Thus, authorities have to encourage banks to develop a risk management process, which is rigorous and comprehensive enough to deal with known risks, and flexible enough to adjust to changes in the type and intensity of the risks.

5.4 Recommendations of the Working Group on Internet Banking

The recommendations cover the risks associated with internet banking, the technology and security standards for internet banking, legal issues involved in this new type of activity and the regulatory and supervisory concerns of the central bank. The recommendations of the Group are given below:

5.4.1 Security Organization: Organizations should make their security plan explicit and document it. There should be a separate Security Officer/Group dealing exclusively with information on systems security. While the Information Technology Division implements the computer systems, the Computer Security Officer will deal with its security and the Information Systems Auditor will audit it.

5.4.2 Access Control: Logical access controls should be maintained on data, systems, application software, utilities, telecommunication lines, libraries, system software, etc. Logical access control techniques should include user-ids, passwords, smart cards and other biometric technologies.

5.4.3 Firewalls: At the minimum, banks should use the proxy server type of firewall so that there is no direct connection between the Internet and the bank's system. It facilitates a high level of control and in-depth monitoring using logging and auditing tools. For sensitive systems, a stateful inspection firewall is recommended to thoroughly inspect all packets of information and to compare both past and present transactions. These generally include a real-time security alert.

5.4.4 Isolation of Dial up Services: All the systems supporting dial up services through modem on the same LAN as the application server should be isolated to prevent intrusions into the network and to bypass the proxy server.

5.4.5 Security Infrastructure: At present, PKI is the most preferred and used technology for safe Internet banking services. However, it is yet to become available commonly. Though it is recommended strongly for the transition period, until Institute for Development and Research in Banking Technology (IDRBT) or Government puts it in, the following options are recommended for its adoption and use. Usage of SSL, which ensures server authentication and the use of client side certificates issued by the banks themselves using a Certificate Server. The use of at least 128-bit SSL for securing browser for web server communications and, in addition, encryption of sensitive data like passwords in transit within the enterprise.

5.4.6 Isolation of Application Servers: It is also recommended that all unnecessary services on the application server such as ftp, telnet should be discouraged. The application server should be isolated from the e-mail server.

5.4.7 Security Log (Audit Trail): All computer accesses, including messages received, should be logged. All computer access and security violations (suspected or attempted) should be reported and follow up action taken as the organization's policy.

5.4.8 Penetration Testing: The information security officer and the information system auditor should undertake periodic penetration tests of the system, which should include:

- Attempting to guess passwords using password-cracking tools.

- Search for back door traps in the programs.
- Attempt to overload the system using DDoS (Distributed Denial of Service) & DoS (Denial of Service) attacks.
- Check if commonly known holes in the software, especially the browser and the e-mail software exist.

The penetration testing may also be carried out by engaging outside experts (often called 'Ethical Hackers').

5.4.9 Physical Access Controls: Though generally overlooked, physical access controls should be strictly enforced. The physical security should cover all the information systems and sites where they are housed and have secured against both internal and external threats.

5.4.10 Back up and Recovery: The bank should have a proper infrastructure and schedules for backing up data. The backed-up data should be periodically tested to ensure recovery without loss of transactions in a time frame as given out in the bank's security policy. Business continuity should be ensured by having disaster recovery sites where backed-up data is stored. These facilities should also be tested periodically.

5.4.11 Monitoring Against Threats: The banks should acquire tools for monitoring systems and the networks against intrusions and attacks. These tools should be used regularly to avoid security breaches.

5.4.12 Education and Review: The banks should review their security infrastructure and security policies regularly and optimize them in the light of their own experiences and changing technologies. They should train their security personnel and their end-users on a continuous and consistent basis.

5.4.13 Log of Messages: The banking applications run by the bank should have proper record keeping facilities for legal purposes. It is necessary to keep all received and sent messages both in encrypted and decrypted form. (When stored in encrypted form, it becomes possible to decrypt the information for legal purpose by obtaining the keys with the consent of the owner.)

5.4.14 Certified Products: The banks should use only those security solutions/products which are properly certified for security and for record keeping by independent agencies (such as IDRBT).

5.4.15 Maintenance of Infrastructure: Security infrastructure should be properly tested before using the systems and applications for normal operations. The bank should upgrade the systems by installing patches released by developers to remove bugs and loopholes, and upgrade to newer versions which give better security and control.

5.4.16 Approval for Internet Banking: All banks having operations in India and which intend to offer Internet banking services to public must obtain prior approval for the same from RBI. The application for approval should clearly cover the systems and products that the bank plans to use as well as the security plans and infrastructure. RBI may call for various documents pertaining to security, reliability, availability, auditability, recoverability, and other important aspects of their services. RBI may provide model documents for Security Policy, Security Architecture, and Operations Manual.

5.4.17 Standing Committee: RBI may set up a standing Committee to monitor security policy issues and technologies, to review prescribed standards, and to make fresh recommendations on a regular basis.

5.5 Advantages of Net Banking

Costs of banking service through the Internet come to only a fraction of costs incurred in conventional methods. Rough estimates assume cost of teller at Re.1 per transaction, ATM transaction cost at 45 paisa, phone banking at 35 paisa, debit cards at 20 paisa and Internet banking at 10 paisa per transaction. The cost-conscious banks in the country have therefore actively considered and accepted use of the internet as a medium for providing services. Fully computerized banks, with better management of their customer base are in a better position to cross-sell their products through this channel.

Internet banking, both as a medium of delivery of banking services and as a strategic tool for business development, has gained wide acceptance internationally and is fast catching up in India with more and more banks entering the fray. India can be said to be on the threshold of a major banking revolution with the unleashing of net banking. At present, 22 banks in India provide internet-banking services at different levels, 11 banks propose to offer Internet banking in the near future and the remaining banks have no immediate plans to offer such facility. However, many scheduled commercial banks in India still remain in the initial stage of Internet banking operations.

Further incentives provided by banks would dissuade customers from visiting branches personally and thus get 'hooked' to the convenience of armchair banking. The facility of accessing their accounts from anywhere in the world by using a PC with internet connection is doubly fascinating to account holding Non-Resident Indians and high net worth Individuals in particular.

With gradual adoption of Information Technology, most banks maintain their own web sites that provide general information pertaining to the banks and its location, NRI and other services available e.g., loan and deposit products, application forms which can be downloaded and e-mail option for enquiries and feedback. It is largely a marketing or advertising tool. Customers are required to file and fill in applications on the Net and can also receive loans or other products requested for from their local branch.

A few banks allow customers to enquire into his demat account (securities/shares) holding details, transaction details and status of instructions given by him. These web sites still do not allow online transactions for their customers.

Some of the banks permit customers to interact and transact with them electronically. Such services include request for opening of accounts, requisition for cheque books, direction for stop payment of cheques, perusing and printing statements of accounts, inter account movement of funds within the same bank, querying on status of pending requests, instructions for opening of Letters of Credit and Bank Guarantees etc. Banks like ICICI

Bank Ltd., HDFC Bank Ltd. Citibank, UTI Bank Ltd., Federal Bank Ltd. etc have initiated these services. Recent entrants to Internet banking are Allahabad Bank, (for its corporate customers through its 'Allnet' service) and State Bank of India, which announced that it will provide such services soon. Certain banks like ICICI Bank Ltd., have gone a step further within the transactional stage of Internet banking by allowing transfer of funds by an account holder to any other account holder of the bank.

Some of the more aggressive players in this area such as ICICI Bank Ltd., HDFC Bank Ltd., UTI Bank Ltd., Citibank offer the facility of receipt, review and payment of bills on-line. These banks have tied up with a number of utility companies. The 'Infinity' service of ICICI Bank Ltd. also allows online real time shopping mall payments to be made by customers. HDFC Bank Ltd. has made e-shopping online and real time with the launch of its payment gateway. It has tied up with a number of portals to offer business-to-consumer (B2C) e-commerce transactions. HDFC bank carried out the first online real time e-commerce credit card transaction in the country on a visa card at the Easy3shoppe.com shopping mall.

Banks like ICICI Bank Ltd., HDFC Bank Ltd. etc. are thus positioning themselves as one-stop financial shops. These banks have tied up with computer training and manufacturing companies, Internet Services Providers and portals for expanding their Net banking services, and thus widen their customer base. ICICI Bank Ltd. has set up a web-based joint venture for on-line distribution of its retail banking products and services on the Internet, in collaboration with Satyam Infoway, a private ISP through a portal named as icicisify.com. The customer base of www.satyamonline.com portal is also available to the bank. Setting up of Internet kiosks and permeation through the cable television route to widen customer base are other priority areas in the agenda of the more aggressive players. Centurion Bank Ltd. has already taken up an equity stake in the teauction.com portal, with the aim of bringing together buyers, sellers, registered brokers, suppliers and associations in the tea market as an alternative for their physical presence at auctions.

Banks, which provide Internet banking services, enter into agreements with their customers and set out the terms and conditions of the services. These include information on the access through user-id and secret password, minimum balance and charges, authorization to the bank for carrying out transactions performed through the service, liability of the user and the bank, disclosure of personal information for statistical analysis and credit scoring also, non-transferability of the facility, notices and termination, etc.

5.6 Mobile Banking

Mobile banking is relatively a new form of electronic banking product and it is gaining ready acceptance from the customers. It has become one of the customer-friendly facilities, which can have far-reaching implications for the financial sector as a whole. It takes the bank to the customer's cell phone. Its communication facilities are of immense use to even an illiterate user. It is cost effective and assists the rural customers in reaching the customer and banker instantly.

On-line banking is now moving in to the mobile mode, giving everybody with a mobile phone access to real time banking services, irrespective of their location. In India banks with the facility of mobile banking, services at present provide only limited number services to their customers. The potential for mobile banking is endless with the scope for introduction of new services and products on a large scale.

With mobile banking, the concept of anywhere and proximate banking is at the fingertips of the customer literally. In this system, a customer can access his\her account details on a mobile phone by using the Short Messaging Service (SMS) technology through which select data is entered in to the mobile device. The wireless application protocol technology, which allow the user to surf the net on their mobiles to access anything and everything.

Customers can carry out a number of conventional

transactions by remaining in their office, or home, in fact from anywhere with a mobile phone. The following services are made available and accessible through mobile phone:

- Account balance- clear balance and total balance.
- Mobile alerts such as Debits and Credits to the account.
- Registered bill payment.
- Last few transactions statement (mini-statement).
- Request for cheque book
- Password change for mobile banking.
- Suspension of mobile banking services.
- Transfer of funds from one account to another etc.

5.6.1 Benefits of Mobile Banking: Mobile banking is certainly beneficial to the customers. It enables the customers to carry on certain routine business transactions without personally visiting the branch or ATM counters of a bank. Customers can make use of this facility from anywhere in India. When a customer comes to a branch for a routine transaction viz. checking a balance or for getting a cheque book, he has to wait for a while in the bank. Mobile banking is doubly beneficial to the customers i.e. by way of savings in both time and money. Another advantage of mobile banking to the customers is that they can avail reliable information in quickly and easy manner.

Mobile banking is advantageous to the banks also. Mobile banking reduces the number of visits of customers to bank branches and thereby reduces their physical presence. When there are no queues or no waiting of customers in the bank it brings down considerably the cost of banking for the customer over a period of time. The bank also benefits because mobile banking helps them to increase their productivity. It also enables banks to deliver speedy and quality services, which are ultimately beneficial to the banks by way of increasing and retaining their customer base. Thus, Mobile banking dissuades customers from visiting branches personally and they can instead 'hook' on to the convenience of armchair banking.

Customers can adopt any of the following methods of registration for mobile banking services.

A. Registration through ATM: A customer can register for mobile banking service through ATM by inserting the ATM card and by selecting the 'Other Services Menu', and thus select mobile banking registration option, by entering their mobile number and in return receive a receipt as acknowledgement of registration.

B. Direct Submission of Application Form: Application form for mobile banking services is available in most of the bank branches and their ATM counters. A customer has to fill up and submit the application form for mobile banking at any of the bank branches or drop in at an ATM.

C. Opt for On-line Registration: A customer can also register for mobile banking service online. Click on to the web site and Select the mobile banking registration option by submitting the details of the customer.

The mobile will be activated by the bank for mobile banking after 48 hours from the time of registration through any of the above options. Bankers charge a nominal fee per quarter as service charge for providing mobile services.

HDFC Bank is the first bank in India, which introduced mobile banking service in Mumbai, ICICI Bank and UTI Bank followed the lead given by the HDFC Bank. A good number of banks in our country have already started offering the mobile phone technology to extend banking facilities, which has become a convenient, economical and efficient way of transacting the banking business.

5.7 Telebanking

Telebanking is another innovative form of electronic banking introduced by banks through which banking services or products are rendered through telephone to its customers. A customer can access his\her account through the telephone at anytime or at any place throughout the country with the same Telebanking PIN they desire. Customers can carry on a number of transactions from their own home or office; in fact, from anywhere they have access to a phone and in a very convenient and comfortable manner. It is definitely one of the most convenient modes of transacting banking business.

Telebanking is offered by the banks through a technology known as Interactive Voice Response Service (IVRS). Basically this system, accept only 'tone' dialed input from callers telephones instruments and provides suitable voice response messages and information to the caller. Telebanking service is available 24 hours a day and 7days of a week. In other words, it provides "round the clock banking. The potential of Tele banking is limitless and it is often projected as a future potential growth area. Telebanking came into vogue in USA in the 1970s. Now many banks in India provide this facility to their customers to carry on their transactions with the banks.

To obtain account related information under Telebanking dial the BSNL\MTNL or any land line number, which is given by the banker to their customers for availing telebanking service. (1) Dial * (star) button on the telephone when directed by the bank (after their welcome message). (2) Select language of choice. (3) Dial customers ID when directed. (4) Dial Telebanking PIN when directed. (6) Dial-1- To access customer account, Select the account form from the list of accounts they hear in the phone:

Then Dial as shown below:

(1) Current balance,

(2-1) Balance on a particular date,

(2-2) Previous few transactions,

(2-3) Statement for a particular period - by fax on same call\ on another number\ by e-mail (e-mail address) registered with the bank,

(2-4) Today's statement- by fax on same call\ on another number\by e-mail,

(3) Status of the cheque issued by the customer etc.

Besides delivering information relating to the customers account, banks also provide the following information under telebanking service.

1. Information on deposit interest rates,

2. Information on locations of Branches and ATM,
3. Receiving of following forms by fax or e-mail:

- *i c*onnect Registration and declaration form,
- Debit Card application form,
- Travel Currency Card Application form,
- Registration form for LIC Premium Payment through ATM,
- BSNL Bill Payment Registration form and
- Encash Declaration form.

5.8 Phone Banking

Under Phone banking, service a customer can talk to a Phone Banking Officer for transacting a banking business. It is generally provided to customers from Monday to Saturday (except on National Holidays). The number of days and working time for transacting banking business through Phone Banking vary in individual banks and their branches.

Under Phone Banking service, a customer can interact directly with a telephone-banking officer appointed by the bank. Under this scheme, a customer can obtain information about their accounts and can prefer their requirements before the telephone-banking officer. Following are the facilities available in a Phone Banking Service.

1. Balance and transaction in customers account.
2. Status of cheques issued or deposited by the customer and information relating to clearing.
3. Location at which cheque\ cash was deposited in the account.
4. Transactions at ATMs or merchant establishments.
5. Charges related to customers account.
6. Account statement by fax or e-mail or printed statement of account.
7. Status of Debit card swallowed \ captured in ATM and request for sending it to any branch for collecting it.
8. Requisition for cheque book.
9. Requisition for new PIN for Debit card or new password for internet banking.
10. Queries regarding non-receipt of cheque book, statement of

account, debit card PIN, welcome kit etc.

11. Internet banking, funds transfer facility, bill payment facility, mobile refill transactions, e-Broking and mobile banking.
12. Travel Currency Cards – Balance and Transactions.
13. Information about Demat account etc.

Apart from the account related requirements, a customer can also seek and get the following information from the Phone Banking Officer:

1. Products and services of banks with the facility for forwarding the customers requirements to the appropriate branch office of bank.
2. Deposit interest rates.
3. Locations of ATMs and branches.
4. Facilities for Non – Residents Accounts.
5. Travel Currency Cards.
6. Receiving the following forms by fax or e-mail; *i* Connect registration and declaration form, debit card application form, registration form for Life insurance premium payment through ATM, BSNL Bill payment registration form etc.

6

Payment and Settlement Systems in India

Introduction of reforms in the financial sector combined with globalization and liberalization measures and the emergence of new private sector and foreign banks have increased the level of competition in the banking business. Technology has also played a significant role in improving the efficiency of the banking industry in India. Technology is also recognized as an excellent tool for providing an exhaustive range of new products/services and extending banking facilities to the vast multitude of unbanked population.

Technology upgradation is taking place both in the Public and old private sector banks in a phased manner. New private sector and foreign banks are well equipped with the latest technology to meet challenges of global competition. The entry of new private sector banks and foreign banks has posed a challenge to the monopoly hitherto enjoyed by the nationalized banks. RBI took several initiatives with the broad objective of providing systems, which would be beneficial for the bank like efficient housekeeping, better customer service and overall systemic efficiency.

6.1 Clearing and Settlement Systems

Payment and settlement systems play a pivotal role in the development of an economy. Adoption of an efficient, modern and global electronic payment and settlement system beneficial to everyone viz. the customers, business undertakings, bankers, the government and to the economy as whole.

Electronic Payment and settlement systems are cheaper because they have lesser production cost than paper-based instruments. The clearing operation can also be carried out faster in comparison with paper-based transactions. The increased use of electronic payments will enhance the efficiency of the payment and settlement system. It helps the process of capital formation and money management.

The evolution of electronic payment system can be traced back to the 1950's, with the introduction of ERMA (Electronic Record Method of Accounting) and MICR (Magnetic Ink Character Recognition) based cheque-clearing systems in USA. Thus, these systems are considered as the initial innovations in the field of electronic clearing. Stanford Research Institute and Bank of America developed and introduced ERMA in 1951 for automation and recording of transactions in accounts. Several countries implemented these two systems in various forms and it remains as the backbone for payment systems. Later, many payment systems came into existence.

As part of restructuring of the banking sector, RBI has accorded special emphasis to improvements in payment and settlement systems. Prominent payment and settlement systems in India are Electronic Funds Transfer (EFT), National Electronic Funds Transfer System (NEFT), Special Electronic Fund Transfer (SEFT), Real Time Gross Settlement System (RTGS), MICR Cheque Clearing System, Magnetic Media Based Clearing System (MMBCS), Centralized Funds Management System (CFMS) and Cheque Truncation System (CTS). The SFMS would be the backbone for all message-based communication in the Indian Financial Network (INFINET).

Reserve Bank of India has initiated a number of steps in 1997-98, to improve the efficiency of the financial system by way of ensuring safe, secure and effective payment and settlement systems for the whole country. The work relating to the satellite-based Wide Area Network (WAN), to provide reliable communication framework for the financial sector commenced its operation by the end of 1998-99. The upgradation of cheque clearing activity in the banking industry and the existing cheque processing systems at the 4 National Clearing Centres (NCC) has also been taken up.

To facilitate banks to formulate their plans for implementing effective payment systems within their own area of activities, RBI published a 'Vision Document' in December 2001. The document summarized the vision of RBI in respect of payment and settlement systems for the immediate future and the medium term.

To strengthen further the payment and settlement system, RBI prepared another Vision Document or an action plan for three years from April 2005 to March 2008. It sets out the roadmap for implementation of the vision of the RBI for payment and settlement systems. The key themes of the action plans identified in the 'Vision Document' are Safety, Security, Soundness and Efficiency (Triple-S and E).

The vision document indicates the broad framework of the initiatives taken by the RBI and the approach adopted for time bound implementation of the various projects. The vision document is prepared in consultation and discussion with the officials of various banks, technology solution providers, members of the public and experts from the fields of banking and technology. The main action points for payment and settlement systems, 2005-08 as set out in the Vision Document are indicated below:

First Year: During the first year, *i.e.* 2005-06, the vision document envisaged the following;

- Persuade Indian Banks' Association and major banks for setting up of a national level entity, which will operate all retail payment systems in the country.
- Operationalising National Settlement System for all clearings at four metro centres by December 2005.
- Finalizing the proposed Electronic Funds Transfer (EFT) regulations.
- Implementing Stage-2 of RTGS System, *i.e.* Integrated Accounting System (IAS)-RTGS rollout during which all inter-bank transactions at all major centres would be settled on RTGS platform and paper-based inter-bank clearing will be closed.
- Take up with RTGS participants coverage of all their networked branches under RTGS framework paving way for

RTGS-based customer related transactions at about ten thousand branches in the country.

- Implementing image-based Cheque Truncation System (CTS) at the National Capital Region (NCR) on a pilot basis.
- Ensuring minimum standard of operational efficiency at MICR Cheque Processing Centre (CPC).
- Making available EFT facility at 500 capital market intensive centres identified by BSE and NSE.
- Setting up of Customer Facilitation Centre (CFC) at the Reserve Bank for various segments of national payment systems.
- Public disclosure by each payment service provider of its standards terms and conditions under which the payment will be effected and also compensation policy and procedure for any deficiency in services including the setting up of CFC.
- Drafting the Red Book on Payment Systems in India and
- Drafting a comprehensive legislation on payment system.

Second Year: During the second year, *i.e.*, 2006-07, it is envisaged to:

- Complete the tasks initiated during 2005-06.
- Extend MICR clearing to 20 identified additional centres.,
- Ensure that every cheque issued follows MICR format and standards.
- Implement EFT systems at the national level through a new retail payment institution.
- Make all payment systems in India compliant with the Core Principles for Systemically Important Payment Systems (SIPS).
- Increase the reach of payment services by means of tie-up and collaboration with other large coverage entities such as the post offices; and
- Facilitate government payments and receipts through electronic mode.

Third Year: During the third year *i.e.*, 2007-08. The vision will be for:

- Creating off-city back-up arrangements for large value

national payment systems such as RTGS and G-Sec Clearing.

- Making fully functional the new organization for retail payment systems bringing all such payments under its umbrella.
- Regulating various payment systems.
- Ensuring cheque truncation based clearing at Mumbai, Chennai and Kolkata.
- Making National Settlement System, cover all major clearing houses/clearing organizations in the country.

6.2 Electronic Fund Transfer (EFT)

Electronic Funds Transfer system (EFT) is one of the important electronic banking services offered by commercial banks to attract and retain their customers. Electronic funds transfer system is an easy and speedy mechanism to facilitate the transfer of funds from one place to another. Compared to all other existing systems of funds transfer, EFT is the most convenient system, which facilitates the instant transfer of funds from one end to the other.

Electronic Fund Transfer system enables the customers to transfer money instantly from one bank account to another one of the same or another customer, from one branch or the other of the same bank or a different bank not only within the country but also within anywhere else of the world through electronic message.

With the introduction of EFT system, the existing systems of funds transfer namely Cheques, Demand Drafts (DD), Mail Transfers (MT) and Telegraphic Transfers (TT) and Money Orders (MO) have lost their significance. These traditional systems of funds transfer have their own limitations. EFT system offers is advantageous to the banker as well as the customer.

EFT system enables the beneficiary to receive money on the same day or on the next day of money transfer. Because money is transferred instantly, EFT system minimizes the loss of interest as far as the customer is concerned. More over MT and TT systems does not facilitate the transfer of money from one bank branch to another branch of a different bank. EFT eliminates paper cheques and late payments. It also liberates the customer from worry and fear of theft or loss of money during transit.

It is also beneficial to the banks that it helps to reduce their cost of administration by around forty per cent. Electronic Fund transfer is a completely paperless transaction mechanism, which accelerated the speed of transfer or exchange of money.

The Electronic Fund Transfer system was introduced on the basis of the recommendations of the 'Saraf Committee' appointed by RBI on 'Technology Issues' in 1994. The scheme has been in operation since February 1996.

The Vasudevan Committee on "Technology Upgradation in the Banking Sector" submitted its report in July 1999. The Committee made wide-ranging recommendations based on which the Reserve Bank drew up an Action Plan for implementation of the recommendations. The committee recommended amendments to the Reserve Bank of India Act, 1934 and assign the regulatory and supervisory powers on payment and settlement systems to RBI. Simultaneously, the RBI was to pronounce a new legislation on Electronic Funds Transfer System to facilitate multiple payment system which was, to be set up for banks and financial institutions. The RBI and IBA should take up with the Department of Telecommunications (DoT) or other competent authorities to permit encryption of data files/messages transmitted through communication channels for facilitating easier access to remotely located branches to the INFINET network.

The EFT scheme for funds transfer, operated by the Reserve Bank is available in thirteen major cities in the country, as on September 30, 2001. The scheme was originally intended for small value transactions. The electronic funds transfer was extended during the year 2002, to 15 centres of the country viz. Ahmedabad, Bangalore, Bhopal, Bhubaneshwar, Chandigarh, Chennai, Guwahati, Hyderabad, Jaipur, Kanpur, Kolkata, Mumbai, Nagpur, New Delhi and Thiruvananthapuram. All banks and branches in these locations are mandatory participants. The maximum limit for any single transaction under the EFT, which was Rs. 5.00 lakh, was enhanced during the year to Rs. 2.00 crore.

Some banks for security reasons impose limit on the amount per transaction and per day transactions.

In order to encourage electronic funds transfer system, the processing charges for all the electronic funds transfer services have been waived till March 31, 2006. This is expected to give a fillip to the scheme, apart from making it an ideal means of funds settlement for the securities market, which has migrated, to the rolling settlement. The credit which was being accorded to the beneficiary's account on the second working day – using the T+0 or T+1 process cycle, has since been made to be completed on the same day and multiple settlements – at 12:00 noon, 2:00 p.m., and 4:00 p.m. have been introduced from January 2, 2002. Inward EFT is mandatory for all banks and outward EFT is optional. The facility is available for any customer. No sign up process is required and can be initiated by anyone. Once the transaction is uploaded to the RBI system and it is not returned, then the settlement is treated as final.

Substantial efforts are being made through the National Clearing Cells of the RBI to increase the scope, coverage and usage of both the Electronic Clearing Service (ECS) and EFT facilities. Few banks have integrated their funds transfer schemes with that of the RBI-EFT Scheme. In addition to the above, the EFT software has been integrated with Public Key Infrastructure (PKI) so as to provide for increased levels of security. Banks are encouraged to use the PKI by creating the required registration authority.

6.3 Special Electronic Fund Transfer (SEFT)

To provide for transfer of funds electronically across a large number of bank branches in the country as a forerunner to the nation-wide funds transfer system (NEFT), the Special Electronic Fund Transfer (SEFT) System was introduced from April 1, 2003. SEFT is a system with the settlement being centralized at Mumbai and providing for same day funds settlement with multiple settlements (three settlement Cycles per day) during the day. SEFT covers 2,312 branches of 29 banks situated in127 centres across the country. This scheme facilitated the introduction of the T+2-settlement system by the capital markets. While inward SEFT is mandatory for all banks outward, SEFT is optional.

In order to ensure that the benefits of electronic modes of funds transfer are available across almost all the locations of the country and to provide for transfer of messages relating to EFT in a safe and secure manner, it is proposed to commence a National EFT using the facilities available under the SFMS over the INFINET. This would result in EFT being available from any branch of a bank, which has connectivity to INFINET with the settlement-taking place in the books of account of the RBI at a single location.

In November 2005, banks were advised to develop appropriate delivery channels of electronic payment services using the payment systems developed by the Reserve Bank such as RTGS, ECS, Electronic Fund Transfer (EFT) and National Electronic Fund Transfer (NEFT) with no further delay. Banks, which fulfill the eligibility criteria for participation in RTGS, were invited to participate in the NEFT.

6.4 National Electronic Funds Transfer System (NEFT)

The Reserve Bank of India introduced a payment system called the "RBI National Electronic Funds Transfer System" which is referred as "NEFT. The operationalisation of the NEFT in November 2005 was a major step in the direction of setting up and operating a national level payment system. The NEFT is a secured network, which uses the Structured Financial Messaging Solution (SFMS) messaging format with Public Key Infrastructure (PKI) enabled digital signatures retail electronic payment system having a nation-wide network.

NEFT brings greater efficiency in the movement of funds and reduction in risks relating to the transfer of funds. All the SEFT clearing banks were advised to migrate to NEFT system by December 15, 2005. With the implementation of NEFT, the SEFT system was discontinued from February 2006.

6.4.1 Operational Guidelines of NEFT: Important

operational Guidelines to the Banks for the implementation of NEFT system are as follows.

1. Banks, which would like to participate in the scheme, have to obtain an approval from the RBI and only the branches authorized by participating banks can receive and send money under the scheme.
2. The parties to a fund transfer under NEFT system are the 'sending bank', the 'sending service centre', the 'NEFT clearing centre', the 'receiving service centre', and the 'beneficiary branch'.
3. A bank customer who is willing to avail of the remittance facilities offered by a sending bank shall submit an "NEFT Application Form" authorizing the bank to debit the sender's account and transfer funds to the beneficiary specified in the NEFT application form.
4. The sender's request for transfer of funds should contain no condition other than dates on which funds transfer process should be initiated.
5. The relationship between the customer and the sending bank will be based on an agreement executed by them.
6. NEFT transactions may be made for amounts inclusive of paisa component.
7. There is no upper value limit for putting through an individual NEFT transaction.
8. A transaction with the NEFT system will be said to have been initiated when the sending bank accepts a payment order issued by the sender by issuing a "receipt" indicating the date of initiating funds transfer operation.
9. A bank may reject a customer's request for funds transfer under the following circumstances;

- The customer has not placed funds at the disposal of the sending bank; or funds placed is not adequate to cover the sum to be remitted and the service charge, or
- Beneficiary details given in the NEFT application form are not adequate to identify beneficiary by the beneficiary bank.

10. The clearing settlement for NEFT takes place at RBI in four

batches, during the day i.e. at 9.30 a.m., 10.30 a.m. 12.00 noon, and 4.00 pm. The cut off time for final batch of settlement at RBI is 4.00 pm. Branches must complete the transactions in CBS at least 30 minutes before the final cut-off at RBI.

11. Branches must display at its premises prominently the cut – off time schedules up to which they will receive the NEFT Application Form from its customers for different settlements.
12. A payment order issued for execution shall become irrevocable when it is executed by the sending bank. Any revocation after the payment order is executed by the sending bank shall not be binding on any other party in the NEFT system.
13. No acknowledgements are envisaged under NEFT scheme.
14. If the beneficiary specified in the sender's payment order fails to get payment through the NEFT system for some valid reasons, the sender should informed immediately after the sending branch gets the returned NEFT.
15. After crediting the account of the beneficiary, the branch shall advise the beneficiary about payments made. The statement of account\pass book entry or any online messaging system shall indicate briefly the source of funds as well.
16. The sending branch should be responsible for the accuracy of the name of the beneficiary, the nature of account and account number of the beneficiary, the name of the beneficiary bank etc.
17. The sending branch should bear the liability for loss, if any, caused to any participant in the NEFT system on account of the acceptance by it of any revocation of a payment order after it has executed it.
18. The service charge for outward remittance is Rs. 1.50 per Rs. 1,000 or a part thereof subject to a minimum charge of Rs. 25 and a maximum of Rs. 1,500. For inward remittances Rs. 50 per remittance irrespective of the amount.

6.4.2 Rights and Obligations of Customers:

- The customer shall be responsible for the accuracy of the

particulars given in the payment order issued by him and shall be liable to compensate the bank for any loss arising on account of any error in his payment order.

- The customer shall be bound by any payment order executed by the Bank if the bank had executed the payment order in good faith and in compliance with the security procedure. Provided that the customer shall not be bound by any payment order by the bank if he proves that the payment order was not issued by him and that it was caused either by negligence or a fraudulent act of any employee of the bank.
- The customer shall ensure availability of funds in his account properly applicable to the payment order before the execution of the payment order by the bank. Where, however, the bank executes the payment order with out properly applicable funds being available in the customer' account the customer shall be bound to pay to the bank the amount debited to his account for which an NEFT was executed by the bank pursuant to his payment order, together with the charges including interest paying to the bank.
- Customer agrees that the payment order shall become irrevocable when it is executed by the bank.
- Customer agrees that any notice of revocation does not bind the bank unless it complies with the security procedure.
- Customer agrees that he should not be entitled to make any claim against any party in the RBI NEFT system except the bank.
- Customer agrees that in the event of any delay in the completion of the fund transfer or any loss on account of error in the execution of the funds transfer pursuant to a payment order, the bank's liability shall be limited to the extent of payment of interest at the Bank Rate for any period of delay in the case of delayed payment and refund of the amount together with interest at the Bank Rate up to the date of refund, in the event of loss on account of error, negligence or fraud on the part of any employee of the bank.
- Customer agrees that no special circumstances shall attach to

any payment order executed under the NEFT facility under this agreement and under no circumstances customer shall be entitled to claim any compensation in excess of that which is provided in clause (g) above, for any breach of contract or otherwise.

6.4.3 Rights and Obligations of the Bank: The Bank shall execute a payment order issued by the customer duly authenticated by him as verified by the security procedure, unless:

- The funds available in the account of the customer are not adequate or properly applicable to comply with the payment order and the customer has not made any other arrangement to meet the payment obligation.
- The payment order is incomplete or it is not issued in the agreed form.
- The payment order is attached with notice of any special circumstances.
- The bank has reason to believe that the payment order is issued to carry out an unlawful transaction.
- The payment order cannot be executed under the RBI NEFT system.
- No payment order issued by the customer shall be binding on the bank until the bank has accepted it.
- The bank shall upon execution of every payment order executed by it, be entitled to debit the designate account of the customer, the amount of the funds transferred together with charges payable thereon, whether or not the account has sufficient balance.
- If the funds transfer is not complete before of business of the third business day following NEFT the bank shall advise the same to the customer.
- The Bank shall issue to him a duly authenticated record of the transaction after completion of the funds transfer and also issue at the end of each month, a statement of account. The customer shall, within a period of 2 days from the date of receipt of the record of transaction or as the case may be, with in the period of ten days from the date of receipt of the

monthly statement report to the bank if any discrepancies in the execution of the payment order. The customer agrees that he shall not be entitled to dispute the correctness of the execution of the payment order or the amount debited to his account if he fails to report the discrepancy within the said period of days.

The credit which was being afforded to the beneficiary's account on the same or second working day – using the T+0 or T+1 process cycle with four settlement batches in a day, which is ideal for retail customers. A message, which is not returned unaffected before the next settlement day is treated to have been completed and credit afforded to the beneficiary's account by the beneficiary branch.

The NEFT scheme operated by the Reserve Bank of India for funds transfer is at present available in 3,800 branches of 24 banks across 100 locations in the country. The scheme had originally no restrictions in the transfer of amounts. However, banks impose certain restrictions in the number of transfer and amount transferred per day for reasons of security.

6.5 Electronic Clearing Services

Indian Banks are competing with one another to offer new products and services to their customers. Banking service and products in India witnessed transformation on a large scale in the last few years. Technology has played a significant role in facilitating the transformation in the banking sector. Electronic Clearing Services (ECS) is one of the new electronic banking services.

Electronic Clearing Service (ECS) is a non-paper based movement of funds, which is encouraged by the Reserve Bank of India on a wide scale. Indian banking sector has made a quantum leap forward in terms of switching over from paper-based transactions, like use of currency notes, cheques, drafts or challans, to electronic means, like Real Time Gross Settlement (RTGS), National Electronic Fund Transfer (NEFT) and other electronic modes.

In November 2005, banks were advised to develop appropriate delivery channels of electronic payment services using the payment systems developed by the Reserve Bank such as RTGS, ECS, EFT and NEFT with no further delay. Emphasis on widespread usage of Electronic Clearing Services (ECS) is being prescribed by the Reserve Bank of India to encourage non-paper based funds movement. The prime thrust areas forming part of this vital activity include the extension of ECS to more centres, inclusion of more customers under the ambit of the scheme and provision of a centralized facility for making payments. Electronic Clearing Service consists of:

- Electronic Credit Clearing Service and
- Electronic Debit Clearing Service

6.6 Electronic Credit Clearing

RBI introduced the Electronic Credit Clearing Services in April 1995. At the time of introduction, the facility was available only at National Clearing Centre Mumbai and Chennai and later it was extended to New Delhi and Kolkata. However, at present this facility is available across the country at 58 centres. All banks and branches in these locations are mandatory participants.

Electronic Credit Clearing Service is a reliable device used for bulk and repetitive credit-push payments such as salary, pension, dividend, commission, IPO refunds, interest etc. ECS facility is largely utilized by the public and private limited companies and Government departments, which makes bulk and recurring payments. Electronic Credit Clearing Services brings down administration cost and ensures more profitability and productivity to the bank.

Organizations, which desire to make bulk payments frequently to a large number of beneficiaries, can avail the ECS facility by registering for it with their bank. The bank will forward a copy of the registration form to RBI after allotting a register number. Institutions availing this facility have to prepare the credit instructions on the magnetic media and submit the same to RBI, through their bankers. Bank would present the payment data for clearing through its local service branch. Clearing house debits its account and credit the account of the banks where the beneficiaries of the transactions maintain their accounts. RBI process the data arrived at inter-bank settlement and provide bank and branch wise reports containing the details of payments to facilitate fast payment to the beneficiaries. Dates to be fixed for bulk payments. The maximum limit for ECS credit clearing facility is limited to Rs. 5,00,000 and below. It is an electronic bulk transfer, using the values in T+3-process cycle.

In the Electronic Clearing System, the ECS credit volumes are much higher than the ECS debit volumes. In the year 2005-06, ECS credit had 442 lakh transactions amounting Rs. 32,324 crore. The ECS credit were higher than the ECS debit by 1.2 times in volume and 2.5 times in terms of value.

6.7 Electronic Debit Clearing

Electronic Debit clearing facility was initially introduced by the RBI at Chennai in August 1994 and at Mumbai in March 1996 and later was extended to New Delhi and Kolkata. At present, this facility is available at 43 centres across the country and all banks and branches in these locations are mandatory participants.

Electronic Debit Clearing service was introduced by RBI to facilitate the payment of credit-pull transactions such as payment of utility bills, insurance premium and repayment of loans installments. Under ECS debit clearing, customers authorize their bank to deduct directly from their account the amount of their utility bills such as telephone, electricity bill etc. and regular payments of insurance premium and installments of loan amount. Under this scheme, on receipt of the bill from the utility or service providing company the customer can approach his banker and authorize the bank branch to debit his account for the amount of the bill and transfer the amount to the bank account of the utility company. In this scheme, the branch has to prepare a floppy File through a table top MICR Reader of all such transfer advices and this floppy is received by the service branch, which would consolidate it for onward submission to the clearinghouse. The

RBI would debit the individual bank and credit the sponsor bank of the utility company. The system facilitates electronic transfer of bulk amounts using T+3-process cycle. Dates to be fixed in advance for bulk debits. Only after the cycle is complete, finality of the settlement would be known.

With effect from June 14, 2005, processing charges for all electronic transactions under EFT, SEFT and ECS facility amounting to Rs. 2 crore and above, were waived up to the period ended March 31, 2007. In terms of the guidelines issued on October 17, 2005, banks were advised to provide details to the customers in their Pass book/Account Statement regarding the credits affected through ECS.

In order to start a robust state-of-the-art nationwide ECS, both debit and credit, covering more branches and locations with centralized data submission system, Scheduled Commercial Banks (SCBs) including co-operative banks were advised to furnish information indicating their level of preparedness for the project as on June 27, 2006. To take the effort further, all SCBs were directed on July 4, 2006 to initiate steps for incorporating an appropriate mandate management routine for handling ECS (Debit) transactions.

In order to make available ECS at more centres, bank operated Cheque Processing Centres (CPCs) have been advised by the Reserve Bank to commence ECS operations at the earliest. Banks already operating ECS services were also advised to have a uniform two-day processing cycle at all the centres and also to adhere to the return clearing on the same day of the presentation.

In the Electronic Clearing System, the ECS debit volumes and values are lower than the ECS credit debit volumes and values. In the year 2005-06, ECS Debit had 359.58 lakh transactions amounting Rs.12,986 crore. However, the rate of growth of debit clearing was substantial in the year 2006, when compared to previous years.

6.8 MICR Cheque Clearing Facility

Magnetic Ink Character Recognition (MICR) technology is

used for automatic listing and sorting of cheques and arriving at a settlement position of the member banks. Before the introduction of MICR, technology cheques were cleared manually. MICR cheques were introduced with a view to automate the labour intensive business of clearing cheques and to facilitate to strengthen, and speed up the payment and settlement system in the economy.

Banks, which indent to avail the automated cheque clearing facility, would issue MICR cheques to their customers. MICR instruments are made of special quality paper and have a number of specifications, which the MICR equipment can read. The code line at the bottom of MICR cheques contains a lot of information, which are in the code line and are printed in magnetic ink enabling the machine to read it instantly. Following are the pieces of information in the MICR cheques: a) first six numbers indicate the cheque number, b) next three numbers each indicate city code, c) bank code, d) and branch code. Then after some space, there is the number for transaction code, viz. savings or current account.

The conversion or transaction period from a non-MICR based cheque system to MICR, based clearing usually takes two years because member banks continue to issue the available stock of non-MICR cheques. In order to speed up the MICR based clearing facility all over India RBI advised banks to issue MICR cheques irrespective of whether cheque clearing centres use MICR cheque format or not.

MICR based clearing system was initially introduced in USA in 1959. Different countries have implemented this system in various forms and it remains the main mode of payment systems in many of those countries. Even though, a lot of other, which are highly advanced systems, comes in to existence, MICR based payment system continue to be a prime payment option.

The first phase of mechanized cheque clearing using Magnetic Ink Character Recognition technology has been completed in June 1986 with the introduction of high-speed reader sorter system for processing local as well as inter city MICR cheques at the clearinghouse managed by Reserve Bank of India.

MICR cheque clearing facility has introduced by RBI initially in four Metropolitan cities namely Mumbai (1986), Chennai, New Delhi (1987) and Kolkata (1989). At the end of March 2006, MICR cheque clearing system is in operation at 60 cities across the country.

The progress in MICR based clearing system both in terms of volume and value for the last three years are given in Table 6.1.

Table 6.1: Progress in MICR based Cheque Clearing (2002-06)

Year	Count (lakh)	Value (Rs. crore)
2002-03	5980	1,09,78,762
2003-04	6241 (4.4)	91,78,751 (-16.4)
2004-05	9726 (55.8)	96,18,065 (4.8)
2005-06	10331 (6.2)	94,72,367 (-1.51)
Percentage of Value in Total Cheque Clearing (2005-06)	75.45	82.85

Figures in brackets indicate percentage of change over the previous year.

Table 6.1 depicts the physical cheque clearing volumes and value in MICR centres during a period of four years from 2002 to 2006. The percentage of increase in volume was 55.8 in 2004-05, whereas the corresponding percentage for the year 2005-06 was only 6.2. The value of cheque clearing in MICR centres also shows a decline in 2005-06. In 2005-06, the value of cheque clearing shows a decline of 1.51 per cent over the previous year. During the year ending March 31, 2006, total clearing turnover under MICR facility covers about 75 per cent in terms of volume and 83 per cent in value of the total clearing in the country. The declining trend in the MICR clearing centres can be attributed to:

- Inter bank settlement happens now only on RTGS,
- High value cheque clearing is slowly being phased out and
- EFT\ECS are prominently available in MICR clearing locations and the customers in these locations are shifting to

electronic payment modes.

In order to ensure the smooth operations of the MICR cheque processing, RBI framed a Minimum Standards of Operational Efficiency for the MICR cheque processing centres. The standards mainly relate to encoding of instruments, time schedule, operational procedures, speed and accuracy of On-Line Reject Repair (OLRR), checking of settlement reports for supervisory signals, enabling banks to download reports/data on-line, reconciliation and business continuity plan. The MICR cheque processing centres have to submit a self-assessment report-certifying adherence to the minimum standards ensuring operational efficiency to the Reserve Bank.

6.9 Magnetic Media Based Clearing System (MMBCS)

RBI introduced magnetic Media Based Clearing System (MMBCS) with the goal of improving the efficiency and speed of the paper-based system of clearing. Even though the rate of growth in cheque volumes has decelerated over the last few years, cheque clearing still continues to be the largest mode of settlement in terms of the volume of processing.

For further improving the efficiency of the paper-based system, a plan has been drawn up by the Reserve Bank for computerization of clearing operations at centres where there are more than 30 banks apart from the 60 centres where magnetic ink character recognition (MICR) cheque processing centres have already been set up.

Magnetic Media Based Clearing System (MMBCS) is a clearing system in which the member banks present their claims in the form of an electronic file, which gets processed on the computer. This enables arriving of settlement figures within a quarter of an hour as compared with three or four hours under the manual system.

6.10 Cheque Truncation System (CTS)

The Reserve Bank of India took several measures periodically to develop and improve the efficiency of the payment and settlement system in the country. The implementation of Cheque Truncation System (CTS) is yet another effort from the side of RBI for improving the efficiency of paper-based clearing systems.

The Working Group appointed by RBI under the Chairmanship of Dr. R. B. Barman on "Cheque Truncation and e-cheques" recommended Cheque Truncation System (CTS) at the presenting bank. Under CTS, paper instruments do not travel beyond the presenting bank. The system would entail the physical cheques being truncated within the presenting bank to derive maximum efficiency. It is up to banks to take a decision on the point of truncating the cheque – at the branch or service branch or gateway level. Electronic images would be used for payment processing. Grey Scale technology for image capture would be used for imaging.

The CTS enables banks to handle the payment instruments in an easier way. Customers also enjoy the benefit of encashing their cheques faster. Apart from reduction in transaction costs, for banks as well as customers, the full implementation of CTS would make it possible, to achieve T+1 clearing cycle as CTS is straight-through processing and automated payment processing enabled system. Moreover, with CTS, banks also have the additional advantage of getting reduced their reconciliation problems and incidents of clearing frauds. In order to ensure that banks gear up with the desired infrastructure well in time, detailed guidelines were issued to banks regarding the hardware communication requirements.

The preservation period of paper instruments would be one year and that of the electronic images would be eight years. Settlement will be generated based on the current structure of the MICR fields. A Centralized Agency per clearing location would act as an image warehouse for the banks. Minimum entry norms recommended for Warehouse Agency are technical competency, efficiency orientation and size of resources.

This system was introduced on a pilot project basis in the national capital region of Delhi by the end of December 2006. RBI in its 2005-08 'vision document' on the payment and settlement system, ensured the extension of Cheque Truncation Based Clearing immediately to Mumbai, Chennai and Kolkata and the rest of the country in a phased manner.

6.11 Real Time Gross Settlement (RTGS)

The smooth functioning of the payment and settlement system is a pre-requisite for the financial stability of an economy. RBI constituted a National Payments Council (NPC) in May 1999, with Deputy Governor Shri S.P. Talwar as the Chairman with a broad representation from commercial banks and other financial sectors. NPC was constituted with the objective of providing perspectives and recommendations on broad policy issues to help design, develop and maintain an integrated and robust payment and settlement system for the country. Of the different policy decisions, which were taken by the NPC, the most important decision was the one to introduce Real Time Gross Settlement (RTGS) System.

For giving vital importance to the payment and settlement system, Reserve Bank of India constituted an apex body called Board for Regulation and Supervision of Payment and Settlement Systems (BPSS) in March 2005. BPSS is entrusted with the task of giving policy directions in the area of payment and settlement systems. One of the important policy directions given by the Board for Regulation and Supervision of Payment and Settlement Systems was setting a target for using the RTGS system. Other directions were publishing the charges levied by banks for electronic payment systems; setting up of an umbrella organization for all retail payment systems in the country; and preparing the Electronic Funds Transfer Regulations under the Reserve Bank of India Act.

Reserve Bank of India introduced Real time Gross Settlement (RTGS) System with a view to enhance the efficiency of the cheque clearing system. The Real Time Gross Settlement System was implemented by the Reserve Bank of India after a comprehensive audit and review of the software and also by conducting extensive training of users at commercial banks on

March 26, 2004. The Real Time Gross Settlement system is being designed to provide large value funds transfer and settlement in an on-line real time environment to the banking industry, with settlement on a gross basis. An integral component of the Real Time Gross Settlement system will be the Delivery versus Payment module for trading and settlement in Government Securities transactions. The system would have link with other netting systems like Clearing, Automated Clearing House transactions comprising of Electronic Clearing Service, Retail Electronic Funds Transfer, all Plastic Money and Smart Card transactions and Electronic Funds Transfer at Point of Sale (EFTPOS).

RTGS is an electronic based settlement of inter-bank and customer based transactions, with intra-day collateralized liquidity support from the Reserve Bank to the participants of the system. The RTGS system has also enabled banks to opt for straight through processing (STP) of customer transactions without manual intervention.

The RTGS System will be fully integrated with the Accounting System of the Reserve Bank and other settlement services such as Deferred Net Settlement Systems, (DNS) the settlement of which will be performed as RTGS transactions through a facility for Multi Lateral Net Settlement batch processing.

The RTGS System has several unique features. It is a single, all-India system, with the settlement being effected in Mumbai. The payments are settled though a transaction-by-transaction method. The settlement of funds is final and irrevocable. The settlement is done in near real time (maximum of 2 to 4 hours); the funds settled can be further used immediately. When required it will be available only through specific time window during the day. The RTGS system will have no restrictions on the amount to be settled. It is a fully secure system, which uses digital signatures and PKI based encryption, for safe and secure message transmission. It provides for intra-day collateralized liquidity support for the member banks to smoothen the temporary mismatches of fund flows and thereby ensuring smooth settlements.

Under the RTGS System, inter-bank transactions, customer based inter-bank transactions and net clearing transactions can be settled. Both high value and retail payments can be effected through the RTGS system. Thus, it provides less risk-based funds transfers for both banks and for their customers, apart from providing for more efficient funds management at the treasuries of banks.

RTGS system which was initially started (March 26, 2004) with four banks, besides the Reserve Bank, as participants, at present has 109 direct participants (the Reserve Bank, 94 scheduled banks and 14 Primary Dealers) of which 84 banks are offering RTGS based customer services from more than 11,280 branches in 508 towns/cities across the country. The target is to have RTGS based customer services in 15,000 bank branches by March 2006. As against this, RTGS payment services were offered only by 51 banks through their 1,451 branches located in 152 cities and towns on November 19, 2004.

Performance of the RTGS based settlement system for the last three financial years are given in Table 6.2.

Table 6.2: Growth in RTGS based Settlement (2003-06)

Year	RTGS-Count (in lakh)	RTGS-Amount (Rs. crore)
2003-04	0.001	1,965.49
2004-05	4.600	40,66,183.91
2005-06	17.670	1,15,40,835.84
Percentage of Growth in 2005-06	384.13	183.82
Percentage of Share in Various Payment Systems in 2005-06	0.129	50.23

Table 6.2 reveals that RTGS scheme introduced in the year March 2004, has shown a spectacular growth both in terms of

volume and in value. In a short span of three years, it has been in existence, it has bypassed the cheque based clearing volume in terms of amounts. The growth of RTGS ahs been prominent in the year 2005-06 compared to 2004-04. Its count grew by 384 per cent and volume by 183 per cent. Table further reveals that RTGS constitute about 50 per cent of the overall payment volumes in the year 2005-06. It is clear from the table that RTGS will emerge as the principal payment system in India for wholesale payment.

With the implementation of RTGS, the paper-based Inter-Bank Clearing had been discontinued in a phased manner beginning with the closure of inter-bank clearing at Mumbai in November 2004. The inter-bank paper-based clearing was terminated in eleven centres from June 2005. High Value Clearing available to both wholesale and retail customers, based on Deferred Net Settlement (DNS) system, would be phased out slowly and should be transferred to RTGS. All RTGS member banks have now been settling their inter-bank transactions only through RTGS. Non-RTGS member banks have been asked to make use of the electronic platform as customers of some RTGS participants.

6.12 Clearing Corporation of India Limited (CCIL)

Recognizing the greater impetus ascribed towards payment and settlement systems, a clearing corporation known as Clearing Corporation of India Ltd. (CCIL) was established in April 2001 for clearing and settlement of government securities and foreign exchange transactions. It was promoted by SBI (chief promoter) and co-promoted by Bank of Baroda, HDFC Bank, ICICI, IDBI, and LIC in April 2001 with an authorised and paid-up capital of Rs. 50 crore.

SBI subscribed Rs. 13 crore as share capital of the corporation representing 26 per cent in the equity. Bank of Baroda and HDFC Bank have subscribed a share capital of Rs. 2.5 crore each. Central Bank of India subscribed Rs. 2 crore in the equity of CCIL, one crore rupees were subscribed by Punjab National Bank and Oriental Bank of Commerce and Rs. 50 lakh each by

Citibank, Bank of India, Canara Bank, Corporation Bank and Union Bank of India. Other banks, financial institutions, primary dealers and mutual funds contribute Balance equity.

Clearing Corporation of India which was set up by banks is the Central Counter Party (CCP) for clearing of transactions in Government securities and foreign exchange. The CCIL operates the G-Sec clearing while the settlement for both the securities and funds takes place in the Reserve Bank. CCIL acts as the CCP for all the transactions, guarantees both the securities, and funds legs of the transaction. Dv PIII mode of settlement has been adopted, whereby both the securities leg and the fund leg are settled on a net basis. CCIL guarantees settlement of trades on the settlement date by acting as a central counter party to every trade through the process of novation. Another large value segment operated by the CCIL is the forex clearing. Every eligible foreign exchange contract entered into between members, gets novated and is replaced by two new contracts between CCIL and each of the two parties, respectively. The rupee leg is settled through the member's current account with the Reserve Bank and the USD leg through CCIL account with the designated settlement bank at New York. The settlement through CCIL has reduced the gross dollar requirement by more than 90 per cent.

7

Credit Information Bureau Services

7.1 Credit Information Bureau

The financial sector is becoming more complex and the Non-Performing Assets (NPAs) have become the most critical factor affecting the performance of banks. NPAs have various implications on profitability, liquidity and solvency of the banks. The level of NPAs of a bank is considered as an indication of its asset quality and in turns its performance and rating. The financial sector reforms of 1991 brought about several measures for the reduction of NPAs. The Narasimham Committee fixed a target for bringing the gross NPA level of banks to the international standard of three per cent by the year 2002.

It became very urgent to thwart the accumulation of fresh NPAs in the banking sector through an efficient system of credit information on borrowers as a first step towards risk management. The development of an efficient credit information system is considered as crucial for the development of a sound financial system. The Credit Information Bureau (CIB) is expected to speed up credit and investment decisions by banks and financial institutions, and a CIB provides an institutional mechanism for sharing credit information on borrowers and potential borrowers among banks and FIs. It acts as a facilitator for credit dispensation and helps to mitigate the credit risk involved in lending and curb the accumulation of fresh NPAs.

Credit Information Bureau is a company registered under the Indian Companies Act 1956, to collect credit information related to customers of banks, financial institutions or other authorities and maintain data on such information and also for the provision to disseminate such information on request to the specified users of the Bureaus, with a view to facilitate efficient distribution of credit and matters connected therewith and incidental thereto.

Credit Institutions includes Commercial banks, Regional Rural Bank, Co-operative banks, Financial institutions, Non-banking financial companies, Export Credit Guarantee Corporation of India Ltd., and such other Lending Institutions as may be specified by the Reserve Bank in its direction issued as per this Act.

7.2 Credit Information Bureaus: International Scenario

Credit Information Bureaus were set up in well developed financial economies like. USA, UK, Australia, New Zealand, France, Germany and Belgium and have been functioning for many years in all these countries. CIBs have also been in operation even in many less developed economies like Sri Lanka, Mexico, Bangladesh and Philippines. But in our country the proposal for setting up a CIB was put forward only at the end of nineties.

An analysis of the organizational set up of Credit Information Bureaus in foreign countries, reveals that there is no uniformity in their number, ownership and operational aspects. Countries like USA, UK, New Zealand, Sri Lanka and Philippines have separate Credit Information Bureaus for collecting information on individual borrowers and corporate borrowers. For example in USA 'Equifax' and 'Trans Union' collect and maintain credit information on the retail sector and bureaus like The 'Dun and Bradstreet' (D&B) on the corporate sector. In some other countries there is no separate CIBs for collecting the credit information on individual borrowers and the corporate sectors and in some others CIBs were established as a separate division of the Central Bank of the country which is publicly owned. In USA, UK, Australia and New Zealand, credit information bureaus were operating under the private ownership.

The biggest privately owned Credit Information Bureaus in the world are 'Dun & Bradstreet', 'Equifax' and 'Experian'. 'Dun & Bradstreet' (D & B), headquartered in USA and they operate through 217 offices. It has a credit information data base on about 53 million business establishments. D&B generates 6,70,000 data updates per day. 'Dun & Bradstreet' has set up bureaus, in partnership with Trans Union, in Canada, Mexico, Spain, Hong Kong and South Africa.

'Equifax' based in USA, serves the financial services, retail credit card and telecommunications sectors. Equifax provide the following services:

- consumer and commercial credit information.
- fraud detection and prevention services.
- card marketing services.
- account acquisition services.
- mortgage information.
- out sourcing of collection services.
- authentication of buyers and sellers.
- issuance and management of digital certificates and directories.

Equifax is a leading provider of consumer and commercial information in USA, Canada, UK, Spain, Portugal, Brazil, Argentina, Peru, Columbia, El Salvador and Mexico Equifax has 13,000 employees on its roll and operates in 18 countries. It has sales of US$ 1.70 billion and a data base of 400 million consumers and businesses around the world. 'Experian' is the largest Credit Information Bureau in the UK handling approximately two thirds of all credit enquiries there.

In some countries the operation of CIB is not limited to a single institution and in some other countries there is only a single bureau which operates for the collection of credit information. 'Experian' is the leading credit referencing agency in UK, and there are also a good number of smaller bureaus formed through private initiatives. In New Zealand, several companies are providing credit information services and most of them are under private ownership. These private companies supply credit reports on individuals and corporate borrowers. 'Baycorp' is the leading company in New Zealand. In Australia, while 'Credit Reference Ltd'. provides information on small and medium-sized businesses, 'Dun and Bradstreet' (Australia) provides commercial credit information on big corporates.

In several countries CIBs were set up under the direct ownership and control of the Central Bank of the country. The CIB of France is under the ownership of Banque de France, which collects monthly credit information from banks pertaining to the corporate lending. In Belgium, credit information offices, set up as divisions of the central bank, which collect information on default in installment payments, consumer credit, mortgage agreements, leasing and corporate borrowings. Banks and financial services institutions in Germany are required to notify the details of those borrowers whose indebtedness exceeds DM 3 million during the three preceding calendar months of the reporting date.

7.3 Development of Credit Information Bureau in Asian Countries

The CIB in Sri Lanka was set up in 1990 by an Act passed in Parliament incorporating the directives of the Central Bank of the country (Credit Information Bureau of Sri Lanka Act). The equity pattern of the CIB in Sri Lanka reveals that 51 per cent of the issued share capital of the Bureau was held by the Monetary Board, 30 per cent by commercial banks and the remaining 19 per cent by other lending institutions. In Bangladesh also the CIB was formed as a division of the Central Bank. The CIB in Bangladesh collects credit information from commercial banks about their corporate customers. It also provide to commercial banks credit information on their request.

The CIB in Philippines was established in 1982 by the Central Bank, jointly with the Securities and Exchange Commission and the Financial Executives Institute. The CIB in Philippines provides information on both corporate and individual customers. The CIB collects from commercial banks on a monthly basis information on all corporate borrowers who have availed facilities exceeding Taka ten lakh (INR = 1.15 BDTK) and furnishes on demand to any commercial bank a CIB report. The information is updated monthly on customers with facility above Taka 100 lakh and quarterly on customers with facility above

Taka 10 lakh. The database consists of over 50,000 files. The Individual Report provides information on the individual's identity, background, business affiliations, assets, financial standing and negative records. The database consists of 1,50,000 individual records.

7.4 Credit Information Services in India: A Historical Perspective

The amendment of the Reserve Bank of India Act 1934 is considered to be the first step towards the introduction of credit information services in the country. The RBI Act of 1934 was amended in the year 1962, by inserting Chapter III A and by amending Section 45C. Section 45C of the Reserve Bank of India Act, 1934 provides that the Bank may, at any time, direct any banking company to submit to it such statements relating to such credit information and in such form and within such time as may be specified by the Bank from time to time and that the banking company shall be bound to comply with any direction issued in relation thereto.

Credit information has been defined in sub-section (c) of Section 45 A as relating to:

- The amounts and the nature of loans or advances and other credit facilities granted by a Credit Institution to their borrower or class of borrowers as the case may be.
- The nature of security secured by a Credit Institution from its borrower or class of borrowers, as the case may be for credit facilities granted to him or to such class.
- The guarantee or any other non-fund based facility furnished by a Credit Institution for any of its constituent or any class of constituents.
- The means, antecedents, history of financial transactions and the credit worthiness of any borrower or class of borrowers of a Credit Institution.
- Any such information which the Reserve Bank in its opinion may consider as relevant to be included in the data to be collected and maintained by the Credit Information Bureau

and specified in its directions issued periodically for the purposes of this Act.

The Reserve Bank of India introduced a Credit Information Scheme in the year in 1962. Through the amendment of the Act, the Reserve Bank is empowered to collect credit information of borrowers on banks and financial institutions on a half yearly basis. Under this scheme banks and notified financial institutions are enforced to submit complete details of borrowers of whose secured credit limit aggregates Rs. 5 lakh and above and unsecured credit limits Rs. 1 lakh and above. The details to be submitted are name of the borrower, amount of credit sanctioned, credit disbursed, securities provided, period of credit, outstanding credit and its overdue etc. The cut-off limits for collection of information under the scheme were later revised to Rs. 10 lakh and Rs. 5 lakh respectively for secured and unsecured advances.

The information was pooled on a borrower-wise basis and furnished to banks and institutions which sought it, without disclosing the names of the banks which submitted such information to the Reserve Bank. The law provides that the information so furnished shall be treated as confidential and shall not be used for any other purpose other than specified. Likewise, the information collected by the Bank can be published if it is considered necessary in public interest to do so and only in a consolidated form, without disclosing the names of any banking company or its borrowers. Hence, the exchange of such information among bankers has, not served the purpose for which it was intended. As a result, the process of exchange of information among banks has been reduced to a mere formality which one has to observe while processing the loan applications.

In the case of corporate customers, some attempts have been made to collect and codify information and make them available to other lenders. The Investment Research and Information Services Ltd., (IRIS), Mumbai, brings out the 'Investor's Guide to Indian Corporates' incorporating half-yearly results of the companies selected on the basis of such criteria as, market capitalization, total sales, etc. The booklet published by IRIS, apart from giving industry review, provides tit bits on business performance of the company based on broad parameters like cash flow analysis, balance sheet data, raw material consumption, capital structure, etc. Although the booklet provides information on the credit rating obtained by the companies, it does not, however, provide information on borrowings of the company from various sources which will facilitate the intending lending institution to from a view on further dealings with the corporate.

In accordance with the Budget Speech of the then Finance Minister on February 28, 1994, the Reserve Bank of India put forward a scheme for collection and dissemination of information of non-payment accounts from banks and notified financial institutions. Under this scheme banks and all financial institutions were directed to submit the details of defaulting borrowers on floppy diskettes to the RBI. The names and details of defaulting borrowers above a thresh hold will be circulated among banks and financial institutions. Reserve Bank of India would also publish a list of defaulting borrowers in cases where suits have been filed by banks and financial institutions. Based on the information submitted under the above schemes, RBI has been publishing bank- wise lists of suit-filed accounts of Rs. 1 crore and above and suit-filed accounts of willful defaulters of Rs. 25 lakh and above as on March 31 every year which are also put on the website of RBI. Quarterly update of suit-filed accounts of Rs. 1 crore and above is also put on the above website.

In the present set up, information on defaulted customers is collected from all public sector banks, private sector banks, foreign banks operating in India and 10 notified all India Financial Institutions viz., ICICI, IDBI, IFCI, IIBI, EXIM Bank, NHB, UTI, LIC, SIDBI and GIC.

In the present set up the RBI collects detailed information about defaulting customers of banks and specified institutions at particular intervals. The RBI collects the details of borrowers of the following categories.

Category I: Where the outstanding of a borrower aggregate Rs. one crore or above and be classified as doubtful or lost. The institutions are required to submit the details of defaulted borrowers at half yearly intervals ending March 31 and September 30 and the due dates for submission were 15th of April and October every year.

Category II: All suit filed accounts of Rs. one crore and above. The details of the second category of borrowers must be informed at yearly interval ending March 31, every year and the due date is April 15.

Category III: Banks and financial institutions are requested to update the suit filed accounts showing additions to and deletion from the list. Under this category, institutions must submit information at quarterly intervals ending June, September, December, and March. The information must be submitted with in a period of 15 days from the due date.

7.4.1 Collection and Dissemination of Information on Cases of Willful Default: This Scheme was introduced in February 1999. Banks and notified all India Financial Institutions (FIs) were advised to report to Reserve Bank of India the cases of wilful default of Rs. 25 lakh and above on a quarterly basis with effect from the quarter ended June 30, 1999. Reserve Bank of India had advised the banks and other notified FIs that wilful default will broadly cover the following:

- Deliberate non-payment of the dues despite adequate cash flow and good net worth.
- Assets financed have either not been purchased or have been sold and proceeds have been misutilised.
- Misrepresentation/falsification of records.
- Disposal/removal of securities without bank's knowledge.
- Fraudulent transaction by the borrower.

The cases of wilful default will be reported to the RBI on a quarterly basis.

7.5 Setting Up of Credit Information Bureau in India

The RBI constituted a Working Group in June 1999, under the chairmanship of Shri N.H. Siddiqui, to explore the possibilities of setting up a full-fledged "Credit Information

Bureau" in our country. The working Group consisted of representatives from select public sector banks, IDBI, ICICI, Indian Banks' Association and Reserve Bank of India. The Working Group held detailed discussions and sought the views of Chairmen of banks, financial institutions and experts in the field of banking regarding modalities and the need for setting up a credit information bureau. The Chairmen of various banks got convinced of the need and importance of a credit information bureau in the country. They unanimously opined that the establishment of a credit information bureau would help in reducing the growth of NPAs in the banking system.

The Working Group submitted its report in November 1999. After wide discussions, the Group arrived at a conclusion that there was an urgent imperative need for setting up a Credit Information Bureau in the country. The Group opined that under the existing legal framework, it would not be possible to set up a world class Credit Information Bureau in our country. The law permits the banks to supply financial information of a borrower to outside agencies only with the explicit consent of the party or only when where the lending institution has filed suits. Hence, formation of a Credit Information Bureau under the present legal set up, will not accomplish its full purpose. The recommendation of the Working Group was for a complete modification or suitable amendments of the existing banking regulations Act.

However, the group suggested that pending the amendment of the Act, a honest beginning could be made by setting up a Credit Information Bureau which can operate initially by pooling the limited information under the existing legal framework and share such information among its members. The scope of the proposed Credit Information Bureau (CIB) under the present set up is thus limited to suit filed accounts and those cases where the borrowers have given consent for disclosure.

Based on an examination of the various aspects of bureaus at international level, the group stated that there was no uniformity in the number of bureaus and operational aspects. The Group also examined the ownership pattern of bureaus in different countries and assessed various options of setting up of the bureau in the private sector like setting it either as a fully owned subsidiary of the RBI or jointly with other banks, or permitting a group of banks and financial institutions to set up a bureau as a statutory body or as a division of the central banks etc.

The Group is of the view that in spite of the provisions contained in Chapter III A of the RBI Act, 1934 enabling to collect credit information from banking companies and furnish such information to any banking company, it would not be desirable to establish Credit Information Bureau within the Reserve Bank. During the course of discussions with experts, the Group arrived at a unanimous conclusion that the Reserve Bank should not take the lead role in the setting up of the Bureau either as a major promoter or as a participant in the equity share capital of the Bureau. The Group also opined that if the Bureau was established under an Act of Parliament, it would lead to the establishment of one single statutory corporation, closing the door for other private initiatives. The Group is of the view that the legislation enacted for the purpose should provide for establishing Bureaus to cater to the needs of different market segments and covering the large geographical area of the country.

The Group took in to consideration the interest of some of the leading public sector banks such as, SBI and institutions like DFHI and IBA which were keen to set up a Credit Information Bureau, they taking the lead role as a promoter with equity participation from its member banks. Accordingly, the Group concluded that the role of the Reserve Bank should be that of a facilitator and instrumental in putting in place an appropriate legal framework for the Bureau.

The Group suggested that the proposed Credit Information Bureau would function as a separate company registered with RBI, under the provisions of the Companies Act of 1956. The proposed company would have equity participation of banks and financial institutions and non banking finance companies. The proposed company can obtain foreign expertise by co-opting a foreign technology partner or a collaborator. An appropriate legal framework be put in place to provide adequate protection to the Bureau as also the credit institutions sharing information with the Bureau. The Bureau should inherit the best international practices with regard to collection of information, processing of data and sharing of information and it should build up an effective system to ensure the secrecy of data maintained by it and restrict access to its data base to institutions accredited by it and evolve an appropriate mechanism to ensure the same. The Bureau should collect and share credit information on corporate consumer and retail segments.

The Group proposed that in order to enhance the efficiency of its operation, the Credit Information Bureau should resort to state of the art information technology solutions as and when the need arises for the same. Likewise, the Credit Information Bureau should also follow automated data collection method and telecommunication solutions. On-line updating of data and information enquiry will be preferable. The software needed for the Bureau should be capable of creating and maintaining a credible, reliable and accessible database. It should guarantee reliability of data with adequate features for validation and security. The Credit Information Bureau should build up through a reputed service provider, an appropriate technology platform to ensure it effective functioning. The technology partner should preferably be one of the reputed international bureaus, which is well experienced in using information and communication technology pertaining to the area of credit information collection and dissemination. The selection of hardware also needs to be decided in consultation with the technology partner. The central server of the Bureau may be positioned at Mumbai or any other convenient location in India. Operational connectivity could be established through a Wide Area Network (WAN) with major financial centres in the country.

The Group recommended that the Bureau should be a technology-driven and professionally managed company and it should develop into an institution of excellence for which it should be capable of speedy processing, periodic updating and have error-free data at all times in the system. It should not function in a bureaucratic style and manner but should basically be a commercial organization. The equity participants of the Bureau should not be allowed to interfere in the day-to-day operations of the Bureau. A strong market research group could be organized in the initial or second stage of its operation, which will collect information on industry profiles, major economic trends, market information including the business/investment plans of individual corporate, etc. The Bureau would require a high degree of professional skills in data management, financial analysis and information technology. Therefore, care should be taken by the Bureau during selection process to ensure that a suitable professional with the requisite qualifications is selected for the post. The foreign collaborator could meet the training requirements for the staff.

The source of income of the Bureau consists of membership fee, annual renewal fees and charges levied for enquiry by member organizations such as banks and financial institutions. International experience shows that such a Bureau took one to two years for getting itself established and it would break even only after 3 years.

On the basis of the report submitted by the Working Group, the Government of India realized the importance and need for a separate institutional arrangement to obtain and share data on borrowers in a systematic manner for sound credit decisions. The Union Government in its 2000-01 Budget announced the establishment of a Credit Information Bureau.

On the basis of the recommendations of the Working Group in its report to explore the possibilities of setting up a Credit Information Bureau, the RBI in its Monetary and Credit Policy (2000-2001), announced the setting up of the Credit Information Bureau in India. With a view to developing an institutional mechanism for sharing and dissemination of credit information on borrowers/ potential borrowers a Credit Information Bureau (India) Ltd. (CIBIL) was set up in August 2000. Subsequently, in the Monetary and Credit Policy of April 2000, the Reserve Bank advised banks and financial institutions to make the necessary in-house arrangement for transmission of required information to the Bureau.

Under this institutional mechanism a scheme has been put in place to collect and disseminate, amongst banks/notified all- India FIs, the details about borrowers of banks and FIs with outstanding aggregating to Rs. 1 crore and above which are classified as 'doubtful' or 'loss' or where suits have been filed. The list of borrowal accounts against which banks and FIs have filed suits for recovery of their dues aggregating to Rs. 1 crore and above as on March 31, 2001 is available on the Reserve Bank website. Information on cases of willful default with outstanding balance of Rs. 25 lakh and above up to the quarter ended March 31, 2001, has also been furnished to the banks and notified all India FIs. The list of wilful defaulters of Rs. 25 lakh and above against whom suits have been filed is published along with the list of suit filed accounts of Rs. 1 crore and above and is also available on the RBI website.

7.6 Legal Obligation of Banks and FIs

Under the present set up RBI will not be held responsible for any false information supplied by banks and financial institutions about their customers. The RBI reproduces only the information furnished by the banks. Under Section 45 B of the Reserve Bank of India Act, 1934, the banks and FIs should ensure that while furnishing the information they are to discharge their statutory duty by way of ensuring the accuracy of the data furnished to the Reserve Bank of India. The banks and FIs concerned would be held responsible for any leakage of the information to any of its constituents or any outside agency. Any disclosure of the information contained in the floppy diskette to any outside agency except with the prior permission of the Bank or under the compulsion by a Court of Law or authority having powers of a Civil Court for summoning and examining any person on oath, requiring discovery and production of documents and receiving evidence on affidavit, would attract penal provisions contained in

Section 58 B (4) and (6).

7.7 Credit Information Bureau (India) Ltd. (CIBIL)

The State Bank of India (SBI) has entered into a Memorandum of Understanding (MOU) with the Housing Development Finance Corporation (HDFC), with M/s. Dun and Bradstreet Information Services (India) Pvt. Ltd. and Trans Union International Inc. USA as foreign collaborate, to set up a Credit Information Bureau (CIB) within the existing provisions of the legislation. The modalities for setting up of the Bureau and its ownership, equity participation, management composition, rights and liabilities are being worked out. Banks and financial institutions were advised to make necessary in-house arrangements for gathering and collection of such information and transmitting it to the Bureau as and when it was established.

State Bank of India set up the Credit Information Bureau (India) Ltd., (CIBIL) in association with HDFC in January 2001, with an authorised capital of Rs. 50 crore and a paid up capital of Rs. 25 crore, with equity participation of 40 per cent each. The two foreign technology partners have an equity participation of 20 per cent. The CIBIL was to be technology driven to ensure speedy processing, periodic updating and availability of error-free data at all times. CIBIL's technical partners have already commenced their preliminary work relating to customization of software based on the information furnished by some banks.

Pending the enactment of CiB Regulation Bill, a Working Group was constituted in December 2001, under the Chairmanship of Shri S.R. Iyer, to examine the possibility of the CIB performing the role of collecting and disseminating information on suit-filed accounts and the list of defaulters, including the willful defaulters and the feasibility of dissemination of on-line information to members.

The Working Group submitted its Report in January 2002 and its recommendations which accord with the existing legal framework are being implemented by the RBI. The Working Group which examined the legal, technical and other aspects of collection and dissemination of information and the extent, periodicity, coverage and feasibility of supplying such information on-line to members.

The RBI issued directives regarding credit information to banks and financial institutions on October 1, 2002, and February 10, 2003. Under the directives, banks and financial institutions are required to obtain the consent of their eligible borrowers regarding the supply of credit information and dissemination in case of failure to repay the loan. The CIBIL which was established in 2001 began functioning from March 2003, by collecting details of suit filed accounts of customers of banks and notified financial institutions. The data on suit filed accounts is available on the website of CIBIL'. The RBI directed banks and financial institutions to take immediate steps for the submission of data relating to credit information of borrowers to the CIBIL. Reserve Bank also advised the Director Boards of the banks and financial institution to ensure the supply of necessary information to the CIBIL and a progress report to the Reserve Bank at specified intervals.

Based on the recommendations of the above Working Group, banks and FIs have been directed under Section 35 A of the Banking Regulation Act, 1949 that they should submit the list of suit-filed accounts of Rs. 1 crore and above as on March 31, 2002 and quarterly updates thereof till December 2002 and suit-filed accounts of wilful defaulters of Rs. 25 lakh and above at the end of March, June, September and December 2002 to the RBI as well as to the CIBIL for a period of one year till March 31, 2003. Thereafter, the aforesaid information should be submitted only to CIBIL and not to the RBI.

Banks and notified FIs would, however, continue to submit the data relating to non suit-filed accounts of Rs.1 crore and above, classified as doubtful and loss, as on March 31 and September 30 and also quarterly list of wilful defaulters (Rs.25 lakh and above) where suits have not been filed only to RBI as hitherto. Thus, the statement on non suit-filed accounts need not be sent by banks/FIs to CIBIL.

The Reserve Bank of India drafted a legal amendment regarding collection, processing and sharing of credit information on the borrowers of the banks and also the rights, responsibilities, obligations and safeguarding of privacy rights of the members of credit institutions. The drafted amendments were submitted to the Government for approval on May 2001. The Bill was passed by the Rajya Sabha and the Lok Sabha in May 2005 and received the assent of the President in June 2005. The role of CIBIL in dissemination of credit information was clarified. CIBIL should move towards a sufficiently diversified ownership structure with no single entity owning more than 10 per cent of its paid-up capital. The Bill empowers CIBIL to collect information of all borrowers and confers upon the Reserve Bank the power to determine policy in relation to functioning of credit information companies.

As announced in the Annual Policy Statement for the year 2004-05, the Credit Information Bureau of India Limited (CIBIL) was advised to work out a mechanism, in consultation with the Reserve Bank, Small Industries Development Bank of India (SIDBI) and Indian Banks Association (IBA), for development of a system of proper credit records to enable the banks to determine appropriate pricing of loans to Small and Medium Enterprises (SME). CIBIL is currently in the process of exploring solutions in association with its technology partner, Dun & Bradstreet Information Services India (P) Ltd. (D&B) either by modifying the existing system of CIBIL to segregate small and medium enterprises data or creating a separate system for drawing information from database of both CIBIL and D&B.

CIBIL held discussions in this regard with IBA, SIDBI and the Reserve Bank. The proposed small and medium enterprises solution will provide a consolidated report comprising SME loan related data, SME vendor payment related data and a consolidated SME score. With a view to strengthening the legal mechanism and facilitating credit information bureaus to collect, process and share credit information on borrowers of banks/FIs, the Credit Information Act was passed in May 2005. Subsequently, the

Reserve Bank released the draft rules and regulations under the Act for feedback on April 5, 2006. On the basis of the responses received, the draft rules and regulations have been revised and would be notified shortly in consultation with the Government of India giving directions to credit information companies.

By introducing the scheme RBI expected that such a measure would effect greater discipline among the borrowers. The bank wise details of defaulting customers will be published by the Reserve Bank on its website. The system facilitates banks to obtain reliable confidential information from the reporting bank instead of obtaining directly from the defaulting customers. The information supplied by RBI will be helpful to the bankers and other financial institutions to avoid sanctioning of new loans to an existing defaulting\suit filed customer of some other banks. The system helps banks to be more vigilant on requests from the defaulting borrowing units or their proprietors\partners\directors for new or additional credit. The system also prevents obtaining of loans in the name of some other units owned or associated by a suit filed defaulting borrower of a bank. Exchange of credit information among banks would be of immense help to avoid possible NPAs. The system should provide a mechanism to ensure that the unscrupulous borrowers are not in a position to play one bank against the other. It would help banks ultimately to enhance the quality of credit decisions and improving the asset quality of banks, apart from facilitating faster processing of credit request and disbursal of the same.

8

Mergers, Acquisitions and Bank Failures

The terms merger and amalgamation are generic terms used interchangeably to denote different types of business combinations wherein two or more firms combine to form one legal entity. A merger is a combination of two or more firms in which only one firm would survive and the other would dissolve. The assets and liabilities of the firm are taken over by the surviving firm.

The term amalgamation is used when two or more companies carrying on similar business go into liquidation and a new company is formed to take over their business. The outcome of amalgamation is that the amalgamated firm gets dissolved and loses its identity and its shareholders become shareholders of the amalgamating firm.

In principle, merger and acquisition provide an opportunity to banks to share their resources, reduce intermediation costs, and expand delivery platforms and to improve chances for economies in their operations.

The banking sector in India shows a high degree of fragmentation. The market share of top five banks in India is approximately 42 per cent and the share of top ten banks is only 57 per cent whereas the corresponding percentage in China is 75 per cent and 85 per cent respectively. The entry of new private sector and foreign banks has further fragmented the Indian banking industry.

In the Indian Banks Association document "Banking Industry: Vision 2010", it is envisioned that mergers between public sector banks or public and private sector banks, could be the next logical thing to happen as market players try to consolidate their position and there by to remain competitive. Mergers and acquisition route provided to banks a quick method to acquire competitive size and an opportunity to share markets and reduce cost of product development and delivery. Thus, consolidation in the banking industry has become unavoidable.

A recent trend in the Indian joint stock banks is the attempt on the part of the regulators to strengthen the banking system by eliminating the weak banks and to merge strong banks to make the banking sector more vibrant and to meet the international challenges and competitions. India is now moving in the direction of fewer banks of mega size in tandem with the Global-banking scenario. At least five to six Indian banks can be among the 100 large global banks. Then only can India become an economic powerhouse. At present SBI in the only bank in India, which finds 82nd place among the big hundred, banks in the world. Five other Indian banks now occupy a position among 500 larger banks in the world setting.

8.1 Brief History of Bank Failures in India

8.1.1 Bank Failures during the Colonial Period: In the first phase of banking development in India, commercial banks combined banking operations with their trading activities. The commercial banking in India had its origin in the seventeenth century by the agency houses and primary concern was trade. The East India Company encouraged the establishment of agency houses in India, which combined banking with general trading. With the increase in banking business, many agency houses started commercial banks mostly on the basis of unlimited liability. The General Bank of India, one of the earliest joint stock banks was voluntarily dissolved by liquidation on March 1791. The Bank of Hindustan (1770) founded by agency houses went into liquidation in 1833. The Union Bank of Calcutta and the United Service Bank promoted by agency houses went in to liquidation in 1848. Important causes identified for the failure of colonial banks were combination of banking with trading business, speculation in business, mismanagement, fraud, laissez faire policy of the government in economic matters etc. Banks with efficient management and which were bankers to the government like Bank of Hindustan and General Bank of India also failed due to the collapse of their main trading business. Bank of Banaras failed due to fraudulent and mismanagement behaviors on the part of its employees.

8.1.2 Failure of Joint Stock Banking with Limited Liability: The principle of limited liability was made applicable to joint stock banks in India in 1860. At the time of introduction of this principle, it was believed that failure of banks with limited liability would be lesser in the case of banks with unlimited liability. In 1860, (Act VII) for the first time certain enactments were also made to ensure the stability of banks and protection of depositors. This enactment was for creation of reserves and an added assurance to the depositors that a portion of the share capital was to be kept uncalled, which would be called up only in the event of winding up of the bank. Consequent to the effect of American Civil War, The Bank of Bombay collapsed in 1865. Between 1870 and 1894, three banks out of the seven started during this period failed. The Bank of Burma established in 1904 failed in 1911 due to misappropriation of money by its general manager and directors. A Commission was appointed to probe the causes of bank failures. The Commission found that the old Act was unnecessarily restrictive. However, the Commission did not think it advisable to remove all restrictions because the Bank had opened its door to the practice of ruinous and lax system of banking, and was in fact, the chief cause of its failure.

The number of bank failures increased from 12 in 1913 to 42 in 1914. The important failures were those of Indian Spice Bank, Peoples Bank, Credit Bank of India, Standard Bank and Bank of Upper India. An accountant was appointed to report the causes for the failure of Indian Spice Bank. The report disclosed that the books of accounts of the bank were incomplete and the management committed only limited forms of fraud.

Between 1912 and 1923 the number of bank failures was 143 and the total authorized capital involved was Rs. 4,789 lakh with a paid up capital of Rs 659 lakh. During 1938- 47 the number of bank failures were 547 and the total authorized capital was

Rs. 3,394 lakh and the paid up capital Rs.186 lakh only. The noted failure was that of Travancore National and Quilon Bank Ltd. in 1938. This failure affected adversely the functioning of banks in South India to a great extent. But the timely interference of the Reserve Bank of India helped a lot in creating confidence among depositors of the scheduled banks. Between 1947 and 1952, the number of failures was 236 and authorized capital was Rs. 4,069 lakh and paid up capital Rs. 519 lakh. In 1946-47, the failures witnessed were those of ABC Bank, the Exchange Bank of India and the Nath Bank, Calcutta. The Reserve Bank took action against these banks by way of ordering them they should not accept further deposits.

8.1.3 Banks Failures during the Post Independence Period (1947-1991): The liquidation of two scheduled banks Palai Central Bank and the Laxmi Bank in 1960 necessitated urgent action to stabilize and strengthen the weaker segments of the banking structure. Following the failure, the Reserve Bank found that a large number of small and medium-sized banks had still not come up to the eligibility standard required for the grant of license under section 22 of the Banking Regulation Act. The existence of a number of weak banks all over the country placed the banking system in a vulnerable position. Refusal of licenses further to so many banks would lead to undesirable consequences in the banking system. In order to strengthen the weak banks and to revitalize public confidence in the banking system, a new Section 45 was inserted in the Banking Companies Act in September 1960. The Act was amended with the object of eliminating weak and non-viable banking units through a process of amalgamations and mergers.

Section 45 empowers the Government of India to compulsorily amalgamate weak banks with strong banks. The Government can exercise this power only on the basis of a recommendation from the Reserve Bank of India for merger. Prior to merger, the RBI is empowered to recommend to the Central Government for issue of an order to place the bank a moratorium under Section 45 (1) of Banking Regulation Act,

1949. According to Section 45, the Reserve Bank of India is required to submit to the Government a scheme for amalgamation of the weak bank with a strong one. After a proper investigation in to the affairs of the weak bank, a scheme for reconstruction and amalgamation should be prepared and the scheme should be submitted to the Central Government within a period of not more than six months. After accepting the scheme for amalgamation, the Government of India will issue notification in terms of sub-Section (7) of Section 45 of the BR Act 1949. The scheme of amalgamation will come into force from the date of notification. The bank mergers in India increased considerably from 22 in 1963 to 79 in 1964.

The unpublished report of Travancore Banking Enquiry Committee in 1963 expressed serious concern over the existence and spread of many local, small, weak and substandard banks through out Kerala. The committee recommended immediate take over of these banks through the process of mergers, or transfer of assets and liabilities. As a result of the recommendation of this committee bank mergers gained substantial momentum in Kerala.

During the period of 1950 to 1970 as many as 255 banks went under voluntary liquidation, 36 were voluntarily amalgamated 49 were compulsorily merged and 143 banks transferred their assets and liabilities to. As result of mergers and transfers, the number of functioning scheduled banks declined from 92 to 72 and that of non- scheduled banks declined from 474 to15 during the period of 1951 -1970.

During the year, 1989 Reserve Bank of India issued an order of moratorium in respect of United Industrial Bank Ltd. Calcutta by invoking the provisions of Section 45 of the Banking Regulations Act. The bank was later merged with Allahabad with full protection to the depositors. On August 22, 1989, RBI issued moratorium in respect of four more private sector banks. These banks were Bank of Tamil Nadu Ltd., Bank of Thanjavur Ltd., The Parur Central Bank Ltd., and the Purbanchal Bank Ltd. Purbanchal Bank Ltd. was amalgamated with the nationalized Central Bank of India on August 1990. During the period of 1985 to1991, the government sanctioned a scheme for. amalgamation of 10 banks.

8.1.4 Bank Failures and Bank Mergers during the Post Financial Sector Reforms Period: Since 1992 several initiatives steps were initiated by the Reserve Bank and the Government of India to strengthen the banking system. In order to formulate and equip with banks to meet the global challenges many proposals were put forward by committees appointed for the same.

The Narasimham Committee in its first report of 1991 recommended measures to refurbish the structure of the Indian banking system. An important recommendation in the Report of this Committee was for the revamping of the structure of the banking system. The committee suggested a substantial reduction in the number of public sector banks through mergers and acquisitions. The committee gave following recommendations for the restructuring of banks.

- Formation of three or four large banks like State Bank of India, which could become global in character and competitiveness.
- Eight to ten national banks with a net work of branches spread throughout the country engaged in universal banking.
- Local area banks whose operations would generally be confined to a specific area or region.
- Rural banks including Regional Rural Banks whose operations would be confined to the rural areas and their business would predominantly be in engaged in financing of agriculture and allied activities.

The Narasimham Committee recommended merger of strong banks, in the public and private sectors between themselves and in some cases and even with development financial institutions and non-banking financing companies.

In India, mergers are being proposed as a measure to surmount the financial crisis. Instead of mergers, the committee recommended market lead mergers, which may gain momentum in the coming years to overcome the financial crisis of the weak banks. A perusal of international banking scenario shows that most of the global banks have got themselves transformed completely through consolidation, competition and convergence.

8.2 Mergers in Banking Sector in India: 1992 to 1994

During the year 1991-92, 28 banks under liquidation were treated as dissolved and 2 banks were placed under liquidation. On 31st March of 1992, 96 banks were under liquidation. During the year under review, 2 banks namely the Bank of Credit and Commerce International, (Overseas) Ltd. Bombay (BCCI) and the Bank of Karad Ltd. got liquidated.

On July 6, 1991, RBI suspended all payments and other transactions of BCCI (O) Ltd. and State Bank of India was appointed as the provisional liquidator of BCCI. In February 1993, the Grand Court of Cayman Islands approved the terms and conditions for the sale of BCCI (O) Ltd., to the SBI. The SBI offered to purchase the business of Bombay branch for a consideration of Rs. 40 crore. Following the promoters agreement a wholly owned subsidiary of SBI viz. SBI Commercial and International Bank Ltd. (SBICI) was incorporated on October 1993. After obtaining the license from RBI on November 1993, SBICI commenced its business from January 31, 1994.

Due to large-scale irregularities in the transactions relating to certain stockbrokers, the Bank of Karad Ltd. fell into financial crisis of a huge liability, which the banks found unable to meet. The financial crisis was likely to affect the survival of the bank and the interest of the depositors and public. Then RBI took over the matter and issued an interim order for liquidation of the bank on May 27 1992. The Scheme of Amalgamation with Bank of India thus came into force on July 20, 1994.

8.2.1 Bank Mergers: 1995 to 2000: An important bank merger of the early nineties was that of a nationalized bank viz. New Bank of India (NBI) with another nationalized bank (Punjab National Bank). The New Bank of India had incurred losses during the last four preceding years. With the introduction of prudential accounting standards and new NPA norms, the financial position of the New Bank of India worsened further. The cumulative losses and the erosion of deposits weakened the liquidity and financial position of New Bank of India and threatened its existence. In order to protect the interest of depositors and to convey greater strength to the banking system RBI took a decision in September 1993 for merging the weak New Bank of India with a strong nationalized bank viz. Punjab National Bank (PNB).

Kashinath Seth Bank Ltd. a non-scheduled bank was placed under moratorium in June 1994 and was amalgamated with State Bank of India in January 1996. Private sector small banks like the Punjab Co-operative Bank Ltd. and Doab Bank Ltd. were placed under moratorium initially for a period of three months with a subsequent extension in for the same period by an order of the Government of India on 30th September 1996. These two banks were amalgamated with the Oriental Bank of Commerce Ltd. on April 8, 1997. The number of banks under liquidation as on June 30, 1997 was 88.

The 20th Century Finance Corporation Ltd. was merged with the new private sector bank viz. Centurion Bank with effect from January 1998. Bareily Corporation Bank Limited merged with Bank of Baroda in June 1999 and Sikkim Bank with Union Bank of India on December 1999. The new generation private sector bank, the Times Bank merged with another new generation private sector bank viz. HDFC Bank on February 2000.

8.2.2 Varma Committee Report on Bank Mergers: The RBI in consultation with the Government of India appointed in February 1999 a "Working Group on Restructuring of Weak Public Sector Banks" under the chairmanship of Shri M.S. Varma, which was to identify weak public sector banks and to suggest a scheme for restructuring and strengthening the weak banks. For identifying the weak public sector banks, the Working Group listed out important parameters, which were essential for a financially strong bank. The Group submitted its report in October 1999, identified and recommended seven parameters covering three important areas viz. solvency, profitability and earning capacity of a bank. The norms selected for identifying weak banks were the following.

- Capital adequacy ratio.
- Coverage ratio.
- Return on assets.
- Net interest margin.
- Ratio of operating profit to average working funds.
- Ratio of cost to income.
- Ratio of staff cost to net interest income plus all other income.

On the basis of the aforesaid parameters public sector banks were classified into three categories. Banks where none of the seven parameters were present were grouped one category, banks where all the parameters were present in another category and banks where some of the seven parameters were present in yet another.

The Working Group made an exhaustive case-by-case examination of the financial strength and weakness of all public sector banks and identified the Indian Bank, UCO Bank, and United Bank of India as weak banks, which wanted to meet the seven parameters. The Group suggested a two-stage operation for restructuring of weak banks.

The Group opined that the option for merger or privatization will be relevant only after enhancing the operational efficiency of the banks. The Working Group recommended that the privatization and mergers of weak bank with other banks should consider only at the last stage. The committee recommended operational, organizational, financial and systemic restructuring during the first stage. The operational efficiency can be attained only by adopting modern technology, reducing cost of operations, reducing the level of non-performing assets, improving practices of corporate governance, change of the legal system, adopting staff rationalization measures, enhancing the efficiency and involvement of bank management etc.

The Working Group in its recommendation estimated that an overall cost of restructuring the weak banks in the next three years will be Rs. 5,500 crore of which capital infusion will be Rs. 3,000 crore, NPA buyout process Rs. 1,000 crore, staff rationalization measures Rs. 1,100 to 1,200 crore and for technology up gradation Rs. 300 to 400 crore. As part of the restructuring process, the Working Group also recommended the constitution of a Financial Restructuring Authority (FRA). Of these, the amounts for technology up gradation and staff rationalization would be provided in cash. For speeding up the recovery process in weak banks, the Committee suggested that an arrangement should be made for the Debt Recovery Tribunals (DRTs) to take their cases on a priority basis.

As against the recommendations of the Varma Committee the then Finance Minister, in his 2000-01 Budget announced the constitution of a Financial Restructuring Authority (FRA) for each weak banks instead of a single Authority for all weak banks. Under the proposed framework, the statutes governing public sector banks would be amended to provide for suspension of the Board of Directors on the basis of recommendations of the Reserve Bank and constitution of a FRA comprising experts and professionals. The amendments would also enable the FRA to exercise special powers, including all powers of the Board of the bank. The Government would consider recapitalization of the weak banks to achieve the prescribed capital adequacy norms.

8.2.3 Bank Mergers: 2000 to 2005: The year 2001 witnessed the merger of the 57-year-old Tamil Nadu based private sector commercial bank "Bank of Madura Ltd." with a new generation private sector bank viz. ICICI Bank. The bank with a net work of 264 branches on March 31, 2000 had assets worth Rs. 3,988 crore and deposits of Rs. 3,395 crore. The Board of Directors of ICICI Bank Ltd. and Bank of Madura Ltd. approved the scheme of merger on December 11, 2000 and its share holders subsequently approved the same in its extraordinary meeting on January 19, 2001. The RBI approved the merger of Bank of Madura with ICICI Bank Ltd. with effect from March 10, 2001. As per the scheme of amalgamation, the swap ration was fixed at two equity shares of ICICI Bank for every one equity share of Bank of Madura Ltd.

The RBI accorded approval for merger of ICICI Ltd. with

ICICI Bank Ltd. on April 26, 2002 subject to the following conditions:

- ICICI Bank Ltd. would have to maintain SLR/CRR as prescribed on the net demand and time liabilities of the bank on the post merger liabilities even though the liabilities of ICICI Ltd. existing prior to merger did not attract the reserve requirements;
- The assets and liabilities of ICICI Ltd. would be taken over by ICICI Bank Ltd through the process of merger. In the post merger period ICICI Bank Ltd. would have to comply with all prudential requirements, guidelines and other instructions concerning capital adequacy, asset classification, income recognition and provisioning requirements as applicable to other banks.
- ICICI Bank Ltd. would have to deploy an additional 10.0 per cent, over and above the requirement of 40.0 per cent, on the residual portion of its advances after the merger till such time as the aggregate priority sector advances reach a level of 40.0 per cent of the total net bank credit of the bank.

RBI accorded approval for merger of Benares State Bank Ltd (BSBL) with Bank of Baroda (BoB). The Central Government on June 19, 2002 sanctioned the scheme of amalgamation of the Benares State Bank Ltd. with BoB. Accordingly, the BSBL has been merged with BoB with effect from June 20, 2002 and all the branches of the BSBL started functioning as branches of BoB from July 19, 2002.

A notable instance of bank collapse during the year 2002-03 was that of the Nedungadi Bank of Kerala, which reported a loss of Rs. 67.8 crore for the firs time for the year ended in March 2001. The financial position of the bank was progressively getting weakened and the banks capital got fully eroded in the year ended March 2003. The capital to risk weighted assets ratio recorded an alarming level of -1.9 per cent as against the statutory minimum requirement of 9 per cent. The net worth of the bank amounting to Rs. 60.4 crore got fully eroded due to accumulated losses. The bank required approximately Rs. 125 crore to achieve the CRAR of 9 per cent. Because the financial position and solvency of the bank got fully worsened the RBI had no alternative other than to consider the amalgamation of Nedungadi Bank with a nationalized bank.

For the purpose of amalgamation, Nedungadi Bank was placed under moratorium for a period of three months from November 2nd, 2002. During this interim period, the Reserve Bank prepared a Draft Scheme for the Amalgamation of the Nedungadi Bank Limited with Punjab National Bank and it was forwarded to both the banks on November 30, 2002 for their comments, suggestions and objections. The Scheme of amalgamation was sanctioned by the Central Government in terms of sub-section (7) of Section 45 of the Act, through a notification dated January 31, 2003. The scheme of amalgamation of Nedungadi Bank Limited with Punjab National Bank came into effect on February 1, 2003. There were 77 banks under liquidation as on December 31, 2003.

The notable bank failures during the year 2003-2004 were the newly formed local area bank viz. 'South Gujarat Local Area Bank Ltd' and the new generation private sector bank viz. 'Global Trust Bank Ltd.'. The Government of India issued orders of moratorium in respect of Gujarat Local Area Bank Ltd, for the period from November 13, 2003 to August 12, 2004. Government of India sanctioned the Scheme of amalgamation of South Gujarat Local Area Bank Ltd. with Bank of Baroda. The Scheme of Amalgamation came into force on June 25, 2004.

The Global Trust Bank Ltd. (GTB), one of the new generation private banks, which was granted license in September 1994, began showing adverse growth in 2002. The RBI instructed the GTB to adopt prudential norms for reducing its adverse futures like high growth of risk-weighted assets, high NPA, high exposure to capital market etc. The bank reported some progress in making recoveries and also the efforts underway to have equity infusion. However, the bank was not able to finalize to the programme of capital expansion from domestic sources as advised by RBI.

In July 2004, the GTB submitted a proposal from an overseas

equity investor for capital augmentation to RBI for its consideration and the proposal was as not feasible from the point of view of prudential norms and other considerations. As the financial condition of the bank was steadily deteriorating and its solvency getting seriously affected, the Reserve Bank had placed the bank under moratorium on July 24, 2004 to protect the interests of its small depositors and that of the banking system. Of the various merger proposals, the one proposed by the Oriental Bank of Commerce (OBC) was found acceptable by the RBI and was forwarded it to the Central Government for approval. Before finalizing the proposal for merger RBI evaluated the strategic advantages, branch network, interest of depositors of GTB and strengths and weaknesses of both banks. As per Government notification, the GTB got merged with OBC on August 14, 2004.

An important event related to the amalgamation of banks during the year 2005 was the proposal for voluntary amalgamation submitted by two new generation private sector banks. The scheme of amalgamation of "Bank of Punjab Ltd." with the Centurion Bank Ltd. was approved by the Reserve Bank in terms of Section 44A of the B. R. Act, and became effective from October 1, 2005. The Centurion Bank subsequently changed its name to Centurion Bank of Punjab Ltd.

8.2.4 Bank Mergers during the Year 2006: The net worth of the Ganesh Bank of Kurundwad Ltd. turned negative and failed to maintain the capital adequacy requirements for several years and the bank declared moratorium for a period of three months effective January 7, 2006. During this interim period, the Reserve Bank prepared a Draft Scheme of Amalgamation of the bank with the Kerala based old private sector bank viz. Federal Bank Ltd., which was sanctioned by the Government on January 24, 2006. But the proposed scheme for amalgamation drafted by RBI was challenged by shareholders of Ganesh Bank of Kurundwad Ltd. and others before the High Court of Bombay. Following the Supreme Court's dismissal of Petition filed by the bank on August 28, 2006, the Central Government issued the necessary notification on September 1, 2006 to effect the merger from

September 2, 2006.

The Capital to Risk Weighted Assets Ratio (CRAR) of the United Western Bank Ltd. (UWB) had turned negative and failed to maintain it, the Reserve Bank placed the bank under moratorium for a period of three months with effect from September 2, 2006 (under Subsection (2) of Section 45 of the B. R. Act, 1949). During the period of moratorium, the Reserve Bank of India received from 17 banks the willingness of acquisition of the business of UWB. Subsequently, the Government notified the Scheme for amalgamation of United Western Bank Ltd. with Industrial Development Bank of India Ltd (IDBI Bank), which came into effect on October 3, 2006.

Another development related to the merger of banks during the year 2006 was the merger proposal of an old private sector bank with a new generation private bank. The shareholders of the Kerala based Lord Krishna Bank (LKB) and Centurion Bank of Punjab (CBP) were approved their merger proposals. Both the banks are planning to submit applications to the Reserve Bank of India for the requisite regulatory approvals.

During the year 2005-06, two domestic banks and one foreign bank were amalgamated and the business of another foreign bank was closed. Among foreign banks ING Bank NV closed its business in India. The number of scheduled commercial banks thus got reduced from 88 at the end of March 2005 to 84 at the end of March 2006.

Merger and amalgamation of weak banks with strong banks, as a policy measure for strengthening the structure of the banking system, resulted in its merger of 23 banks during a seven-year period. The number of scheduled commercial banks excluding RRBs, decreased from 107 on March 31, 1999 to 84 at the end of March 31, 2006.

8.2.5 Bank Mergers during the Year 2007: The year 2007 witnessed the merger of an old private sector bank "Bharat Overseas Bank Ltd." with a nationalized bank viz. Indian Overseas Bank. The bank was established in the year 1974 was originally owned by the Indian Overseas Bank and other six private sector banks in India viz. Bank of Rajasthan Ltd., South Indian Bank Ltd., Karnataka Bank Ltd., Vysya Bank Ltd., Karur Vysya Banks Ltd. and Federal Bank Ltd. The bank with a net work of 103 branches was taken over by the Indian Overseas Bank in April 3, 2007.

With effect to this merger, the number of old private sector banks in India reduced from 19 to 18. Scheduled Commercial Banks comprises 28 public sector banks (State Bank of India and its 7 associates, 19 nationalized banks and the Industrial Development Bank of India Ltd.), 8 new private sector banks, 18 old private sector banks and 29 foreign banks.

8.2.6 Merger of Subsidiaries with Parent Bank:

- The Bank of Rajasthan Ltd. was given the approval to merge with itself its wholly owned subsidiary viz., Rajasthan Bank Financial Services Ltd. with itself.
- Andhra Bank was given 'in principle' approval to merge its housing finance subsidiary i.e. Andhra Bank Housing Finance Ltd. with itself.
- Bank of India was given approval to merge its wholly owned subsidiary viz., Bank of India Finance Ltd. and Band of India Asset Management Company Ltd. with itself.

8.2.7 Recommendations of the Joint Parliamentary Committee and the Working Group: On the basis of the recommendations of the Joint Parliamentary Committee (2002), The Reserve Bank of India constituted a Working Group to prepare guidelines for voluntary merger of banking companies. On the basis of the recommendation of the working Group the Reserve Bank issued guidelines for merger of banks on May 11, 2005, containing the details of the process of merger. The guidelines for merger were to deal with merger proposals between two banking companies or between a banking company and a non-banking financial company, which were applicable to both private and public sector banks.

A. Guidelines on Merger and Amalgamation of Commercial Banks

- The draft scheme of amalgamation must be approved

individually by two-thirds of the total members of the Board of Directors of both banking companies.

- The draft scheme of amalgamation must be approved by the shareholders of both the banking companies by passing a resolution in its special meeting. The resolution requires the approval of majority of shareholders representing not less than two-thirds in value of shares, present and to be in person or by proxy at the meeting.
- The exchange ratio must be determined by proficient and experienced independent valuers.
- The value to be paid by the banking company to its dissenting shareholders is to be determined by the Reserve Bank.
- The shareholding pattern and composition of the Board of the amalgamating banking company are to be in accordance with the guidelines of RBI.

B. Guidelines on Merger of a Non Banking Finance Company with Banking Company

On the basis of the recommendations of the Joint Parliamentary Committee, the Working Group also framed guidelines for the voluntary merger of a Non Banking Finance Company (NBFC) with a banking company. Accordingly the Reserve Bank issued guidelines for the merger of a NBFC with a banking Company.

- When a NBFC is proposed to be amalgamated with a banking company, the Board should see and ensure that the NBFC has not violated or not likely to violate any of the norms of the Reserve Bank of India and the Securities and Exchange Board of India (SEBI) They should also ensure that the norms are complied with before approval of the scheme of amalgamation;
- In case of amalgamation of a non-banking finance company with a banking company, the banking company is required to obtain the approval of RBI before the scheme of amalgamation is submitted to the High Court for approval.
- Ensure that the NBFC has complied with the Know Your Customer (KYC) norms for all the accounts, which will

become accounts of the banking company after amalgamation; and

- The NBFC has availed of credit facilities from banks/FIs and if so, whether the loan agreements mandate the NBFC to seek consent of the bank/FI concerned for the proposed merger/amalgamation.

8.3 Strategy for Strengthening Weak Banks: International Experience

The bank crisis of the 1980s and 1990s weakened the banking system of several countries. Reconstruction of banking institutions through merger and amalgamation gained momentum in many developing countries. In many developing countries the banking system remains uneven by way of the number and size of institutions, ownership, liquidity, profitability, operating efficiency, financial innovations, prudential norms, use of modern technology etc. and needs to improve their strength and financial viability.

Experience across countries reveals that several strategies were adopted in emerging economies to restructure the banking systems. These are government capital injection, establishment of asset management corporations, domestic bank mergers and foreign bank takeover. Bank consolidation in many countries took place because of capital adequacy. In some other economies government led consolidation received good response because of the failure of small banks.

Andrew Sheng (1996) lists the necessary conditions for the successful bank restructuring as clear links with enterprise restructuring, stable macroeconomic environment, strong political will, effective restructuring agency, transparent accounting standards, legal framework, financial discipline, incentives favouring private sector growth and competition, availability of professional bankers and effective bank supervision and enforcement.

For instance in Hungary, some 40 institutions are presently competing in the retail and corporate markets. At the same time,

Belgium's KBC and ABN Amro merged their Hungarian operations to exploit the synergies of the market.

After a large number of bankruptcies of private banks particularly in Poland and Czech Republic, the number of commercial banks dwindled significantly.

Malaysia established in June 1998 a public company Danaharta owned by the Ministry of Finance, whose objectives were to acquire, manage, finance and dispose of assets and liabilities of financial institutions and to allow them to focus on the core business of lending. The Malaysian authorities announced plans for the country's banks and finance companies to be merged into six large groups by September 1999. The obvious example of this approach is Malaysia's Danamodal, a special purpose institution established with the twin objectives of consolidation and rationalization of the banking system. Malaysia also setup Asset Management Corporations (AMCs) to manage bad assets and introduced schemes to inject public money into the banks as capital.

In Indonesia, the Asset Management Unit is a component of the Indonesia Bank Restructuring Agency (IBRA). In September 1998, the authorities of Indonesia announced that, four of the seven state owned banks would be consolidated into a new state bank called Mandiri. Their bad assets will be transferred to the Indonesian Bank Restructuring Agency. In addition, eight private banks, which were taken over by the Indonesian Bank Restructuring Agency (IBRA), were merged into a new institution during 2000.

Thailand was the first country in the region to set up an asset management company (AMCs) to manage bad assets. In Philippines, a range of incentives is being offered to the merging banks, including better access to rediscount facilities and temporary relief from certain prudential requirements.

In Argentina, largely the domestic and external financial liberalization launched in the early 1990s, and the progressive tightening of prudential regulations drove bank consolidation.

In China, both commercial and co-operative banks as well as

non-banking institutions are also restructured as part of their programme for revitalization of the financial sector. From 1995 to 1998, more than 2000 urban credit co-operatives were merged with 88 city commercial banks on the basis of assessing their assets and capital, writing off of some bad debts, estimating net worth of equity and encouraging new shareholders. During 1997 and 1998 one insolvent bank and three trust and investment companies were closed down in China. The asset management company for dealing with non-performing loans of state banks was established in April 1999.

The Government of Korea proposed several schemes for restructuring and strengthening their financial sector. Government permits viable banks to recapitalize and write off non-performing loans by bringing public funds. The Government advised the viable banks to increase equity by attracting foreign capital, enhancing the expertise and efficiency of management and reducing the staff strength. An asset management fund was also established by the government in KAMCO in November 1997, which was entrusted with the task of disposing off the non-performing assets of the financial institutions.

In Saudi Arabia, the government put forward several schemes for strengthening the banking system viz. tax holidays, tax deductibility of provisions for doubtful accounts, withholding tax on inter-bank transactions, setting up of banking disputes committee, strengthening of the technological infrastructure, good corporate governance and sharing of information on large borrowers and delinquent loans.

9

Commercial Banks in Insurance Business

Insurance sector plays a very important role in the economic development of a nation. Insurance companies enact different roles such as mobiliser of savings, promoter of investment activities, stabilizer of financial markets and as a risk manager. While encouraging saving habits, it also provides a safety net to both enterprises and individuals. According to preliminary estimates published by the Reserve Bank of India, contribution of insurance funds to financial savings was 14.2 per cent in 2005-06, i.e. 2.4 per cent of the GDP at current market prices.

An ever-growing insurance sector is of vital importance for the economic growth. The insurance companies renders some useful financial intermediary services like transferring funds from the insured to capital investment required for continued economic expansion and growth which in turn generates long-term funds for infrastructure development. The graph of insurance business has been changing across the globe and the ripple effects of the same can be seen in the domestic markets also.

During the formative days of insurance, the business of insurance coverage was confined to only a few categories of risks. Because of greater awareness of the usefulness of insurance, the people now extensively use it. In human life and business operations, every individual and business concern is exposed to innumerable risks and accidents. In the case of an individual, he encounters a number of risks like ailments leading to indisposition, accidents and consequent disablements, premature and sudden death etc. On account of such and similar happenings, he may loose his income either temporarily or permanently leaving his dependents in the lurch or forcing them to fend for themselves. In business concerns too, there are risks arising from fire, riots, theft, flood, earth quake, lightening, violence, loss in transit etc. leading to great financial losses to the business. The risks inherent in life and business are very often vary and uncertain, causing tension, stress and strain and unbearable financial losses of grave consequences. Now it is possible to insure against personal risk, accident, sickness, burglary etc. Now different types of insurance like life and general insurance are available and they have become very popular. Thus, insurance is capable of ensuring protection against almost all types of risks to which human beings and business are often exposed to.

9.1 Meaning of Insurance

The whole business of insurance is based on the assumption that only a small proportion of a large group will alone really suffer losses from a given cause within a particular period. Thus, insurance covers the risks involving a large number of people. Therefore insurance may be defined "as a social device whereby a large group of individuals who agree to make small contribution in order to reimburse those who suffer losses that may be foreseen and estimated". Insurance involves the transfer of potential losses to an insurance pool. The pool combines all the potential losses and then transfers the cost of the predicted losses back to the exposures. Thus, insurance involves the transfer of loss exposures of several entities into a common pool, and the redistribution of the cost of actual losses among the members of the pool.

In legal sense, insurance is a contract between two parties, whereby one party covers the risk by paying a specified amount; in return, the other undertakes to indemnify the loss suffered by him. The person who covers his risks by insurance is called the insured, the person who undertakes to protect the risk is called the insurer, and the amount that is paid to insure the risk is called the premium. The insurer is a risk taker who accepts the risks of others and earns a profit by way of the difference between the total premium collected from the buyers of insurance and the total payment made on account of compensation for losses.

9.2 Insurance Business in India: A Retrospect

India is not new to insurance business. It prevailed in India right from the 19th century i.e. with the arrival of British Enterprises in India leading to a socio-economic transformation. Bombay Mutual Life Assurance Society was the first insurance company established in India, which opened its business in 1870. Oriental Life Insurance Company began its operations in Kolkata in the year 1818.

In 1905 following the Swadeshi Movement, many Indian entrepreneurs established banking and insurance institutions. Later many insurance companies sprung up like mushrooms. The area of operation of these institutions was mainly confined to cities and urban centres. There were also some banks in the thirties (General Insurance Bank of India Ltd. Mangalore) doing both banking and insurance business simultaneously. However, the business of these institutions did not survive for long for many reasons. Like the history of banking in India, the history of insurance also reveals that insurance industry evolved through a series of trials and tribulations.

The failure of insurance business was mainly due to lack of control over the business by the government because of the absence of legislative measures. The Indian Assurance Companies Act of 1912 was the first statue meant to regulate the life insurance business in India. However, insurance Act of 1938 was the first comprehensive legislation in India intended to control the business of insurance companies in all its totality. The Act was passed mainly with the object of safeguarding the interest of the insuring public. However, the situation changed in total only after the country's independence and through a series of legislative and regulatory measures.

9.2.1 Insurance Business in India: After Independence: Insurance is the only industry in India, which is fully nationalized. The Insurance sector in India was organized as General and Life Insurance with the establishment of the Life Insurance Corporation of India (LIC) and General Insurance Corporation (GIC). LIC was formed through the take over and nationalization of the business of 245 Indian and foreign insurers and provident societies. The Life Insurance Corporation of India was established by an Act of Parliament, which received the President's assent on June 18, 1956. The Act came in to force on July 1, 1956 and the Corporation became functional on September 1, 1956.

The Indian Mercantile Insurance Ltd. formed in 1907 is considered as the first company to transact all types of general insurance business in India. General Insurance Corporation of India (GIC) was established in 1973 after nationalization of general insurance companies in the country. At the time of nationalization, about 100 small companies and a few large companies were operating in the field of general insurance. After nationalization, one holding company named General Insurance Corporation of India (GIC) was set up. Subsequently all the existing companies were merged and reorganized into four subsidiaries of GIC viz. National Insurance Company Ltd., New India Insurance Company Ltd., Oriental Fire and General Insurance Company Ltd., and United India Insurance Company Ltd. These companies used to carry out the business of general insurance in India in a monopolistic manner up to1999 and in that year the insurance business was thrown opened for private players also.

General Insurance Company's supervisory role over its erstwhile subsidiaries was terminated by an administrative order, it was re-designated as the "Indian Reinsurer" in 2000 by an Act of Parliament, and it was to function exclusively as Life and non-Life Re- insurer. Subsequently to the General Insurance Business (Nationalization) Amendment Act of 2002, GIC ceased to be a holding company of its subsidiaries and their ownership got vested with the Government of India.

9.3 Banking with Insurance Business: International Scenario

Historically and generally the banking and insurance activities remain strictly segregated in most of the countries, except by way of ownership linkages. Only licensed insurance companies were allowed to engage in insurance activities and the business of insurance companies was largely confined to insurance and financial activities closely related to it.

The concept of Universal Banking is now adopted by both advanced and developing economies across the world. The concept refers to an integration of commercial banking, insurance and investment banking activities with both equity and debt provided by the same institution under one roof.

Internationally banks now follow one of the following three ways to enter into the business of insurance. Banks either set up either their own insurance company or buy shares of the existing insurance companies or swap shares of banks with insurance companies.

In many countries, insurance companies acquire stakes in some banks. Those shareholdings can be seen as an investment, or as a way of diversifying from the insurance business, or as a method for promoting the distribution of insurance products through branches of banks. Another diversification corridor widely used by banks in recent years for their entry into the insurance industry is either direct or quite often through forming an alliance with an insurance company.

In most European countries, banks are allowed to set up insurance subsidiaries. But in USA and Japan restrictions exist on setting up of subsidiary for insurance business by banks. In Europe, the synergy between banking and insurance has given rise to a novel concept called 'bank assurance'. Also known as 'Alfinanz', bank assurance can be defined as a package of financial services that can satisfy both banking and insurance needs at the same time. For instance, financial services companies offer a gamut of financial products like banking services, motor insurance, home finance, and life insurance and pension schemes. Many European markets have put bank assurance into practice.

In France, more than 50 per cent of life insurance products are marketed through banks. In the United Kingdom a large number of banks deal with insurance and offer divergent insurance products to their customers. In the USA, banks lease space to insurers and retail products of multiple insurers. In India too, banks offer personal accident and baggage insurance directly to their credit card holders as value addition to their products.

In developed economies, the collaboration between banking and insurance is brought about by several means. Banks like the Deutsche Bank and the Credit Agricole entered the insurance market by launching their own insurance companies. Others like SE Banken (Sweden) and Lloyds Bank chose to buy stakes in already existing insurance companies. A third group of banks preferred to swap shares with insurance companies, while some banks resorted to mergers as a means for making inroads into the insurance sector. Initiatives in this direction were not one sided. Insurance companies often try to acquire stakes in some banks.

9.4 WTO and Financial Services

The eighth round known as Uruguay Round lasted around eight years and was the most comprehensive and controversial one. It covered almost all trade, right from matchbox to aeroplane, from banking to telecommunications, from seeds of wild rice to AIDS treatment. After several rounds of discussions, the WTO concluded treaties on financial services in general and insurance, banking, telecommunications, and maritime transport in particular in the context of the General Agreement on Trade in Services (GATS) in December 1997. These negotiations brought under its purview the largest service sector viz. banking, insurance and other financial related services fully subjected to multilateral rules.

Financial services under WTO included two broad categories of services: 1) Insurance and insurance related services, 2) Banking and other financial services. Insurance and insurance related services are further subdivided as detailed below:

Insurance and insurance-related services cover life and non-life insurance, re-insurance, insurance intermediation such as brokerage and agency services, and services auxiliary to insurance such as consultancy and actuarial services.

9.5 Concept of Universal Banking

The concept of universal banking is of recent origin as far as India is concerned. The emerging scenario in the Indian banking system is to ensure a provision for multifarious financial services under a single roof. But, it will at the same time throw challenges in the form of increased competition among banks and cast a strain on the profit margins of banks.

Universal banking is a name accorded to banks, which are engaged in dispensing diverse kinds of banking business. Universal banks in general refers to those banks that offer a wide range of financial services, other than commercial banking and investment banking i.e. issuing, underwriting, investing and trading in securities. In a very broad sense, however, the term 'universal banks' refers to those banks that offer a wide variety of financial services, mainly insurance.

The Reserve Bank of India constituted a "Working Group for Harmonizing the Role and Operations of Development Financial Institutions" (Chairman: Shri S.H. Khan) in 1998 for exploring the possibilities of harmonizing the role and operations of development financial institutions and banks. The committee discussed various issues related with the introduction of universal banking in India. It brought its report out in May 1998 and recommended the introduction of universal banking. The report contains the Reserve Bank's draft proposals for bringing greater clarity in the respective roles of banks and financial institutions and for greater harmonization of facilities and obligations applicable to them. They suggested a gradual move towards universal banking. Universal Banking in India was also elaborately discussed in the Report of the Committee on Banking Sector Reforms (Narasimham Committee-II - 1998).

In the light of the recommendations of the Working Group, the Reserve Bank, in consultation with the Government of India, proposed to prepare a 'Discussion Paper'. As announced in the policy statement of October 30, 1998, the 'Discussion Paper' on "Universal Banking" was circulated among all concerned for their wider comments and debates. The 'Discussion Paper' released in January 1999 contains solutions for some of the issues and problems raised by the Working Group's, so that the development of universal banking takes place in a smooth and orderly manner.

Based on intensive discussions and consultations, some of the desirable directions for evolution of the Universal Banking policy are the following:

- Universal Banking is a desirable goal and some progress has been made by permitting banks to diversity into investments and long-term financing and the Development Financial Institutions (DFIs) to lend for working capital, etc. The process of enabling the provision of diversified services both by banks and by DFIs, either in-house or through the subsidiary route, as a conglomerate should continue to be subjected to appropriate regulation by the Reserve Bank of India.
- Banks have certain special characteristics and as such, any discriminatory dilution of RBI's prudential norms for conduct of banking business would be inadvisable.
- The regulatory framework of RBI in respect of Development Financial Institutions should be strengthened and they have been allowed greater access to short-term resources for meeting their financing activities.
- Though the DFIs would continue to have a special role in the Indian financial system, until the debt market demonstrates substantial improvements in terms of liquidity and depth, any DFI, which wishes to do so, should have the option to transform itself into a bank, provided the prudential norms as applicable to banks are fully complied with. In respect of any DFI, which requires a transition path to fully comply with regulatory requirement of a bank, the DFI concerned may consult RBI for such transition arrangements.
- Banks and DFIs will be encouraged by the Reserve Bank to have appropriate coordinating mechanisms among themselves for exchange of information and sharing of risks particularly in respect of large and capital intensive projects.

The policy regarding Universal Banking was enunciated in the annual monetary and credit policy Statement of RBI in April 2000. The salient operational and regulatory issues to be addressed by the financial institutions for conversion into a universal bank were also communicated through a circular in April 2001. These issues among relate to, others, reserve requirements, permissible activities, disposal of non-banking assets, composition of the Board, prohibition on floating charge of assets, nature of subsidiaries, restrictions on investments, connected lending, licensing, branch network, assets in India, formats of annual report, priority sector lending and prudential norms.

In the Mid-term, review statement of October 2001, the Reserve Bank has stated that the applications received from the concerned institutions would be processed in the light of considerations outlined in Reserve Bank of India's circular to FIs on approach to Universal Banking in April 2001. In India, the concept of bank assurance has been recognized by its inclusion in the broader ambit of Universal Banking.

9.6 Insurance Regulatory and Development Authority (IRDA) Act, 1999

In order to provide better insurance cover to citizens, the government in its budget speech of 1998, pronounced its decision to open up the insurance sector and to set up a statutory Insurance Regulatory and Development Authority (IRDA). IRDA was the outcome of the recommendations of Malhotra Committee. The Insurance Regulatory and Development Authority Act passed in the Indian Parliament, came in to force in the year 1999, opened the insurance business for the private sector. IRDA was established with the object of protecting the interests of policyholders and to regulate, promote, ensure orderly growth of the insurance industry, and for matters connected there with incidental thereto. The Insurance Act of 1938, the Life Insurance Corporation Act of 1956, and the General Insurance Business (Nationalization) Act of 1972 also amended.

The IRDA consist of a chairman and not more than nine members of whom not more than five members are full-time members, to be appointed by the government from among persons of ability, integrity and standing who have knowledge\experience of life insurance\general insurance\actuarial service, finance, economics etc. The IRDA may constitute a 25 member Insurance Advisory Committee (IAC) to represent the interest of commerce, industry, transport, agriculture, consumer forum, member surveyors, agents, intermediaries, including brokers, consultants and loss assessors, organizations engaged in safety and loss prevention, research bodies and employees' associations in the insurance sector, to advise it on matters relating to making regulations by it and on such other matters as may be prescribed.

With the passage of the IRDA Act in 1999, banks were allowed to enter into insurance business. It was a milestone in the history of insurance business in India. The Act also provided statutory backing to the IRDA. The IRDA Act, 1999, has been enacted against the background of the widely recognized need for opening up of the insurance sector. It liberalized the insurance industry by allowing private participation. It also framed a mechanism for issuing of licenses, monitoring, capital adequacy, investment norms and audit. Under this Act, foreign equity will be limited to 26 per cent of the total paid-up capital. Banks, with their wide net work of branches including in rural areas, coupled with available work force, can utilize this opportunity for mobilizing sizeable funds of long-term nature, which can finance infrastructure projects of long gestation periods.

Recognizing the need for reforms in the financial and insurance sectors, the Government appointed a committee under the chairmanship of former finance secretary and the Governor of RBI Mr. R.N. Malhotra. The committee went in to the details of the reforms process and identified the measures required for a reforms process of far reaching results.

With a view to assessing the scope, desirability and eligibility of institutions to take up insurance business, draft guidelines were framed for banks to enter into insurance business with risk participation as also for permitting banks to undertake fee-based business as insurance agents. According to guidelines of Reserve Bank, banks can neither conduct insurance business departmentally-nor can they set up a capitalized subsidiary separately. Relationship between the bank and the insurance entity has to be one of 'arms length', so that risks inherent in insurance business do not discredit the bank's balance sheet. Secondly, the guidelines made a distinction between banks which set up joint venture companies and which can 'underwrite' or perform the principal function and those banks, which can only distribute insurance products, or perform only agency function. Thirdly, insurance companies will benefit from the wide net work of rural branches of commercial banks in India through the agency route, which will enable banks to earn fee income.

International experience in insurance business clearly reveals that it cannot break-even during the formative years of its operations. It is, therefore, necessary for banks to have adequate financial strength to commence this activity. Insurance business also requires product designing skills and actuarial expertise, and banks may be required to enter into joint ventures with foreign insurance partners. The entry of banks into insurance would however, raise a number of issues related to overlap of banking and insurance business, which is recognized as very critical in India.

The issue of regulatory overlap also comes to the forefront when banks enter into insurance business by setting up joint venture companies. The guidelines, however, try to eliminate any concern on this account. Whereas the holding of equity by a promoter bank in an insurance company or participation in any form in the insurance business is subject to compliance with the Government/IRDA regulations, the authority to grant case-by-case permission to banks to enter into insurance business is vested with the Reserve Bank of India.

The Advisory Group on Insurance Regulation (Chairman: Shri R. Ramakrishnan), in its Report submitted to the Chairman of the Standing Committee on International Financial Standards and Codes in September 2000, noted the possible future role of co-operative credit institutions in spreading insurance business in rural areas. Similarly, the distribution of insurance products was one of the areas that co-operative banks could undertake to diversify their portfolios as per the recommendations of the 'Task Force to Study the Co-operative Credit System' and suggest measures for its strengthening (Chairman: Shri J. Capoor).

The guidelines issued by the Reserve Bank in April 2000 permitting banks to enter the insurance market emphasize the symbiotic aspect in the relationship between commercial banks and insurance companies. As per the guidelines, commercial banks, depending on their satisfying specified eligibility criteria, can take any of the following three routes:

- By undertaking the distribution of insurance products as an agent of insurance companies on fee basis or,
- Make investments in an insurance company for providing infrastructure and services support. or
- To set up a joint venture company for undertaking insurance business with risk participation.

9.7 Guidelines Issued by RBI for the Entry of Commercial Banks in Insurance Sector

With a view to assessing the scope, desirability and eligibility of institutions to take up insurance business, draft guidelines were initially framed for banks entering into insurance business with risk participation as also for permitting banks to undertake fee-based business as insurance agents. Based on the feedback received from banks and financial institutions, the Reserve Bank issued final guidelines for banks' entry into insurance business along with the announcements in the Monetary and Credit Policy for the year 2000-2001. The guidelines are as under:

1. A scheduled commercial bank will be permitted to undertake insurance business as an agent of insurance companies on fee basis, without any risk participation. The subsidiaries of banks will also be allowed to undertake distribution of insurance product on agency basis.
2. Banks, which satisfy the eligibility criteria given below, will be permitted to set up a joint venture company for undertaking insurance business with risk participation, subject to safeguards. The maximum equity contribution such a bank

can hold in the joint venture company will normally be 50 per cent of the paid-up capital of the insurance company. On a selective basis, the Reserve Bank may permit a higher equity contribution by a promoter bank initially, pending divestment of equity within the prescribed period. The eligibility criteria for joint venture participant as on March 31, 2000 was as under:

- The net worth of the bank should not be less than Rs.500 crore.
- The Capital to Risk Weighted Assets Ratio (CRAR) of the bank should not be less than 10 per cent.
- The level of NPAs should be reasonable.
- The bank should have net profit for the last three consecutive years.
- The record of accomplishment of the performance of the subsidiaries, if any, of the concerned bank should be satisfactory.

3. In cases where a foreign partner contributes 26 per cent of the equity with the approval of IRDA/Foreign Investment Promotion Board, more than one public sector bank or private sector bank may be allowed to participate in the equity of the insurance joint venture.
4. A subsidiary of a bank or of another bank will not normally be allowed to join the insurance company on risk participation basis. Subsidiaries would include bank subsidiaries undertaking merchant banking, securities transactions, mutual fund, lease finance, housing finance, etc.
5. Banks which are not eligible as joint venture participant, as above, can make investments of up to 10 per cent of the net worth of the bank or Rs. 50 crore, whichever is lower, in the insurance company for providing infrastructure and services support. Such participation shall be treated as an investment and should be without any contingent liability for the bank.

Prior approval of the Reserve Bank is required for banks to enter into insurance business. The Reserve Bank would give permission to banks on a case-by-case basis, keeping in view all relevant factors including the position concerning the level of NPAs of the applicant bank to ensure that NPAs do not pose any future threat to the bank in its present or in the proposed line of activity, *viz.*, insurance business. With a view to ensure insulation of banking business from any risks, which may arise from insurance business, there should be an 'arms length' relationship between the bank and the insurance outfit.

Similarly, in June 2000, Non Banking Finance Companies (NBFCs) registered with the Reserve Bank were permitted, with prior approval of the Reserve Bank, to set up insurance joint ventures for undertaking insurance business with risk participation and also to undertake insurance business as agents of insurance companies on a fee basis, without any risk participation subject to satisfaction of some eligibility criteria. This facility was later extended to financial institutions in November 2001. In February 2004, it was decided to allow NBFCs registered with the Reserve Bank to take up insurance agency business on a fee basis and without risk participation, without the approval of the Reserve Bank subject to certain conditions.

9.8 Guidelines for Entry of All-India Financial Institutions in Insurance Business

On account of the interest evinced by some All-India Financial Institutions for entering into insurance business, guidelines regarding entry of All India FIs into insurance sector were issued in November 2001. The FIs are required to ensure that risks involved in insurance business do not get transmitted to the FI and that any risk that may arise from insurance business does not affect adversely its principal business.

An FI having a net owned fund of Rs. 2 crore is permitted to undertake insurance business as an agent of insurance companies on fee basis, without any risk participation.

An FI, which satisfies the eligibility criteria given below, is permitted to set up a joint venture company for undertaking insurance business with risk participation, subject to safeguards.

The maximum equity contribution that the FI can hold in the

joint venture company will normally be 50 per cent of the paid-up capital of the insurance company. On a selective basis, a higher equity contribution by a promoter will also be allowed.

The eligibility criteria for joint venture participant are:

- Owned fund of at least Rs.500 crore.
- Minimum CRAR of 15 per cent.
- NPAs which are not more than 5 per cent of outstanding loans and advances.
- The FI should have net profit for the last three consecutive years. Further, performance of subsidiaries, if any, should be satisfactory. There should be demonstrated compliance with the regulatory requirement of the RBI for rising of resources.

If a foreign partner contributes 26 per cent of equity with approval of Insurance Regulatory and Development Authority/ Foreign Investment Promotion Board, more than one FI may be allowed to participate in the equity of the insurance joint venture.

No Financial institutions would be allowed to conduct business with risk participation departmentally. A subsidiary or a company in the same group of the FI or of another FI engaged in non-banking or banking business will normally be not allowed to join the insurance company on risk participation basis.

Financial Institutions, not eligible as joint venture participants, can make investments of up to 10 per cent of the owned fund of the FI or Rs. 50 crore, whichever is lower, in the insurance company. Such participation is subject to certain eligibility conditions and will be treated as an investment and will be without any contingent liability for the FI. All FIs entering into insurance business as agents or investors or on risk participation basis have to obtain prior approval of the RBI.

9.9 Modified Guidelines for Entry of Commercial Banks in Insurance Business

With effect from October 2002, commercial banks were allowed to undertake referral business through their network of branches with the prior approval of the IRDA and the Reserve Bank. The requirement of such approval from the Reserve Bank was dispensed with in September 2003. In August 2003, a decision was taken to allow financially strong scheduled primary (urban) co-operative banks having a minimum net worth of Rs.100 crore and complying with certain other norms to undertake insurance business as corporate agents without risk participation.

As per the existing guidelines for entry of banks into insurance business, banks which satisfy certain parameters, i.e., minimum net worth of not less than Rs. 500 crore, CRAR not less than 10 per cent, net profit for the last three continuous years, reasonable level of non-performing assets and with a satisfactory track record of performance of their subsidiaries, if any, are eligible to set up insurance joint venture on risk participation basis.

Banks which are not eligible as joint venture participants, as above, would be allowed to take up strategic investment up to a certain limit for providing infrastructure and services support, if these banks satisfy some of the criteria specified therein. Further, any scheduled commercial bank or its subsidiary would be permitted to undertake insurance business as agent of an insurance company and distribute insurance products without any risk participation. The referral model, by which banks can provide physical infrastructure to insurance companies within their select branch premises and earn fee for each referral made by them, was not specifically indicated in the earlier guidelines. As the referral arrangement is akin to sub-agency and is incidental to the main activities of an agency business, it was decided that banks could undertake this activity with prior approval of Reserve Bank/ Insurance Regulatory and Development Authority.

Entry in insurance business from the year 2004 has been made even more broad-based with the inclusion of other banking entities under its ambit. In October 2004, RRBs have been allowed to undertake, with prior permission of the Reserve Bank, insurance business as corporate agents without risk participation, subject to fulfilling certain terms and conditions such as positive net worth, compliance with prudential norms, NPAs not exceeding 10 per cent, continuous profits in the last 3 years and with no accumulated losses. Besides, subject to certain conditions, they have also been allowed to undertake insurance business on a referral basis, without any risk participation, through their network of branches.

On a review of the matter of banks' entry into insurance business,(2004-05) it was decided that banks need not obtain prior approval of the Reserve Bank for engaging in insurance agency business or referral arrangement without any risk participation subject to their complying with IRDA regulations and certain other conditions. However, banks intending to set up insurance joint ventures with equity contribution on risk participation basis or making investments in the insurance companies for providing infrastructure and services support will have to obtain prior approval of the Reserve Bank.

9.10 Commercial Banks in Insurance Business

The Notification by the Government of India, specifying "Insurance" as a permissible form of business that could be undertaken by banks under Section 6(1) (o) of the Banking Regulation Act of 1949, was issued on August 3, 2000. Based on the above, detailed guidelines were issued by Reserve Bank on August 9, 2000. With the issuance of Notification by the Government of India, specifying "Insurance" as a permissible form of business, applications were invited from banks with supporting documents for their entry into insurance business.

Liberalization in the insurance sector allowed the foreign insurers to enter in to the Indian market with their partners. During the year 2000-01, twelve banks expressed their intention to enter into insurance business by way of either joint ventures or agency arrangements. Of these, "in principle" approval was given to two banks, *viz.*, SBI and Vysya Bank Ltd.

The State Bank of India was permitted to set up a life insurance subsidiary on risk participation basis with 74 per cent equity holding, with Cardiff, France. ING Vysya Bank Ltd. was accorded approval to contribute 49 per cent to the equity of insurance joint ventures on risk participation basis with ING

Insurance, Netherlands. Jammu & Kashmir Bank Ltd. was also given approval to contribute 25 per cent to the equity of insurance joint venture with Met Life USA on risk participation basis.

During the year, 2001-02 Punjab National Bank and Vijaya Bank were permitted to make strategic investment to the extent of 15 per cent and 8 per cent, respectively, in the life and non-life insurance joint venture and in a distribution and services company.

One private sector bank was given approval for participating in insurance joint venture on risk participation basis in the year 2002-03. A few banks were permitted to enter into referral arrangements with insurance companies subject to certain conditions to protect the interests of their customers. Up to the end of the year 2002-03, seventeen public sector banks, nine private sector banks and one foreign bank and a subsidiary of a private sector bank were given 'in principle' approval for acting as corporate agents of insurance companies to undertake distribution of insurance products on non-risk participation basis

Further, ICICI Bank Limited was given approval for making an additional contribution of up to Rs. 81 crore to the share capital of ICICI Lombard General Insurance Company Limited. The bank was also given approval for making an additional investment of Rs. 259 crore in the equity of ICICI Prudential Life Insurance Company Limited. Citibank, American Express, Standard Chartered Bank, HSBC, ABN-Amro, HDFC Bank, , Reliance, Deutsche Bank etc. were also given approval to act as corporate agents of insurance companies for distribution of insurance products on fee basis.

IDBI Bank and Federal Bank Ltd. was permitted to set up an insurance joint venture in the year 2006. As per the agreement, IDBI Bank will hold 48 per cent equity in the new venture while the balance 52 per cent equity will be held equally by the Federal Bank and the Holland based Fortis Insurance International. It secured the permission of the Insurance Regulatory and Development Authority. The new joint venture christened 'IDBI Fortis' is likely to start its operation in the year July, 2007.

During the year February 2007, Canara Bank and Oriental Bank of Commerce joined hands with HSBC to set up a life insurance joint venture in India. The new joint venture with a projected paid up capital of Rs. 325 crore was purported to offer innovative products that will suit all sections of the society. Canara Bank will hold 51 per cent stake, while Oriental Bank of Commerce 23 per cent and HSBC the balance of 26 per cent that is the maximum permissible limit for foreign partners under the present regulatory system. The name of the joint venture is yet to be decided. SBI Life Insurance Company was the first private sector company to turn around with net profit of Rs.2.03 crore in 2005-06.

9.11 Scope of Insurance Business in India

Because of the geographical reach and access to customers, banks could be used as best channels for the distribution of insurance products in India. The banks with their network can be effectively utilized for the distribution of insurance products and thus for drawing the resources for the development of the nation.

Studies revealed that Life Insurance Corporation covers only 8 per cent of the Indian population with insurance. In spite of its best efforts, Life Insurance Corporation has not been able to penetrate more than 15 per cent of the insurable population, which comes to more than 300 million people. Insurance penetration as a measure of percentage of GDP is very low for India and countries like South Korea has a much higher rate than India. India is the twenty-third largest markets for insurance business in the world with approximately US$ 7 billion of premium collected annually. It is at the 18th position among Life Insurance markets and 28th in Non Life Insurance markets in the world. This indicates that there is a huge untapped potential for insurance business.

Finance Minister Mr. P. Chidambaram speaking on the occasion of formalization of the tie-up of an Indian Commercial Bank with a foreign company for insurance services in the year 2007 opined that "Eighty per cent of Indians do not have any access to any insurance product neither accident, nor home, fire, riot, or theft. In fact, insurance products are unknown to millions of people in the country".

The Indian commercial banking system has a sprawling network of 69,400 branches spanning the country. Many banks have more than 1,500 branches and about fifty per cent of its branches are in rural areas. The commercial banks with a wide network of branches in both rural and urban areas and having one million staff can be effectively utilized for the distribution of insurance products and collection of premium. While the LIC has, only a limited number of branches with lakh of agents operating through out the country.

The rural economy is yet to relish the benefits of life insurance on a wide scale. In the case of LIC, its businesses from rural areas still constitute only less than 50 per cent. About 47 per cent (30776) branches of commercial banks are in the rural areas. Commercial banks can use their distribution network to sell all types of insurance products including life insurance, to their solid customers in the rural areas. The spread of insurance is thus very thin and therefore there is more than enough leeway for many players to operate in the insurance sector.

9.12 Benefits of Insurance Business to Commercial Banks

Banking is a key industry of the service sector and it is indeed the financial nerve centre of the economy. Banks are the chief providers of financial services to a very large number of individuals and small borrowers. With the introduction of liberalization measures in the banking sector and the emergence of new private sector and foreign banks equipped with latest technology, there is intense competition and consequent reduction in costs in the banking sector. Diversifications thus become imperative and insurance sector offers many opportunities for the banks to widen their business of financial intermediation.

The surplus work force available as a result of the computerization programme in the banking industry can be effectively redeployed for the insurance business. Since banking services, insurance selling and fund management are all interrelated activities and have inherent synergies, selling of insurance by banks would be mutually beneficial for banks and insurance companies. The banks with their rich experience in dealing with a diversified mix of business portfolios can make insurance service with in easy reach of poor people and that too with minimum cost. Insurance companies have experience in designing certain complex financial products and offer financial products for keeping the savings of private customers who will find them very attractive. This would accelerate pace of growth of business of both banks and insurance companies and thus enable the banks to capture market, which is captive.

9.13 Indian Insurance Business at a Glance

Up to 1999, Life Insurance business was carried out in a monopolistic manner by the government owned Life Insurance Corporation of India and Non-Life Insurance by the General Insurance Corporation of India and its four subsidiaries. The IRDA Act, enacted in 1999, liberalized the insurance industry by allowing private participation. Liberalization and Globalization have also allowed the entry of foreign players in to the Indian insurance business. Saturation of markets in many developed economies has made the Indian market even more attractive for global insurance majors. Most of the foreign insurers have entered the local market. Since 1999, the insurance business in India has been witnessing a dynamic change with presence and participation of a good number of insurers in both life and non-life segment.

The insurance business in India grew at 47.93 per cent in 2005-06, exceeding the growth of 32.49 per cent achieved in 2004-05. Compared to other developing economies, the insurance penetration in the country continues to be still very low. In the year 1990 the life insurance penetration was between one and two per cent and from 2001 onwards it came to over 2 per cent. Insurance penetration or premium volume as a share of a country's GDP, for the year 2005 stood at 2.53 per cent for life insurance and 0.62 per cent for no-life insurance. The penetration ratios of health and other non-life insurances in India is also well below the international level.

The insurance sector in India, which was opened up for private participation in the year 1999, and it has completed seven years in a liberalized setting. Table 9.1 portrays the growth of insurance companies in India. It is revealed that since the enactment of the IRDA Act in 1999, there was a tremendous growth in the number of insurance companies. The number of Life Insurance Companies increased from one at the end of September 2000 to 16 at the end of July 2006. During this seven-year period, IRDA granted registration to fifteen new private life insurance companies, which commenced their operations.

General Insurance Corporation of India and its four subsidiaries used to carry out the business of general insurance in India in a monopolistic manner till 1999. During October 2000 to September 2006, 11 non-life insurance companies (2 in public sector and 9 in private sector) were given registration and they commenced their operations during this period.

At the end of July 2006, 16 life insurance, 15 general insurance and 1 re-insurance company were functioning in the area of insurance as a whole. Since the opening up of the insurance sector in 1999, 24 private companies and 2 public companies were given licenses by the IRDA.

Insurance sector has become more competitive because of new entrants in the field of Life and Non Life insurance. Insurers are introducing increasingly by innovative products to meet the specific and particular needs of the prospective policyholders. The Market shares of LIC and major Private life insurance companies at the end of March 2006 are given in Table 9.2.

The market share of the business of state owned LIC got reduced from 100 per cent at the end of the year 1999 to 79.00 per cent at the end of March 2006. Among the private players ICICI Prudential leads with 4.02 per cent market share followed by Baja Allianz with a market share of 2.95 per cent. HDFC Standard is in the third position with a market share of 1.48 per cent followed by Birla Sunlife (1.19 per cent) and SBI Life (1.01 per cent).

Table 9.1: Number of Registered Insurance Companies in India as in July 2006

Type of business	Public Sector					Private Sector				
	2000*	2002*	2005*	2006#	Total	2000*	2002*	2005*	2006#	Total
Life Insurance	1	-	-	-	1	3	9	2	1	15
General Insurance	4	2	-	-	6	3	6	-	-	9
Re-insurance	1	-	-	-	1	-	-	-	-	-
Total	6	2	-	-	8	6	15	2	1	24

*December; #July

Table 9.2: Market Shares of Major Life Insurance Companies (March 31, 2006)

1.	Life Insurance Corporation of India	79.0
Major Private Sector Life Insurance Companies		
1.	ICICI Prudential Life Insurance Company Limited	4.02
2.	Bajaj Allianz Life Insurance Company Limited	2.95
3.	HDFC Standard Life Insurance Company Limited	1.48
4.	Birla Sunlife Life Insurance Company Limited	1.19
5.	SBI Life Insurance Company Limited	1.01
6.	Tata AIG Life Insurance Company Limited	.831
7.	Max New York Life Insurance Company Limited	.744
8.	Kotak Mahindra Old Mutual Life Insurance Company Limited	.58
9.	Private Sector Total	21.00
10.	Public Sector Total	79.00

Other companies which operate the area of life insurance are the following; (1) ING Vysya Life Insurance Company Private Ltd., (2) Metlife India Insurance Company Pvt. Ltd., (3)AMP Sanmar Life Insurance Company Ltd., (4) Aviva Life Insurance Co. India Pvt. Ltd., (5) Sahara India Insurance Company Ltd., (6) Shriram Life Insurance Company Ltd. and (7) Bharti Axa Life insurance Company Ltd. The market share of each of these companies continues to be less than one per cent. It is clear from the table that private and foreign companies operating in the life insurance business made it difficult LIC to retain their business.

Table 9.3 discloses that market share of leading non–life insurance companies both in the private and public sector.

Table 9.3 depicts that the market share of private non life insurance companies during the year 2005-06 represent 26.33 per cent of the total non life insurance business in India. However, during the year 2005-06 public sector general insurance companies' market share declined to 73.67 per cent from 73.90 in 2004-05. The leading public sector New India Assurance Companies market share dwindled from 24.09 per cent in 2004-05 to 23.54 per cent in 2005-06. Oriental Insurance Co. had a market share of 17.32 per cent, followed by National Insurance Company with 17.31 per cent and United India Assurance Co. with 15.50 per cent for the year ended 2005-06. The market share for the year 2004-05 relating to these three companies were in the order of 17.26 per cent, 21.74 per cent and 16.84 per cent respectively.

Among private insurance companies, ICICI Lombard is leading with 7.77 per cent market share with a growth rate of 81.13 per cent, followed by Bajaj Allianz with a market share of 6.25 per cent. IFFCO Tokio is in the third position with a market share of 4.38 per cent. Newly formed public sector general insurance company viz. Export Credit Guarantee Corporation Ltd (ECGE) has a market share of 2.70 per cent, occupying a fifth position among the newly started companies.

Table 9.3: Market Shares of Leading Non-Life Insurance Companies (March 31, 2006)

1.	New India Assurance Co.	23.54
2.	Oriental Insurance Co.	17.32
3.	National Insurance Company	17.31
4.	United India Assurance Co.	15.50
5.	Total of Old Public Sector Insurance Companies	73.67
6.	Export Credit Guarantee Corporation Ltd.	2.70
Major Private Sector General Insurance Companies		
1.	ICICI Lombard General Insurance Company Ltd.	7.77
2.	Bajaj Allianz General Insurance Company Ltd.	6.25
3.	IFFCO Tokio General Insurance Company Ltd.	4.38
4.	Tata AIG General Insurance Company Ltd.	2.68
5.	Royal Sundaram Alliance Insurance Company Ltd.	2.15
6.	Cholamandalam General Insurance Company Ltd.	1.04
7.	Total Private Sector	26.33

During the year 2005-06, the market share of Tata AIG and Royal Sundaram accounted 2.68 per cent and 2.15 per cent respectively of the total non-life insurance business in India. The market share of other players' viz. HDFC Chubb General Insurance Company Ltd., Reliance General Insurance Company Ltd. and the public sector Agriculture Insurance Company of India Ltd. (AIC) continued to be less than 1 per cent. Star Health and Allied Insurance Company Limited commenced its business only in the month of March 2006.

10

Banking Ombudsman Scheme

10.1 Introduction

Complaints and grievances against banks are handled by the Reserve Bank of India at two levels. Banking Ombudsman maintain and handle such complaints that will come under the provisions of the Banking Ombudsman Scheme. Regulatory Departments in the Reserve Bank of India handle those complaints that do not come under the provisions of the Banking Ombudsman Scheme.

Banking Ombudsman Scheme was introduced to safeguard the interest of customers and to redress their grievances. It is a speedy and inexpensive system of redressal of grievances of customers against banks. Banking Ombudsman system is very popular in many countries like United Kingdom, Australia, New Zealand etc. The word Ombudsman in general means a 'grievance man' a public official who is appointed to investigate complaints against the administration.

The scheme is introduced with the object of resolving disputes relating to deficiency of services in banks. It facilitates settlement of disputes between a bank and their customers and between banks. The Scheme envisages expeditious and satisfactory disposal of customer complaints in a time-bound manner through methods of conciliation, mediation and arbitration.

The RBI notified the Banking Ombudsmen Scheme on June 14, 1995 and the Scheme has been in operation since then. As per the recommendations of the Informal Group constituted by the Reserve Bank of India to recommend steps to improve upon the effectiveness of the Scheme, the Banking Ombudsman scheme, 1995 was reviewed. The revised Banking Ombudsman Scheme (BOS) 2002 came into effect on June 14, 2002. To enlarge the extent and scope of the authority and functions of Banking Ombudsman, the RBI partially modified both the Banking Ombudsman Schemes of 1995 and 2002 in the year 2005. The revised scheme came in to force on January 1, 2006.

As per the revised scheme Banking Ombudsman has been authorized by the Reserve Bank of India to receive complaints from the customers of the bank in the following new areas of banking services such as issue of credit cards, failure to provide the promised facilities, non- adherence to the Fair Practices Code and levying of excessive service charges with out prior intimation or notice.

The revised BO scheme also relaxed the mandatory requirement of filing complaints in the application format as prescribed prior to 2006. Complaints can also be filed on-line as well as by sending an e-mail. The complainants can also appeal against the award of the Banking Ombudsman. The secretariat of the office of the Banking Ombudsmen, which earlier consisted of officers from State Level Bankers Committee Convener banks, will now consist of only officers deputed from the Reserve Bank of India. Furthermore, in order to enable the Banking Ombudsman to concentrate more on the complaints, rather than on arbitration of inter bank disputes, the arbitration option enjoyed and exercised by the Banking Ombudsman was removed.

The Banking Ombudsman Scheme is executed and enforced by the Banking Ombudsmen appointed by Reserve Bank of India at 15 centres spanning the whole country.

10.2 Scope of the Scheme

At the time of its introduction in 1995, it was applicable only to Commercial Banks and Scheduled Primary Co-operative Banks conducting business in India. Regional Rural Banks were exempted from the purview of the scheme. The Banking Ombudsman Scheme, 2002 covered all the Regional Rural Banks in addition to all Commercial Banks and Scheduled Primary Co-operative Banks, which were already covered by earlier Banking Ombudsman Scheme, 1995.

The Banking Ombudsman Scheme was operationalised by Reserve Bank of India by establishing Banking Ombudsman Offices at 15 centres across the country.

The offices and area of operation of the Banking Ombudsman are given below:

- Ahmedabad (Gujarat, UT of Dadra and Nagar Haveli, Daman and Diu).
- Bangalore (Karnataka).
- Bhuvaneswar (Orissa).
- Bhopal (Madhaya Pradesh and Chattisgarh).
- Kolkata (West Bengal and Sikkim).
- Chennai (Tamil Nadu and UT of Pondicherry and Andaman and Nicobar Islands).
- Chandigarh (Himachal Pradesh, Punjab, and UT of Chandigarh).
- Guwahati (Assam, Arunachal Pradesh, Manipur, Meghalaya, Mizoram, Nagaland and Tripura).
- Hyderabad (Andhra Pradesh).
- Jaipur (Rajasthan).
- Kanpur (Uttar Pradesh excluding District of Ghaziabad and Uttaranchal).
- Patna (Bihar and Jharkhand).
- Mumbai (Maharashtra and Goa).
- New Delhi (Delhi, Haryana and Jammu and Kashmir and Ghaziabad district of Uttar Pradesh).
- Thiruvananthapuram. (Kerala and Union Territory of Lakshadweep).

The Scheme is executed by Banking Ombudsmen who are appointed by Reserve Bank of India. The Reserve Bank of India is entrusted with the responsibility of framing the guidelines for operationalising the Scheme. It also monitors and supervises the running of the Scheme and administrative arrangements, budget and expenditure of the Banking Ombudsmen Offices.

The Banking Ombudsman should be a reputed person having experience in the legal, banking, financial services, public administration or management sectors and if such person is a civil servant he should be in the rank of Joint Secretary or above in the Government of India and in case of such person being from banking sector, he should have experience of working as a whole time director of a public sector enterprise or one holding equivalent position.

The Governor of the Reserve Bank of India is entrusted with the task of appointment of Banking Ombudsman in each area to carry out the functions of the Banking Ombudsman Scheme. The appointment of Ombudsmen is on the basis of the recommendations of the Selection Committee constituted by the Governor of RBI. The Selection Committee consists of four members. All the three Deputy Governors of the RBI are members of the committee. The Additional Secretary of the Department of Economic Affairs (Finance) is a Special Invitee to the committee meetings.

The Banking Ombudsman is appointed for a period not exceeding three years. The minimum age of a person to be considered for the post of a Banking Ombudsman should be 55 years. Subject to the recommendations of the Selection Committee the tenure of the Banking Ombudsmen can further be extended for a period of maximum of two years with an age limit of 65 years.

10.3 Power and Duties of Banking Ombudsman

10.3.1 General Powers and Duties: Following are the powers and duties of the Banking Ombudsman:

- To receive complaints regarding provision of banking services;
- To process such complaints and facilitate their settlement by agreement, through conciliation\ mediation between the bank and the aggrieved parties or by passing an Award in accordance with the Scheme; and
- To resolve by way of arbitration inter bank disputes and those between a bank and its constituents as may be agreed upon by the disputed parties in accordance with the provisions of the Scheme and the Arbitration and Conciliation Act of 1996.

10.3.2 Other Powers and Duties: The other powers and duties of Banking Ombudsman are listed below:

- The Banking Ombudsman shall exercise general powers of superintendence and control over his Office and shall be responsible for the conduct of business thereat.
- The Banking Ombudsman shall have the power to incur expenditure on behalf of the Office. The expenditures incurred should be with in the limits of budget provision, which is prepared by the Ombudsman and finally approved by the Reserve Bank of India. The Reserve Bank will indicate the share of expenditure to be borne by the concerned banks.
- The Banking Ombudsman shall send to the Governor, Reserve Bank of India, by May 31, of every year, a report containing a general review of the activities of his Office during the preceding financial year and shall furnish such other information as the Reserve Bank call for:
- The Reserve Bank may, if it considers necessary in the public interest to do so, publish the report and the information received from the Banking Ombudsman in such consolidated form or otherwise as it deems fit.

The remuneration and other perquisites payable to a Banking Ombudsman will be determined by the Reserve Bank from time to time and shall be borne by the banks in such proportion and manner as may be decided by the Reserve Bank.

10.4 Grounds of Complaints on Banking Services

Banking Ombudsmen have been authorized by the Reserve Bank of India to receive complaints from the customers of the bank in the following areas of banking services:

- Deficiency in banking service.
- Sanction of loans and advances as they relate to non-observance of the Reserve Bank directives on interest rates, delay in sanction or non-observance of prescribed time schedule for disposal of loan applications or non-observance of any other directions or instructions of the Reserve Bank as may be specified for this purpose, from time to time, and

- Such other matters as may be specified by the Reserve Bank.

10.4.1 Deficiency in Banking Services: Banking Ombudsmen receive complaints on deficiency in any one of the banking services, which are specifically listed below:

1. Non-payment /inordinate delay in the payment or collection of cheques, drafts, bills etc;
2. Non-acceptance, without sufficient cause, of small denomination notes tendered for any purpose, and for charging of commission in respect thereof;
3. Non-issue of drafts to customers and others;
4. Non-adherence to prescribed working hours by branches;
5. Failure to honour guarantee/letter of credit commitments by banks;
6. Claims in respect of unauthorized or fraudulent withdrawals from deposit accounts, or fraudulent encashment of a cheque or a bank draft etc.
7. Complaints pertaining to the operations in any savings, current or any other account maintained with a bank, such as delays, non-credit of proceeds to parties' accounts, non-payment of deposit or non-observance of the Reserve Bank directives, if on rate of interest for deposits.
8. Complaints from exporters in India such as delays in receipt of export proceeds, handling of export bills, collection of bills etc., provided the said complaints pertain to the bank's operations in India;
9. Complaints from Non-Resident Indians having accounts in India in relation to their remittances from abroad, deposits and other bank-related matters.
10. Complaints pertaining to refusal to open deposit accounts without any valid reason for refusal
11. Levying of charges without sufficient prior notice to the customer.
12. Non-adherence by the bank or its subsidiaries to the instructions of Reserve Bank on ATM or Debit card operations or Credit card operations;
13. Non-disbursement or delay in disbursement of pension

14. Refusal to accept or delay in accepting payment towards taxes, as required by Reserve Bank/Government;
15. Refusal to issue or delay in issuing, or failure to service or delay in servicing or redemption of Government securities;
16. Forced closure of deposit accounts without due notice or without sufficient reason;
17. Refusal to close or delay in closing of accounts;
18. Any other matter relating to the violation of the directives issued by the Reserve Bank in relation to banking service.

10.4.2 Complaints Regarding Sanction, Disbursement and Disposal of Loans and Advances: Banking Ombudsmen have been authorized by the Reserve Bank of India to receive complaints on loans and advances, which are specifically mentioned below:

1. Non-observance of Reserve Bank of India directives on interest rates;
2. Delays in sanction, disbursement or non-observance of prescribed time schedule for disposal of loan applications;
3. Non-acceptance of application for loans without furnishing valid reasons to the applicant; and
4. Non-observance of any other directions or instructions specified from time to time by the Reserve Bank for this purpose.

10.4.3 Other Matters as may be specified by the Reserve Bank: Banking Ombudsman may also deal with any other such matter as may be specified by the Reserve Bank from time to time.

10.5 Procedure for Filing Complaint

1. In India, any person having a complaint or grievance relating to the banking services, may himself\herself or through his authorized representative prefers a complaint to the Banking Ombudsman within whose jurisdiction the branch of the complainant bank is located.
2. The complaint should be in a form specified in Annexure-A of the Scheme and duly signed by the complainant or his

authorized representative (other than an advocate). The complainant should state clearly his name and address and also the name and address of the branch or office of the bank against which the complaint is made. The complainant should state clearly the facts giving rise to the complaint and it should be supported by document as proof. Nature and extent of the loss caused to the complainant, the relief sought from the Banking Ombudsman should also be stated clearly in the complaint. He should also file a declaration about the compliance of the conditions referred in Clause (3).

3. No complaint to the Banking Ombudsman shall lie unless:

a The complainant had before making a complaint to the Banking Ombudsman made a written representation to the bank named in the complaint. A person whose grievance against a bank is rejected or no reply received on the complaint from the bank or if the complaint is not resolved to his satisfaction by that bank within a period of two months can approach the Banking Ombudsman.

b The complaint should be made within one year from the date of rejection or final reply given by the bank concerned.

c The complaint is not in respect of the same subject matter, which was settled through the Office of the Banking Ombudsman in any previous proceedings and one not received from the same complainant or along with any one or more complainants or any one or more of the parties concerned with the subject matter.

d The complaint does not pertain to the same subject matter, for which any proceedings before any court, tribunal or arbitrator or any other forum is pending or a decree or Award or a final order has already been passed by any such competent court, tribunal, arbitrator or forum.

e The complaint is not frivolous or vexatious in nature.

4. Notwithstanding the provisions of sub-clause 3(d) of this clause, it would be open to the Banking Ombudsman to entertain a complaint falling under the Scheme provided the Banking Ombudsman is satisfied with the documentary

evidence produced before him by the complainant that;

- The interests of the complainant has suffered adversely on account of lapse or inaction on the part of the bank or due to connivance on the part of any employee of the bank facilitating the unauthorised or fraudulent withdrawal from the bank account of the complainant; or encashment, as the case may be;
- No interim injunction or stay order or any other direction, either restraining, the bank from making payment of the amount of claim as made by the complainant or the complainant from agitating his claim simultaneously, before any other forum, has been passed by any court, tribunal or arbitrator or any other such forum before whom the claim of the complainant is pending adjudication and
- In the opinion of the Banking Ombudsman the disposal of such pending proceeding is likely to take longer time.

10.6 Procedure for Redressal of Grievances

10.6.1 Power to Call for Information: When a complaint is received regarding the banking services, the Banking Ombudsmen will forward a copy of the complaint to the bank named in the complaint. The complainant should also inform the bank named in the complaint or any other related bank to provide any information or to furnish certified copies of any document relating to the complaint which is in possession of the bank. Provided that in the event of the failure of a bank to comply with the requisition without sufficient cause, the Banking Ombudsman may, if he deems fit, draw the inference that such information provided or copies furnished would be unfavourable to the bank. The Banking Ombudsman should maintain complete confidentiality of information or document coming into his knowledge or possession in the course of discharging his duties and should not disclose such information and document to any person except with the consent of the person furnishing such information or document.

10.6.2 Settlement of Complaint by Agreement: On receipt

of the complaint, the Banking Ombudsman shall send a notice of the receipt of the complaint along with a copy of the complaint to the branch of the bank named by the complainant. Be it practicable, the Banking Ombudsman shall try to facilitate a settlement of the complaint by advising the nodal officer of the concerned bank for the same. The banks covered by the Scheme shall appoint Nodal Officers at their Regional/Zonal Offices and inform the respective Office of the Banking Ombudsman under whose jurisdiction the Regional/Zonal Office falls. The Nodal Officer so appointed shall be responsible for representing the bank and furnishing information to the Banking Ombudsman in respect of complaints filed. The Nodal Officer settles the complaint by facilitating an agreement between the complainant and the bank through conciliation or mediation. For the purpose of the same, the Banking Ombudsman may follow such procedure he may consider just and proper and he shall not be bound by any rules of evidence.

10.6.3 Settlement by Award: If a complaint is not settled by agreement within a period of one month from the date of receipt of the complaint or such further period as the Banking Ombudsman may allow the parties, he may, after allowing the parties a reasonable time to present their case, pass an Award or reject the complaint. Before passing an award or rejecting a complaint, the Banking Ombudsman should take into account the evidences placed before him by both the parties. He should also take into account the principles of banking law and practice, directions, instructions and guidelines issued by the Reserve Bank from time to time and such other factors which in his opinion are related and relevant to the complaint.

The Award must contain a summary of valid reasons for passing the award and specific directions to the bank. It must also state clearly the amount if any to be paid by the bank to the complainant by way of compensation for the loss suffered by him. The amount of compensation in any case should not be more than the actual loss suffered by the complainant as a direct consequence of the act of omission or commission of the bank or ten lakh rupees which ever is less.

In the case of complaints arising out of credit card operations, the Banking Ombudsman while determining the amount of compensation payable should take into account the loss of the complainant's time, expenses incurred by the complainant, financial loss, harassment and mental anguish suffered by the complainant.

A copy of the Award must be sent to the complainant and the bank concerned. If the complainant does not accept the Award passed by the Banking Ombudsman or fails to furnish his letter of acceptance within a period of 15 days or within such further time not exceeding a period of fifteen days that may be granted by the Banking Ombudsman, the Award should be cancelled by rejecting the complaint.

The bank concerned should comply with the Award within one month from the date of receipt of the acceptance letter from the complainant or within such time as not exceeding a period of fifteen days that may be granted by the Banking Ombudsman and it should informed it to the Banking Ombudsman.

An Award shall not be binding on a bank against which it is passed unless the complainant furnishes to it, within a period of 15 days from the date of receipt of copy of the Award and a letter of acceptance of the Award in full and final settlement of his claim in the matter. If in the opinion of the bank the Award passed against it is based on wrong appreciation of facts or banking law and practice, or general directions issued by the Reserve Bank; or implementation of the Award is likely to create a bad precedent for the bank or banking companies, the bank can file a review petition to the Review Authority and intimate to the Ombudsman with in one month from the date of the receipt of the copy of the Award. In the event of failure on the part of the bank to implement the Award within the prescribed time limit, the complainant can also approach the Review Authority to pass an appropriate direction to the bank for immediate compliance of the Award.

10.6.4 Appeal before the Appellate Authority: The

aggrieved party i.e. the complainant or the bank not agreeing to the Award passed by the Ombudsman may have the opportunity to file an appeal before the Appellate Authority. The revised Banking Ombudsman Scheme 2002 additionally provides for the institution of a "Review Authority" to review the Banking Ombudsman's Award, when warranted. Deputy Governor in charge of Rural Planning and Credit Department of the Reserve Bank will act as the Review Authority and will be also responsible for the implementation of the scheme. A bank against whom an Award has been passed may with the approval of its Chief Executive, file an application to the Review Authority to seek a review of the Award. The bank can request for such a review only when the Award appears to be patently in conflict with the Bank's instructions and the law and practices relating to banking. The time limit for filing an appeal is 45 days from the date of the receipt of the Award or with in an extended time of 30 days allowed by the Appellate Authority.

10.6.5 Directions issued by the Review Authority: The Review Authority on receiving application should serve a copy of the review application as soon as possible, to the other party. The Review Authority should not accept any additional or new material from any party, which was not produced before the Banking Ombudsman at the time of complaint. The Appellate Authority should give a reasonable time to both the parties to present their case before the authority. After hearing, the Review Authority may adopt any one of the following step:

- Dismiss the appeal.
- Allow the appeal and set aside the Award.
- Return the matter to the Banking Ombudsman for fresh disposal in accordance with such directions as the Appellate Authority may consider necessary or proper.
- Modify the Award and pass such directions as may be necessary to give effect to the Award so modified.
- Pass any other order as it may deem fit. The order of the Appellate Authority should have the same effect as the Award passed by Banking Ombudsman.

The Review Authority on consideration of the review petition, is of the opinion that there is no reasonable ground for review of the Award, then the Authority should issue appropriate direction to the bank to implement the Award with in a period of six weeks from the date of submission of the application or with in such a reasonable time as the review authority may consider necessary. Provided that in the event of the bank failing to implement the Award within the prescribed time limit, the complainant may also, if he so desires, approach the Review Authority to pass an appropriate direction to the bank for immediate compliance of the Award.

10.6.6 Rejection of the Complaint: The Banking Ombudsman may reject a complaint at any stage if it appears to him that the complaint made is:

- Frivolous, vexatious, malafide.
- Without any sufficient cause.
- That it is not pursued by the complainant with reasonable diligence.
- In the opinion of the Banking Ombudsman there is no loss or damage or inconvenience caused to the complainant.
- Beyond the pecuniary jurisdiction of Banking Ombudsman.

The Banking Ombudsman may reject a complaint at any stage if after consideration of the complaint and evidence produced before him the Banking Ombudsman is of the opinion that the nature of the complaint requires consideration of elaborate documentary and oral evidence and the proceedings before the Banking Ombudsman are not appropriate for adjudication of such complaint. The decision of the Banking Ombudsman in this regard shall be final and binding on the complainant and the bank.

10.7 Arbitration and Conciliation Procedure

10.7.1 Banking Ombudsman to Act as Arbitrator: The Banking Ombudsman has also been authorised to function as an Arbitrator. The Banking Ombudsman should assume the office of an arbitrator only if the parties submit the disputes to the Ombudsman by giving their consent through an affidavit duly stamped and notarized. Any dispute between a bank and its constituents or between a bank and another bank can be referred to a banking Ombudsman for arbitration if both the parties agree. The value of the subject matter of individual disputes under arbitration will not exceed Rupees Ten lakh. After assuming charge as an arbitrator, in any dispute, if the Banking Ombudsman considers at any stage that he is unable to perform his function independently and without any personal interest, then he shall decline to continue as an arbitrator.

On receipt of a complaint for arbitration the Secretariat of the Ombudsman direct the claimant to submit his statement of claims along with the list of documents and list of witnesses, with in a period not exceeding three months. The Banking Ombudsman shall be provided with a Secretariat drawn from banks, Reserve Bank, etc., who will be placed on duty with the Office of the Banking Ombudsman. The Secretariat sends a copy of the claim and the documents to the opposite party. The opposite party should submit the reply with the defense supported by relevant documents, to the secretariat with in 15 days from the receipt of the claim. If the opposite party wishes to make a counter claim it should be mentioned in the reply and file the same with in the stipulated time. On receipt of documents the Secretariat should prepare the case for the hearing and seek orders of the Banking Ombudsman for the date for first hearing. The date of hearing should be intimated to the parties. The parties may make new claims or counter- claims before the Banking Ombudsman provided that such new claim or counter-claims remain within the limits of the Terms of Reference. The time limit for award is fixed as six months from the date of first hearing. After signing the award the Banking Ombudsman should send the same to the Secretariat for communicating it to the parties concerned.

10.7.2 Display of Details of Banking Ombudsman Scheme: Bank branches which are covered under the Banking Ombudsman scheme are required to display the features of the scheme for common knowledge of the public.

- The banks covered by the Scheme shall ensure that the

purpose of the Scheme and the name and address of the Banking Ombudsman to whom the complaints are to be made by the aggrieved party are displayed prominently in all the offices and branches of the bank in such manner that a person visiting the office or branch has adequate information of the Scheme.

- The banks covered by the Scheme shall ensure that a copy of the Scheme is available with the designated officer of the bank who is in the office premises and a notice about its availability is displayed at a prominent place in the office.
- The banks covered by the Scheme shall appoint Nodal Officers at their Regional/Zonal Offices and inform the respective Office of the Banking Ombudsman under whose jurisdiction the Regional/Zonal Office falls. The Nodal Officer so appointed shall be responsible for representing the bank and furnishing information to the Banking Ombudsman in respect of complaints filed against the bank.

10.8 Performance of the Banking Ombudsmen

The performance of the Banking Ombudsman Scheme is evaluated by taking into account the variables like the number of complaints received, the grounds of complaints, bank- wise break up of complaints received, complaints settled, complaints pending settlement, awards issued etc.

The number of complaints received and the average complaint received per office of Banking Ombudsman from 1998-99 to 2003-04 is given in Table 10.1.

The Banking Ombudsman Scheme is functioning in the country through Banking Ombudsman Offices established at 15 centres. The number of complaints received by the Banking Ombudsman has been steadily increasing since 1999-2000. More than 5000 complaints are received by the Banking Ombudsmen every year.

A review of the performance of the scheme discloses that complaints received decreased marginally from 6060 in 1998-99 to 4994 in 1999-2000. When compared to the complaints received during 1998-99, there was a decrease in complaints of 2.5 per cent in the year 2001-02 and 11 per cent in the year 2002-03. Compared to 2002-03, (5,399) there was a sharp rise in complaints of 36 per cent (8,246) during the year 2003-04. Average complaints received per year per office also decreased marginally from 404 in 1998-99 to 360 in 2002-03. While during the year 2003-04 on an average 550 complaints were received by the offices of Banking Ombudsman.

Table 10.1: Number of Complaints Received by the Banking Ombudsmen (1998-2004)

Period	No. of Offices of Banking Ombudsman	No. of Complaints Received	Average No. of Complaints Per Office
1998-99	15	6060	404
1999-00	15	4994 (-17.5)	333
2000-01	15	5803 (- 4.2)	387
2001-02	15	5907 (-2.5)	394
2002-03	15	5399 (-11)	360
2003-04	15	8246 (36)	550

Figures in brackets indicate percentage of change in number of complaints compared to the year 1998-99.

10.8.1 Centre-wise Complaints Received: For the year ended March 31, 2002 the maximum number of complaints were received at Jaipur (1021). Other offices of the Banking Ombudsman, which received more than the average number of complaints of 394, were New Delhi (624), Thiruvananthapuram (545), Kolkata (506), Chandigarh (466) and Hyderabad (406). As in the past, majority of complaints during the period emanated from metropolitan and urban centers. Very few complaints were received from rural and semi-urban areas. In order to popularize the Scheme among the rural and semi-urban population, campaigns have been organized by the Offices of Banking Ombudsman apart from inserting advertisements in the local newspapers.

10.8.2 Grounds for Complaints: The grounds of complaints of customers regarding deficiency in banking services are illustrated in Table 10.2. The grounds of complaints of customers regarding deficiency in banking services are analyzed and then classified in to four major heads. The maximum number of complaints dealt with during the period under review pertained to complaints regarding deposit accounts, followed by deficiency in servicing of loans and advances, delay in collection of cheques/bills and miscellaneous complaints. In the year 2003-04 maximum number of complaints dealt with pertained to deposit accounts. It accounted to 26.4 per cent of the total complaints. Complaints regarding loans and advances represent 13 per cent and complaints on delay in collection of cheques\bills represent 10.6 per cent of the total. Miscellaneous complaints represent around 50 per cent of the total.

10.8.3 Break-up of complaints dealt with Bank Group-wise: Bank group-wise break-up of complaints on deficiency in banking services is depicted in Table 10.3.

Table 10.3 reveals that majority of the complaints pertain to the Nationalized Banks followed by the State Bank Group. In 2003-04 the complaints pertained to nationalized banks represent 42.7 per cent of the total complaints followed State Bank Group 29.3 per cent. Thus, around 72 per cent of the complaints are relating to public sector banks. The complaints relating to the private banks represent only 14 per cent of the total.

The RRBs were brought under the purview of the Banking Ombudsman from the year 2002 as per BOS 2002 and the number of complaints against RRBs increased from 33 during the year 2002-2003 to 232 during the year under review. Increasing number of complaints against RRBs also indicate the penetration of the Scheme in rural areas. Compared to 2002-03 the number of complaints of private sector banks in 2003-04 increased by 54 per cent, SBI and group 45 per cent, nationalized banks 28 per cent and foreign banks by 29 per cent.

Table 10.2: Analysis of Complaints Dealt with: Subject-wise (1998-2004)

Particulars	1998-99	1999-00	2000-01	2001-02	2002-03	2003-04
Deposit Accounts	1830 (24.5)	1687 (24.8)	1617 (23.1)	1662 (23.7)	1789 (27.4)	2500 (26.4)
Loans and Advances	1904 (25.5)	1844 (27.1)	1930 (27.7)	1982 (28.2)	1651 (25.4)	1226 (13.0)
Delay in Collection of Cheques/Bills	1198 (16.0)	943 (13.8)	999 (14.4)	1062 (15.1)	908 (14.1)	1001 (10.6)
Miscellaneous	2532 (34.0)	2326 (34.3)	2432 (34.8)	2316 (33.0)	2158 (33.1)	4756 (50.0)
Total	7464 (1404)* (100)	6800 (1806)* (100)	6978 (1175)* (100)	7022 (1115)* (100)	6506 (1107)* (100)	9483 (1237)* (100)

*No. of complaints includes previous year's pending complaints as indicated in brackets. Figures in brackets indicates percentage to total.

Table 10.3: Break-up of Complaints Dealt with: Bank Group-wise (1998-2004)

Bank group	1998-99	1999-00	2000-01	2001-02	2002-03	2003-04
Nationalized Banks	4063 (54.4)	3857 (56.8)	3657 (52.4)	3609 (51.3)	3145 (48.3)	4049 (42.7)
SBI Group	2337 (31.3)	1960 (28.8)	2175 (31.2)	2112 (30.1)	1914 (29.4)	2779 (29.3)
Private Sector Banks	390 (5.2)	417 96.1)	531 (7.6)	629 (9.0)	718 (11.0)	1325 (14.0)
Foreign Banks	219 (2.9)	198 (2.9)	147 (2.1)	254 (3.6)	313 (4.8)	406 (4.3)
Scheduled Primary Co-op. Banks	82 (1.1)	131 (1.9)	122 (1.7)	55 (0.8)	112 (1.7)	166 (1.7)
Others	373 (5.10	237 (3.5)	346 (5.0)	363 (5.2)	304* (4.8)	758** (8.0)
Total	7464 (100)	6800 (100)	6978 (100)	7022 (100)	6506 (100)	9483 (100)

* Includes 33 complaints against RRBs.

** Includes 232 complaints against RRBs.

Figures in brackets indicates percentage to total.

10.8.4 Disposal of Complaints by Banking Ombudsman: The performance of the Banking Ombudsman regarding the settlement of complaints received during the year 1998-99 to 2003-04 is exhibited in Table 10.4.

Table 10.4 reveals that Banking Ombudsman offices disposed around 68 per cent of the maintainable complaints in the year 1998-99. The table further reveals that despite increase in the number of complaints, the percentage of maintainable complaints disposed off also increased steadily except during 1999-2000. During the year 2003-04, the percentage of maintainable complaints disposed represent 73 per cent of the total maintained.

10.8.5 Awards Issued: Details of Awards issued by the Banking Ombudsman during a period of six years are given in Table 10.5.

The Ombudsmen disposed of complaints either by settlement or by issuing an Award. Table 10.5 discloses that during a review of a period of six years (1998-99 to 2003-04), only 430 awards were issued by the Ombudsman, which came to about 2.2 per cent of the total 19,068 maintainable complaints disposed of. During the period under review the percentage of disposal of complaints by settlement to total maintainable complaints disposed of was around 98 per cent. The high percentage of settlement of complaints indicates the effectiveness of the Banking Ombudsmen in disposing of cases.

10.8.6 Other Information: The Banking Ombudsman Scheme 2002 empowered the Banking Ombudsman to deal with cases of disputes between customers and banks and between banks, involving an amount of up to Rs. 10 lakh. During the year 2003-04, the Banking Ombudsmen handled 34 such cases of inter-bank disputes and 19 of those cases were pending disposal at the close of the year. Most of the arbitration cases were handled at Ahmedabad (15) and Mumbai (7) Banking Ombudsman offices.

10.9 Cost Details of Banking Ombudsman

The cost incurred since 1999 in Ombudsman's offices for operating the scheme is presented in Table 10.6

Table 10.4: Disposal of Complaints by Banking Ombudsmen (1998-2004)

Particulars	1998-99	1999-00	2000-01	2001-02	2002-03	2003-04
Complaints Received	7464*	6800*	6978*	7022*	6506*	9483*
Of which not Maintainable	3317	2614	2732	2404	2132	4011
Complaints Maintainable	4147	4186	4246	4618	4374	5472
Complaints Disposed of	2807	2484	3131	3511	3137	3998
Percentage of Maintainable Complaints Disposed of	68	60	74	76	72	73
Complaints Pending	1340	1702	1115	1107	1237	1474

*Includes previous year's pending complaints.

Table 10.5: Awards Issued by the Banking Ombudsman (1998-2004)

Particulars	1998-99	1999-00	2000-01	2001-02	2002-03	2003-04
Total awards	92	74	52	44	47	121
Awards not Implemented by banks	49	34	27	16	20	37
Per cent of Disposal of Complaints by Issue of Awards to Total Maintainable Complaints Disposed of	3.28	2.98	1.66	1.25	1.07	2.21
Per cent of Disposal of Complaints by Mediation/reconciliation/ Recommendation/settlement to total Maintainable Complaints Disposed of	96.72	97.02	98.34	98.75	98.93	97.78

Table 10.6: Cost details of Banking Ombudsman Offices (1998-2004)

Period	Total Cost (Rs. crore)	No. of Complaints Dealt with	Cost per Complaint (Rs.)
1998-99	5.30	7,464	7,108
1999-00	6.15	6,800	9,050
2000-01	6.99	6,978	10,020
2001-02	5.91	7,022	8,425
2002-03	6.36	6,506	9,783
2003-04	7.03	9,483	7,413

The expenditures incurred in Ombudsman's offices for operating the scheme is inclusive of both revenue and capital expenditure. During the period under review the total annual costs of running the 15 Banking Ombudsman offices varied from around Rs 5.30 crore to Rs. 7.03 crore. Since the year 2001-02, the annual cost of the office has been increasing steadily. The average cost per complaint also increased rapidly except in the year 2003-04 which amounted to Rs. 7,413. The average cost per complaint varies from Rs. 7,108 in 1998-99 to Rs. 7,413 in 2003-04.

The Reserve Bank will indicate the share of expenditure to be borne by the concerned banks. As provided in the Scheme, the amount spent is being recovered from participating banks in proportion to the working funds of these banks at the end of the preceding financial year. This is in line with the international practice followed by many Ombudsman Scheme across the world. With effect from January 1, 2006, the cost of the scheme is borne entirely by the Reserve Bank of India.

10.9.1 Fixing of Service Charges: With a view to reduce the number of complaints and representations from the public regarding service charges levied by the banks and to provide a transparent banking service the guidelines on service charges were examined and reviewed by RBI.

Prior to September 1999, the Indian Banks Association (IBA) was entrusted with the task of setting a scheduled benchmark of service charge for the various services rendered by their member banks. Even though it was not mandatory to fix service charges by IBA, all banks adopted this system. Since September 1999, RBI requested IBA to discontinue the practice of fixing service charges for their member banks. With the introduction of liberalization measures in the banking sector, RBI directed individual banks to fix their service charge for various services rendered by them. Individual banks can levy such charges only with the prior consent of their board of directors. In fixing their service charges banks should ensure that, the charges are reasonable and not out of line with the average cost of providing these services.

As per the new guidelines in May 30 2006, banks were advised to post and upload on their website, the details of various service charges in the format prescribed by the RBI. Banks were also directed to display the charges pertaining to certain essential services in their branch office in the local language. Further, banks were also directed to furnish to the RBI by May 31 2006, the details of service charges applicable to enable Reserve Bank of India to place them on its website. A model complaint form along with the name and address of the nodal officer of the bank for settlement of complaints should also be displayed at a prominent site in its website. The complaint form is to indicate that the first point of redressal of complaints is the banks itself and that complainants may approach the Banking Ombudsman only if the complaint is not resolved at the bank level with in a month.

10.9.2 Customer Service Department: In banking industry, the quality of customer service is of prime importance. Customer is now a new watchword and customer service is a new slogan in the Indian banking industry. The Reserve Bank of India took several measures for enhancing the quality of customer service in banks, protecting the rights of customers and for strengthening the grievance Redressal mechanism in banks.

In order to bring all the activities relating to customer service in banks under a single institution, the Reserve Bank of India constituted a regulatory body known as Customer Service Department (CSD) in July 2006. The newly constituted Customer Service Department is entrusted with the task of collection and dissemination of information relating to customer services and grievance redressal mechanism of banks. The CSD of RBI is also assigned with the duty of administering the Banking Ombudsman Scheme and acting as a nodal department of the Banking Codes and Standards Board of India (BCSBI). The Customer Service Department act as a link between Banks, IBA, BCSBI and Banking Ombudsman offices. It is the duty of the Customer Service Department to ensure the redressal of complaints received directly by the RBI regarding customer services in various banks.

11

New Generation Banks

The post independence era witnessed banking industry attaining several milestones. The late sixties were marked by fundamental changes in commercial banking in India. After nationalization, banks effected several diversifications, modifications and innovations in their structure and functioning. These innovations were with a view to expand and extend the reach and range of commercial banks in accordance with the changing needs of the economy.

Banks were nationalized with the aim to usher in social changes by improving the material life of the downtrodden people and through removal of regional economic imbalances and disparities. Nationalization paved the way for extension of retail banking to the rural and semi-urban areas. It brought about a spectacular expansion of bank branches especially in the rural and semi urban areas. There was also noticeable increase in bank deposit, credit disbursement and generation of employment. The growth in bank deposits and advances is an indication of the improvement in the banking habits of the people in the rural, semi urban and unbanked areas. The incredible growth in bank credit also indicates the realization of the goals of nationalization. But these objectives were achieved by sacrificing the profitability and operational efficiency of the public sector banks. The quality of service and that of loan assets decreased as a result of the liberal and lax credit extension policies.

The banking sector in India remained regulated even after the nationalization of major commercial banks in 1969. The most important regulation imposed was the restriction on establishing new private sector banks in the country. The entry of new private sector banks was restricted to prevent destructive competition among them and excessive concentration of their branches in urban and metropolitan cities.

11.1 Paradigm Shift in the Banking Industry

Substantial changes in banking sector began taking place only in the early nineties. The 1991, Budget presented by the then Finance Minister Dr. Man Mohan Singh in parliament unveiled the new economic policy. It contained a plethora of measures aimed at economic stabilization and structural reforms to surmount the shortcomings of the socialistic pattern of economy adopted and followed by India for the last 4 decades.

In accordance with the New Economic Policy, various committees were appointed by Government of India and the RBI to examine the structural, organizational, managerial, procedural, instrumental and functional aspects of the financial sector in general and that of the banking sector in particular. Prominent of these committees were the Narasimham Committee, Goiporia Committee, Varma Committee, Patil Committee, Kohli Committee, and the Rangarajan Committee. They pointed out the weaknesses of the present financial system and recommended radical and drastic changes in the banking system to improve its quality of service and to make it more vibrant to meet international challenges and to retain its competitiveness.

A high-level Committee appointed by the Government of India under the Chairmanship of Narasimham submitted its report in 1993 to the government. It recommended a structural face-lift for the Indian banking system. The Narasimham Committee laid the foundation for far reaching reforms in the banking sector in India and they are termed as the "second banking revolution". It recommended sweeping changes in the financial sector as per international norms to cater to the needs of the sector and to strengthen it. To transform Indian banks from largely domestic ones to truly international ones, and to tackle their internal deficiencies, the Committee put forward several recommendations. The committee went into the entire gamut of banking operations and suggested new norms for accounting practices, prudential standards and capital adequacy requirements.

Deregulation of the interest rate structure, permitting public and private sector banks to access the capital markets, consolidation of the banking industry by merging strong banks, greater emphasis on asset liability management and reduction of government share in banks to 33 per cent were some of its other recommendations.

Apart from these recommendations, the Committee also pointed out the consequences of nationalization. It observed that most of the public sector banks were far from profitable because of social banking which was the aim of nationalization. These banks are not fundamentally strong and are undercapitalized. Revamping their structure was extremely important, because the health of the financial sector in general and the economy in particular would be reflected in its performance. It was against this background, that the financial sector reforms were introduced to usher in a paradigm shift in the banking sector industry, by way of addressing the causal factors for its dismal performance. To introduce competitiveness in the banking sector as a whole the committee recommended that, the industry be opened for participation of private sector banks and foreign banks. Apart from allowing the Indian banks to enter into joint ventures with foreign banks, the foreign banks were also permitted to set up banks in India as branches or as subsidiaries. On the basis of the recommendations of the Narasimham committee and to make banking system competitive, the RBI decided to set up new banks in the private sector.

11.2 Guidelines for Entry of New Private Sector Banks

For a quarter century (1969 -1993), no private bank was allowed to set their business in the private sector. The necessary guidelines were issued by the RBI in this connection on January 22, 1993. The important guidelines in respect of the commencement of new banks were;

1. The bank shall be registered as a public limited company under the Companies Act 1956. The bank will be governed under the provisions of Reserve Bank of India Act of 1934 and Banking Regulations Act of 1949 and other relevant

statues. These new banks shall be subject to the directives, instructions, guidelines and advices given by the RBI from time to time. The decision of RBI with regard to licensing under the Banking Regulation Act of 1949 and its inclusion in the second schedule in the RBI Act 1934 shall be final.

2. The management set up, liquidity requirement etc. are to be governed by the provisions of the RBI Act of 1934 and Banking Regulations Act of 1949. The new banks shall be subject to prudential norms in respect of banking operations, accounting and other policies, norms for income recognition, asset classification and provisioning as well as capital adequacy of 8 per cent and of capital to risk weighted assets ratio from their very beginning.
3. The initial minimum paid up capital for a new bank shall be Rs. 100 crore and the promoter's contribution shall be 25 per cent or 20 per cent where the capital exceeds Rs. 100 cores. NRI participation in primary equity of a new bank shall be to the extent of 40 per cent. In the case of a foreign banking company or finance company as a technical collaborator or a co-promoter, equity participation shall be restricted to 20 per cent. The shares of the bank should be listed in stock exchanges.
4. The new bank shall not be allowed to set up a subsidiary or mutual fund until the completion of three years from the date of commencement.
5. While granting licenses the RBI will give preference to those banks that set up their headquarters in a centre, which does not have the head office of any other bank.
6. Such banks shall be subject to prudential norms in respect of banking operations, accounting policies and the other policies as RBI lays them down. The bank will have to achieve capital adequacy of 8 per cent of the risk-weighted assets from the very beginning.
7. Voting rights of an individual shareholder shall be governed by the ceiling of one per cent. Baking Regulations Act of 1949 was amended in February 1994 for raising the ceiling of

voting rights of an individual shareholder in a private bank from one per cent to ten per cent.

8. A large industrial house should not promote any new bank. Individual companies, directly or indirectly connected with large industrial houses may however, be permitted to participate in equity of a new private sector bank up to a maximum of 10 per cent, but would not have controlling interest in the bank. The bank shall not extent any credit facilities to the promoters and companies investing up to 10 per cent of the equity.
9. The new bank shall not be allowed to have as director any person who is a director of any other banking company and not more than three directors from companies which among themselves are entitled to exercise voting rights in excess of 20 per cent of the total voting rights of all shareholders of the banking company as laid down in the Banking Regulations Act 1949.
10. The bank shall have to observe priority sector loan lending target as applicable to other domestic banks. However, some relaxations in the composition of the priority sector lending may be considered for an initial period of three years.
11. New bank will have to comply with the Reserve Bank instructions in respect of export credit and may be issued an authorised dealer license when applied for.
12. The new banks shall make full use of modern infrastructural facilities and office equipment, computer, telecommunications etc. in order to provide good customer service. These banks should also constitute a high power grievances cell to handle customer complaints. They are also expected to concentrate on core banking activities individually.
13. New banks have to lay down their loan policy with in the overall policy guidelines of the Reserve Bank and shall specifically provide prudential norms covering related party transactions.
14. Branch licensing shall be governed by the existing policy

whereby banks are free to open branches at various centers including urban\ metropolitan centers with out the prior approval of the Reserve Bank once they satisfy the capital adequacy ratio and prudential accounting standards. However, a bank will be required to open rural and semi-urban branches also as laid down by the RBI.

11.3 Commencement of New Private Sector Banks

During the year 1992-93, RBI granted in principle approval for setting up of nine private sector banks. All these banks will be required to raise 60 per cent of their equity capital from the market. In principle, approvals were given to the following institutions. (1) ICICI, (2) UTI, (3) HDFC, (4) Jayanta Madhab & Associates, (5) the 20th Century Finance Corporation Ltd.,(6) Benett Colman & Co. Ltd., (7) Indus Ind. Enterprises & Finance Ltd.,(8) Gujarat State Fertilizer Corporation and (9) IDBI.

During the year 1993-94, ten banks were given 'in principle' approval and six banks commenced their operation. Viz. (1)UTI Bank Ltd., (2) Indus India Bank Ltd.,(3) ICICI Banking Corporation Ltd., (4) Global Trust Bank Ltd., (5) Centurion Bank Ltd. and (6) HDFC Bank Ltd.

Housing and Development Finance Corporation (HDFC) was among the first to receive an 'in principal' approval from the RBI to set up a bank in the private sector. The Bank was incorporated in August 1994 in the name of HDFC Bank Ltd. However, UTI Bank was the first of the new generation banks that commenced its operation in 1994. Unit Trust of India, LIC, General Insurance Corporation of India and its four associates promoted it jointly. ICICI Bank was also promoted in the year 1994, and was promoted by ICICI Ltd. ICICI Ltd was an Indian financial institution established in 1955 at the initiatives of World Bank, Government of India and representative of Indian Industry. The RBI approved the merger of ICICI Ltd. with ICICI Bank Ltd. in the year 2002.

During the year, 1994-95 eight private sector banks out of twelve, which received principle approval, commenced business.

During the year 1995-96 Four more banks viz. (1) Times Bank Ltd., (2) Bank of Punjab Ltd., (3) Development Credit Bank Ltd. (conversion of Development Co-operative Bank Ltd. Mumbai) and (4) IDBI Bank Ltd. become operational taking the total to ten.

11.4 Revised Guidelines for Private Sector Banks

With a view to impart greater competition in the banking system the Reserve Bank set up a committee in January 1998 to review the licensing policy for setting up new private sector banks. Subsequently, the Reserve Bank issued guidelines for entry of new banks in the private sector in January 2001. Following the recommendations of the Working Group to review the licensing policy for setting up new private sector banks, revised guidelines were issued in consultation with the Government of India in January 2001 for entry of new banks in the private sector. The guidelines retained certain existing conditions for the entry of new banks like fixing promoters' capital share at 40 per cent and restrictions on opening of new branches, etc. The proposed bank needs to observe the prescribed targets in respect of priority sector lending (40 per cent of net bank credit) as applicable to other domestic banks. The major changes in the revised guidelines are:

1. The initial minimum paid up capital for a new bank should be Rs. 200 crore, which shall be increased to Rs. 300 crore in the subsequent three years after commencement of business.
2. The guidelines also enable a NBFC to convert into a commercial bank, if it satisfies the prescribed criteria of

- Minimum net worth of Rs. 200 crore.
- A credit rating of not less than AAA (or its equivalent) in the previous year
- Capital adequacy of not less than 12 per cent.
- Net NPAs at not more than 5 per cent.

3. A large industrial house should not promote any new bank. Individual companies, directly or indirectly connected with large industrial houses may however, be permitted to participate in the equity of a new private sector bank up to a maximum of 10 per cent, but would not have controlling

interest in the bank. The bank shall not extend any credit facilities to the promoters and companies investing up to 10 per cent of the equity.

4. Preference would be given to promoters with expertise of financing priority areas and in setting up banks specializing in the financing of rural and agro-based industries.

The guidelines also prescribed March 31, 2001 as the last date for the receipt of fresh applications for the setting up of new banks in the private sector. In the initial stage, the applications received were screened by the Reserve Bank of India to ensure that eligibility of the applicants in general. In the second stage, the applications screened were referred to a High-Level Advisory Committee under the Chairmanship of Dr. I.G. Patel. The Committee was requested to submit its recommendations after scrutiny of application to the Reserve Bank on or before June 29, 2001. "In-principle" approval for setting up of a private bank would be granted by the Reserve Bank only after taking into consideration the recommendation of the Advisory Committee for the same.

The High-Level Advisory Committee recommended two applications as suitable for issue of 'in-principle' approvals for setting up new banks in private sector. The applications recommended were those of Shri Ashok Kapur and two other banking professionals with Rabobank Netherlands, and Kotak Mahindra Finance Ltd., a non-banking financial company.

'In principle' approvals to the above two applicants, valid for one year, were issued on February 7, 2002. On being satisfied that the Kotak Mahindra Finance Ltd. complied with the requisite conditions laid down by the Reserve Bank as part of the 'in-principle' approval, they were granted a license for commencement of banking business on February 6, 2003, under Section 22 (1) of Banking Regulation Act of 1949. The bank commenced its operations on March 22, 2003 and was included in the Second Schedule of the Reserve Bank of India Act of 1934 with effect from April 12, 2003. The other applicant was given extension of time till November 30, 2003 to complete all necessary formalities to commence banking operations.

11.5 Industrial Development Bank of India (IDBI)

Industrial Development Bank of India (IDBI) started functioning as a banking company on October 1, 2004. The Industrial Development Bank (Transfer of Undertaking and Repeal) Bill, 2003 was passed by parliament on December 8, 2003. It provided for the transfer and vesting of the undertaking of the Industrial Development Bank of India in a company to be formed and registered under the Companies Act of 1956 to carry on banking business and for matters connected therewith or incidental thereto and for the repeal of the Industrial Development Bank of India Act of 1964.

With the commencement of the business of IDBI Bank, the number of public sector banks again increased to 28 from 27. The number of branches of IDBI went up from 159 to 181during June 2005 to June 2006. Eighty eight per cent of their branches are located at urban\metropolitan centres. IDBI have 287 ATMs but their branch presence is only 181. The percentage of off-site ATMs to total ATMs of IDBI represents 64 per cent. The Capital Adequacy Ratio of IDBI Bank decreased from 15.51 per cent in 2005 to 14.80 per cent at the end of March 2006, which is above the stipulated limit. Net NPAs as a percentage of total assets also decreased from 1.04 per cent in March 2005 to 0.64 per cent at the end of March 2006.

11.6 Failure\Merger of New Generation Private Sector Banks

The 20th Century Finance Corporation Ltd. got merged with the Centurion Bank Ltd on January 1998. Times Bank Ltd. with a CRAR of 8.45 per cent got merged with HDFC Bank on February 2000. The new generation private sector bank "The Global Trust Bank Ltd." (GTB), which was granted license in September 1994, began showing adverse futures in 2002. The RBI instructed the GTB to adopt prudential norms against its adverse futures like high growth of risk-weighted assets, high NPA, high exposure to capital market etc. The bank reported some progress in making recoveries and also in attempts to have equity infusion.

However, the bank was not able to finalize the programme of capital expansion from domestic sources as advised by RBI. In July 2004, the GTB submitted a proposal from an overseas equity investor for capital augmentation. The RBI later found that the proposal submitted by GTB was not feasible from the point of view of prudential norms and other considerations. As the financial position of the bank was deteriorating steadily and the solvency of the bank was being seriously affected, the Reserve Bank had to place the bank under moratorium on July 24, 2004 to protect the interests of small depositors of the bank and in the interest of the banking system. Among the various proposals considered for merger, the scheme proposed by the Oriental Bank of Commerce (OBC) was found acceptable to the RBI and was submitted it to the Central Government for approval. As per Government notification, the GTB was merged with Oriental Bank of Commerce with on August 14, 2004.

The voluntary amalgamation of the Bank of Punjab Ltd. with the Centurion Bank Ltd. was approved by the Reserve Bank in terms of Section 44A of the B.R. Act, and became effective from October 1, 2005. The Centurion Bank subsequently changed its name to Centurion Bank of Punjab Ltd.

The numbers of new private sector banks in 1993-94, 1994-95 and 95-96 were 6, 8 and 10 respectively. The numbers of new private banks in 1998-99 were 9 and for the years 1999-2000, 2000-01 and 2001-02 were 8 in each year. The number of new private banks in 2002-03, 2003- 04, 2004-05 and 2005-06 was 9, 10, 9 and 8, respectively.

The following are the new private sector banks functioning as on March 31, 2006.

- Centurion Bank of Punjab Ltd.
- Development Credit Bank Ltd.
- HDFC Bank Ltd
- ICICI Bank Ltd.
- IndusInd Bank Ltd.
- Kotak Mahindra Bank Ltd.

- UTI Bank Ltd. and
- Yes Bank Ltd.

11.7 Financial Performance of New Generation Private Sector Banks

The financial performance of the new Indian private sector banks based on some indicators like operating profit, operating profit as a percentage to total assets, net profit, and net profit as a percentage to total assets deposits and advances are depicted in Table 11.1.

The operating profit which is 'the structural measure of profitability', of new Indian private sector banks increased substantially from Rs. 481.02 crore in 1996-97 to Rs. 8,388.25 crore in 2005-06. It shows a 17-fold increase with a compound growth rate of 37.38 per cent over a period of nine years. The table further reveals that the new private sector banks continued to maintain a robust rate in their operating profits. Even though the number of new private banks got reduced to eight from nine, the operating profit, increased by 54 per cent in the year 2005-06 as against an increase of only 8.6 per cent which was recorded in the year 2004-05.

Net profit of new private sector banks also rose steadily from Rs. 280.08 crore in 1996-97 to Rs. 4,108.85 in 2005-06. During the period under review, net profit of new private sector banks registered an upward trend with an increase of 14-fold increase with a compound growth rate of 34.76 per cent. All new private sector banks began to earn profits right from the first year of its operations. The net profits of new private sector banks increased by 32.6 per cent in the year 2005-06, as against a rise of 52.2 per cent in 2004-05.

In tune with the trends in the ratio of operating profits to total assets, there was a reduction in the ratio of net profit to total assets. As a per cent of total assets, the operating profit came down from 2.98 in 1996-97 to 1.99 in 2005-06. The net profit as a percentage to total assets also declined from 1.73 per cent in 1996-97 to 0.97 per cent in 2005-06.

Table 11.1: Financial Performance of New Generation Private Sector Banks: Selected Indicators (1996-2006) (Rs. crore)

Items	1996-97	1998-99	2000-01	2002-03	2004-05	2005-06
No. of Banks	10	9	8	9	9	8
Operating Profit	481.02 (2.98)	684.28 (1.78)	1,368.97 (1.74)	4,432.13 (2.31)	5,442.75 (1.85)	8,388.25 (1.99)
Net Profit	280.08 (1.73	397.05 (1.03)	639.4 (0.81)	1,725.98 (0.90)	3,097.57 1.05	4,108.85 (0.97)
Deposits	-	30,813	62,920	1,15,742	1,97,693	2,97,999
Advances	7,814	13,714	30,086	89,515	1,23,655	2,30,005

Figures in brackets are percentages to Total Assets.

Table 11.1 also gives an idea about the progress in mobilizing deposits by the new private sector banks since 1998-99 to 2005-06. It can be seen from the table that the deposits increased substantially and steadily from Rs. 30,813 crore in 1997-98 to Rs. 2,97,999 crore in 2005-06 recording a 9.6 fold increase with a compound growth rate of 38.2 per cent. The total advances by new private sector banks markedly increased from Rs. 7,814 crore in 1996-97 to Rs. 2,30,005 crore in 2005-06, registering a 29 fold increase with a compound growth rate of 45.6 per cent.

11.7.1 Non-Performing Assets: Table 11.2 gives an idea about the non-performing assets of the new private sector banks over a period of nine years. During 1996-97, the new private sector bank group had the smallest share of NPAs but began showing significant increase in NPAs from the year 1998-99 to 2002-03. The NPAs as a per cent of total assets, which was 1.0 per cent in 1996-97, increased to 1.6 per cent in 1998-99 and 2.2 per cent in 2002-03.

Table 11.2: Non-performing Assets of New Private sector Banks (1996-2006)

Items	1996-97	1998-99	2000 01	2001-02	2004-05	2005-06
NPA as per cent of Total Assets	1.0	1.6	1.2	2.2	0.8	0.4
NPA as per cent to Total Advances	2.00	4.5	3.1	4.6	1.9	0.8

NPAs as a per cent of total advances also got increased from 2 per cent in 1996-97 to 4.5 per cent in 1998-99 and to 4.6 per cent in 2002-03. At the end of the year 2005-06, the new private sector bank group had the smallest share of NPAs compared to all the other types of banks. Net NPA ratio of new private banks was only 0.8 per cent.

11.7.2 Capital Adequacy Ratio of New Private Sector Banks: The capital adequacy ratio of new private sector banks from the year 2001 to 2006 was given in Table 11.3.

Table 11.3: Capital Adequacy Ratio of New Private Sector Banks (2001-2006)

Name of the Bank	2001	2002	2003	2004	2005	2006
Centurion Bank of Punjab Ltd	9.61	4.16	1.95	4.41	21.42	12.52
Development Credit Bank Ltd.	11.28	11.49	10.08	14.14	9.88	9.66
HDFC Bank Ltd	11.09	13.93	11.12	11.66	12.16	11.41
ICICI Bank Ltd.	11.57	11.44	11.10	10.36	11.78	13.35
Indus Ind. Bank Ltd.	15.00	12.51	12.13	12.75	11.62	10.54
Kotak Mahindra Bank Ltd.	-	-	25.97	15.25	12.80	11.27
UTI Bank Ltd.	9.00	10.65	10.90	11.21	12.66	11.08
Yes Bank Ltd.	-	-	-	-	18.81	16.43
Total	11.50	12.30	11.30	10.20	12.10	12.60

Tier I capital adequacy ratio increased significantly to 11.50 per cent in 2001 and to 12.60 per cent at the end of March 2006. Table 11.3 reveals that the Capital Adequacy Ratio of Centurion Bank of Punjab Ltd (12.52), ICICI Bank Ltd. (13.35) and Yes Bank Ltd. (16.43) were above the stipulated limit of 12.6 per cent. The Capital Adequacy Ratio of New Private Sector Banks as a whole remains at the stipulated limit of 12.60 per cent.

The Capital Adequacy Ratio of Development Credit Bank Ltd decreased from 14.14 per cent in the year 2004 to an all time low of 9.66 in 2006 and it is the only one new private sector bank to show a ratio which is below 10 per cent. The table further reveals that the Capital Adequacy Ratio of all new private sector banks decreased in the year 2006 compared to 2005, except ICCI Bank Ltd. which showed an improvement of 1.57 per cent over that of the previous year.

11.7.3 Capital to Risk-Weighted Assets: The capital to Risk-Weighted Assets ratio belonging to the new Indian private sector bank group are given in Tables 11.4.

Table 11.4: Capital to Risk-Weighted Assets Ratio (1996-2006)

Year	No. of New Generation Private Sector Banks	Less than 8 per cent No. of Banks	Between 8-10 per cent No. of Banks	Above 10 per cent No. of Banks
1996-97	9	-	-	9
1998-99	9	-	2	7
2000-01	8	-	1	7
2001-02	8	1	-	7
2002-03	9	2	1	6
2003-04	9	-	1	8
2004-05	9	-	2	7
2005-06	8	-	1	7

Table 11.4 discloses CRAR of new private sector banks from 1996 to 2005-06. From the table it is clear that the CRAR of new private sector banks continues be significantly above the stipulated minimum of 9.0 per cent. At the end of March 2006, the CRAR of all new generation private sector banks except one (Development Credit Bank Ltd. is between 8-10 per cent) is above 10 per cent.

It is conclude that new generation private sector banks expanded their business by opening branches mainly in the metros and cities by providing state of the art services and facilities to their customers. These banks are operating in a highly sophisticated environment with better personnel efficiency were able to win many customers and started making profits from the first year oft its business. ICICI Bank started in 1995 is now, placed as India's second largest bank. In the world setting also, ICICI Bank has a position among the 250 big banks and HDFC Bank among the 500 big banks of the world. Several new generation banks have been positioning themselves as a "one-stop shop" for all financial services with a comprehensive range of products like deposits, loans, credit cards, debit cards, depository services, investment advice, selling third-party products like mutual funds and insurance, utility bill payments and various other transactional services.

12

Corporate Governance in Commercial Banks

A strong financial system is based on sound principles of corporate governance. It lays down the fundamental rules by which companies are governed. The quality of corporate governance has become very decisive for the banking system because of the growing competition and consolidation of the banking system. It also acquires importance as competition among banks becomes intense and they strive to retain their customer base.

In many countries, banks now provide services, which do not come under the field of traditional banking. Throughout the world, old institutional demarcations are getting increasingly blurred. Increasing competition from non-bank intermediaries has paved the way for a decline in traditional banking, wherein banks only accepted deposits and made advances that stayed on their books till maturity.

Traditionally the banking operations were confined to acceptance of deposits, lending of money, payment and transmission of money services. With the introduction of reforms in economic and financial sectors, the operating environment for banks in India witnessed drastic changes. These reforms brought about a number of substantial changes in banking industry by way of diversifications and innovations in their functioning.

Economic Liberalization and globalization has also opened the banking turf to new players. With the entry of foreign and new generation, private sector banks with highly sophisticated inventories have thrown a lot of challenges to the existing Indian banks. Banks are competing with one another to offer multifarious and diversified services to their customers and thereby to widen their customer base. The advancement in information and communication technology also further accelerated and broadened the rate of dissemination of financial services and information.

As a result of reforms, competition and the spread of technology in financial sector different from traditional banking services, banks now offer diversified services such as investment banking, depository service, debit cards, credit cards, securitization, derivatives and all kinds of securities, underwriting of securities, money brokering, asset management, settlement and clearing services, provision and transfer of financial information, insurance, housing finance, managing issue of shares, debentures, bonds, mutual funds, real estate management services, advisory and other auxiliary financial services.

The universalization of banking operations spurred by a combination of factors, such as, the continuing deregulation and heightened competition among banks has transformed the role of banks from one of mere intermediation to one of providing quick, efficient and consumer oriented services. In recent years, the business of banking in India has been moving rapidly to a 'one-stop shop' of varied financial services from that of limited services.

12.1 Genesis of the Concept of Corporate Governance

In the late 1980s in UK, there was growing awareness and serious concern among the business community with regard to frequent failures of corporate entities. Recurring failures and collapse of many companies in United Kingdom raised concerns about corporate governance. The London Stock Exchange took this issue seriously and a committee was constituted. They opined that most practices in publicly listed companies with regard to the system of corporate management were far from good and well. The London Stock Exchange appointed Adrain Cadbury as the Chairman of the Committee. The Cadbury committee with limited terms of reference mainly addressed the issues of corporate failures and the financial issues of publicly listed companies in the London Stock Exchange. Most of the recommendations of Cadbury were accepted by the London Stock Exchange. By way of accepting these recommendations, London Stock Exchange adopted more efficient regulations through appropriate amendments in the listing agreements and company laws and also updated standards of accounting, reporting, disclosures etc.

Apart from the above committee, many other regulators in UK also appointed local committees and commissions, to study similar issues and adopted many recommendations similar to that of Cadbury. The first study in UK on corporate governance made by Berle and Means paved the way for good governance practices by proposing changes in the structure of the boards, processes, shareholder rights, reporting, disclosure standards and legal remedies.

Even though the terms of references of the Cadbury committee were limited, the concept of corporate governance existing in the present day set up was mooted by this Committee. Cadbury is now considered as the 'Guru' of good corporate governance in United Kingdom.

12.2 Conceptual Framework

Corporate governance is the modern expression for an age-old concept called accountability. Corporate governance has as its backbone a set of transparent relationships among an institution's management, board, shareholders and other stakeholders.

Corporate governance is considered as a mechanism incorporating a variety of measures such as protection of shareholders' rights, enhancing shareholders' value, effective balancing of the constitution of Boards (i.e. the role and composition of the board), proactive role of the Non-executive Directors, the efficacy of accounting practices and the control systems, realistic disclosures by the Directors on aspects of compliance with prescribed accounting standards and a code of conduct and adherence to a sound compliance system. Basically, it is about how those assigned the task of day to day management are held accountable to the shareholders and all other providers of funds.

The basic objective of corporate governance is to maximize

long-term shareholder value. Therefore, good governance should address all issues that lead to a value addition for the organization and protect the interests of all the stake and shareholders. The motto of corporate governance is that it is 'of the shareholders, by the shareholders and for the shareholders'. It is a system of structuring, operating and controlling a company with a view to achieving long-term strategic goals to the benefits of shareholders, creditors, employees, customers and suppliers complying with all legal and regulatory requirements. Corporate governance has to become something much broader to include a fair, efficient, and transparent administration to realize certain well-defined objectives with a streamlined system of operation.

There are different set of players in the system of corporate governance. They are the legal system; regulators; the Board of Directors and Executive Directors on the Board; financial intermediaries; markets and self-regulatory organizations. A dynamic balance among them determines the shape and form of the prevailing corporate governance system. The balance varies from country to country depending upon the stage of institutional development and the historical context.

The key pillars of Corporate Governance are Transparency, Accountability and Merit Based Management. Transparency means accurate, adequate and timely disclosure of relevant information to the stakeholders. Without transparency, it is difficult to make any stride towards better governance. There is need to move towards international standards in terms of disclosure of information by the corporate sector and thereby to develop a high level of public confidence in business. Transparency in banking business operations plays an important role in ensuring the needed market discipline. It is also an important mechanism for keeping banks prudent in their operations. Accountability denotes that the promoters and directors of the company remain perennially accountable and responsible to all stakeholders. Corporate governance has to be a top down approach. In companies with good governance, accountability is not just bottom up but in reverse order with the objective of creating shareholder value.

A strong Board of Directors is essential to lead and support merit based management. The Board of Directors must be a strong, independent and non-partisan body that takes crucial decisions with business prudence. It is against this background that the Institute of Chartered Accountants of India (ICAI) observes corporate governance as "embedded configuration of values and ethics". Its appropriate and expected behavior provides the necessary co-ordination for the organizations to perform its role as a societal entity. A code of such corporate governance makes both the available and desirable aspects of such a configuration explicit. It is simply the mode of structure or power that determines the rights and responsibilities of various groups involved in running an organization. Since various corporate governance structures exist in different countries, there are no universally applicable parameters of sound and correct corporate governance.

12.3 Corporate Governance: Indian Scenario

In India, the question of corporate governance has come up mainly in the wake of economic liberalization, deregulation of industry and business and increasing integration of the Indian economy with the rest of the world. With the opening up of the economy and to be in tune with WTO requirements, Indian Companies can succeed and survive amidst increasing competition from multi-national companies only through excellence in their working. The need to conform to internationally accepted norms and standards of corporate governance has become essential for Indian industry, as their stakeholders are no longer confined to this country alone. In the mean time, structural changes effected in the corporate sector also require special attention. Many family owned enterprises are being converted into closely held public limited companies and further into widely held limited companies. The recognition of the need for a code of corporate governance has also moved in line with this trend.

The Standing Conference of Public Enterprises (1996), New Delhi, had first recognized the need to examine the relevant issues of corporate governance of the public sector undertakings in India. The Confederation of Indian Industries (CII) and the Associated Chambers of Commerce and Industry of India (ASSOCHAM) discussed corporate governance in general. In India, the first structural initiative in this regard was initiated by the Confederation of Indian Industry (CII) leading to the issue of a code of governance standards in 1997. The CII issued a code of 17 recommendations titled 'Desirable Corporate Governance – A Code', to be followed on a self-regulatory basis by Indian industries. It is considered as the first Indian Paper of its kind on the subject. It was recognized that the codes, which were referred to the Cadbury's and the Confederation of Indian Industry's at that time were most appropriate to the ills of private sector, its remedies, and the infirmities in the public enterprise governance, which needed a close look.

Yaga Consultants prepared a report titled "Corporate Governance and the Public Sector Undertaking" in October 1997. The report, drawn from the perspectives of several industry leaders and academicians, highlighted the major issues in corporate governance and contained a number of recommendations, to enhance the quality of corporate governance in public sector undertakings. The Administrative Staff College of India, Hyderabad and Yaga Consultants, Hyderabad conducted a Workshop on "Corporate Governance in Bank and Financial Institutions" at Mumbai on June 14, 1999.

12.4 SEBI Code on Corporate Governance

A great deal of attention was given to and intensive and extensive discussions and on the subject of corporate governance took place in India in the late nineties. The Unit Trust of India (UTI) in association with the Securities and Exchange Board of India (SEBI) organized a seminar on Corporate Governance in 1999. The Securities and Exchange Board of India (SEBI) constituted a Committee under the Chairmanship of Kumara

Mangalam Birla, Member, SEBI Board in 2000, to foster and further the standard of corporate governance in respect of listed companies. Amendments were also made in listing agreements in pursuance of the decisions of the Board. These amendments, made in February 2000 came to be known as SEBI Code on Corporate Governance in the country. The above Committee made mandatory as well as non-mandatory recommendations. Its perspective was limited to the typical private sector company. The very composition of the committee reveals its tilt to this sector.

12.4.1 Mandatory Recommendations: Mandatory recommendations made by the Birla Committee were as follows:

- The Board of a Company should meet at least four times a year.
- An Audit Committee should be set up to enhance the credibility of the financial disclosures of the company and promote transparency.
- The Audit Committee will have to investigate the reasons for financial defaults made by companies such as default to depositors, debenture holders, shareholders and creditors.
- A remuneration package for executive directors, including performance-linked incentives, stock options etc.
- A Committee to be formed to study investor complaints.
- The Chairman of these Committees should be present at the Annual General Meeting to answer queries of shareholders.
- The Directors of these Committees cannot be members of more than10 Committees across companies and cannot chair more than 5 companies.
- The Annual Report should have a separate section on corporate governance regarding the status of compliance and
- Significant events in the last 6 months or half-yearly declaration of financial performance should be sent to each shareholder.

12.4.2 Non-mandatory Recommendations: The non-mandatory recommendations made by the Committee were:

- Postal ballot should be used by companies to strengthen shareholder democracy.

- Consolidation of accounts of subsidiaries
- Segment reporting where the company has multiple lines of business and
- Disclosures and treatment of related party transaction and treatment of deferred taxation.

SEBI Code on Corporate Governance has emerged as a strategic tool to strengthen the move towards corporate excellence. It instills a strong sense of commitment and accountability to those who are in the Board towards the stakeholders.

12.5 Significance of Corporate Governance in India

Because of varied reasons, corporate governance is extremely relevant. Of late, the concept has been assuming greater significance, following major business busts across the world. Corporate governance has thus attained vital significance to ensure the stability and soundness of the financial system. Developments in modern business world demands quality, ethics and excellence in right proportions injected into the organization at the level of person, process and product to make them viable. It is closely related to the ISO standards, which guarantees quality practices. To cope with these changes core competency is to be identified and leveraged by Indian companies for success and this is possible through Corporate Governance.

Corporate governance assumes greater significance in Indian context for the following reasons:

- To ensure that promoters of a company remain perennially accountable and responsible to all stakeholders.
- Stresses the need to have transparency in respect of matters relating to Board of Directors, disclosure to shareholders and emphasizes the need to have a close relationship between the promoters/owners and the managers.
- Expounds the need to adhere to ethical business practices.
- Helps to evolve measures for strategic management and to gain credibility.
- Strives to enhance Board performance by emphasizing the

contribution of professionally qualified and experienced Non-executive Directors and Board Committees.

- Tends to monitor and ensure absolute compliance with the laws of the country and
- Ensure adequate disclosures, focused approach, streamlined delegation and professional management which together and ultimately result in maximizing the shareholder values and protecting the interest of creditors and employees.

12.6 Corporate Governance in the Public Sector Banks

In a service industry like banking, corporate governance relates to the manner in which the business and affairs of individual banks are directed and managed by their Board of Directors and higher management. Under corporate governance, banks articulate corporate values, code of conduct and standards of appropriate behavior etc, and have systems and controls to ensure compliance with them. The Board sets the strategic objectives and corporate values of banks and specifies transparent lines of responsibility and accountability, which are communicated across the organization.

Corporate governance in banking sector is important and complex in many ways:

Firstly, the quality of the corporate governance within the bank becomes crucial to the performance and growth of the financial sector. Secondly, an important peculiarity of the Indian banking system is the dominant Government ownership of banking institutions. Since these public sector banks are likely to dominate for some more time in future, these banks have to set a benchmark or standards for the practice of corporate governance in private sector.

Thirdly, in the pre-reform period, most decisions were arrived at externally, i.e., external to the financial intermediary regarding interest rates to be paid or charged and for whom to be lended. Recently, there has been a movement away from micro regulation by the RBI. There is thus, a shift from external regulation to that of internal regulations and therefore, the quality of the corporate governance within the bank or financial institution becomes decisive to the performance of the financial sector and the growth of the financial sector.

Fourthly, the government is no longer the 100 per cent owner of all public sector banks. The financial sector reforms currently underway are aimed at enhanced efficiency and diversified ownership in the form of divestment of its holdings in government owned banks and for maintaining capital adequacy norms, issue of shares to the public. When some additional capital has to be raised by these institutions, they should be able to convince the capital market and shareholders that it is worth investing their money in these institutions. For the survival and existence of private shareholders, issues like enhancing and protecting shareholders value and rights become extremely important. Such a situation did not prevail either in the public or financial sector until a few years ago.

Finally, an efficient market economy presupposes effective corporate governance. Shareholders and other financial stakeholders would expect greater access to information on the bank's overall operations and functions. The government banks must be in a position to assure the market that their system of corporate governance is such that they can be entrusted with shareholders' money. Thus, the corporate governance in the public sector banks needs to be improved and bettered.

12.7 RBI's Initiatives on Corporate Governance in Banks

Reserve Bank of India, as regulator of the financial sector has the responsibility to decide the nature of corporate governance in the financial sector. Corporate Governance in banking sector has been given special focus by the RBI, because banks are playing a very important role in the financial system as a whole. In order to protect the interest of depositors and to protect the integrity of the financial system, it is necessary that owners and managers of banks are persons of sound integrity. Keeping these considerations in mind, the Reserve Bank initiated several measures to enhance transparency and to strengthen the corporate governance practices in the financial sector in India.

12.7.1 The Basel Committee for Banking Supervision (BCBS): The Basle Committee has mentioned in one of its 'Core Principles' that supervisors should promote and pursue market discipline by encouraging good corporate governance (through an appropriate structure and set of responsibilities for a bank's Board of Directors and senior management), and enhancing market transparency and surveillance. The paper of the Basel Committee for Banking Supervision (BCBS) on the subject envisages certain strategies and techniques basic to sound corporate governance in banks. The Committee reported that basic elements of corporate governance are capable and experienced Directors in the Board, efficient management, coherent strategy and business plan and clear lines of responsibility and accountability. The primary responsibility for good corporate governance in banks rests with the Board of Directors. The role of Government, Reserve Bank of India, auditors and banking industry associations are equally important.

12.7.2 Advisory Group on Corporate Governance: The Advisory Group on Corporate Governance (Chairman: Dr. R.H. Patil) had observed that since most of the Indian companies belong to the East Asian insider model, where the promoters dominate governance, it is essential to bring reforms quickly so as to make boards of corporate/banks/financial institutions/public sector enterprises more professional and truly autonomous. As the statutory framework for corporate governance has already been provided in the Companies Act, the Group felt that it was desirable to amend the Companies`Act suitably for enforcing good governance practices in India. The report of the Advisory Group on Corporate Governance conducted detailed studies and assessment and gave its recommendations for good corporate governance practices in the public sector banks.

According to the Group, one of the major factors that directly interrupt the quality of corporate governance is the government ownership in banks. Majority of the banking business is under the control of public sector banks. Under the present circumstance, it would be difficult to implement good corporate governance practices in the public sector banks. Because the Government performs, multiple functions simultaneously in the public sector banks. They are acting in different capacities such as the owner, manager, quasi-regulator, and sometimes even as the super-regulator. The board of directors and top management act merely as functionaries of the government. In addition, the nominees of the RBI and Government in the director board are treated as superior to other directors. The committee opined that it would be difficult to tone up quality of corporate governance practices in the public sector banks with out granting autonomy to the board of directors. The advisory group recommended that for good corporate governance both in the public and private sector, all banks should be brought under a common Act instead of separate Acts.

Another factor that adversely affects good corporate governance practices in the public sector banks is the constitution and appointment of board of directors. At present when directors are appointed in the public sector banks, due representation is given to various sections of the society to protect their interests. Representation is given even to minor sections of economic interest groups. When an individual is nominated in the board for protecting the interest of a particular section, it would be difficult to give due weightage for qualifications and technical expertise. The Advisory Group recommended a major reform in the area of constitution of the bank boards. The chairman, executive directors and non-executive directors on the boards of the public sector banks should be appointed on the advice of an expert body set on the lines of Union Public Service Commission, with similar status and independence. The selection board should be set up jointly by the RBI and Ministry of Finance.

Even if the government dilutes its holding in the Public Sector Banks the efforts to institute good governance practices would be a superficial one if the government does not seriously redefine its role afresh. The changes proposed in the composition of the boards as per legislation under contemplation would result in

Government directly appointing 9 out of the 15 directors including the 4 whole time directors. The rights of private shareholders of SBI and PSBs are reduced considerably by making their approval not required for paying of dividend and adopting of annual accounts. Moreover, the voting rights of the other shareholders will continue to be restricted, thereby negating the basic principle of equal rights to all the shareholders. The subsidiaries of SBI will only enjoy very limited board autonomy because they have to obtain clearance from their parent company on most of the important matters.

The RBI is a regulator exercising tight vigil, control and inspection over the public sector banks, but it does not ensure and enhance the quality of the corporate governance mechanism in these banks. As the regulator, it is not necessary for the Reserve Bank to have representation on the bank boards, given the fact that it often clash with its regulatory functions.

As per current regulatory provisions, a bank cannot lend money to a company if any one of its board members is also a director on the board of that company. The adverse impact of this rule is that banks are not in a position to get good professionals in their boards. For ensuring good governance in banks, it is desirable if government directors abstain from participating in the discussion on such matters and also from voting.

12.7.3 Advisory Group on Banking Supervision: The Advisory Group on Banking Supervision (Chairman: Shri M.S. Verma) put forward several proposals to improve corporate governance without the necessary legislative changes. The Group observed that the nature of a bank's ownership should not be a decisive factor affecting the type and quality of corporate governance. The quality of corporate governance should be uniform in all types of banking organizations, irrespective of their ownership. The Committee made certain other recommendations also pertaining to corporate governance in banks. These are the following:

- All banks should attain an acceptable minimum level of corporate governance. Subsequently, banks are to make sustained progress towards achieving the best international standards within a reasonable timeframe.

- The unions and the management should arrive at a consensus on converting the present performance-unrelated uniform remuneration structure fixed for all management level of Public Sector Banks and into performance-related remuneration structure.
- A comprehensive risk management system should be put in place in all banks within two to three years. Since banks are in different stages of implementation of their risk management systems, small banks, in particular, would require encouragement and technical support to undertake risk management practices.
- The statutory provision (Section 20 of the B.R. Act, 1949) prohibiting connected lending to directors and their connected parties needs to be extended to include large shareholders.
- Banks need to develop mechanisms for ensuring percolation of corporate strategic objectives and set values all over the organization.
- Since Boards of very few banks are known to enforce clear lines of responsibility and accountability for themselves, there is an urgent need to follow the best practices in the banks in respect of constitution and functioning of the Boards. While nominating individuals on banks' Boards, the practice of pre-induction briefing or post-induction orientation can be put in place forthwith to develop a proper appreciation of their role in the banks' corporate governance. A ceiling needs to be imposed on the number of Boards and the number of Committees a Director can work at a time, since members of Board of Directors are required to spend their valuable time for the governance of banks.
- With a view to conducting corporate governance in a transparent manner, public disclosure in respect of details of qualifications of the Directors needs to be revealed in the balance sheet. Banks also need to be encouraged to disclose the senior management structure, basic organizational

structure, information about incentive structure, and nature and extent of transactions with affiliated and related parties.

The Group however noted that the guidelines and norms for good corporate governance in banks are still in a formative stage and laws, which can support corporate governance, are yet to be framed.

The Reports of the Advisory Group on Corporate Governance (Chairman: Shri R.H. Patil) and The Advisory Group on Banking Supervision (Chairman: Shri M.S. Verma) thus outlined several proposals to fine tune corporate governance without the necessary legislative changes. It is, therefore, important to think what improvements in corporate governance practices can be implemented within the existing legislative framework.

12.7.4 Consultative Group of Directors of Banks and Financial Institutions: Following the announcement of the Monetary and Credit Policy Statement of October 2001, RBI constituted a "Consultative Group of Directors of Banks and Financial Institutions" (Chairman Dr. A.S. Ganguly) to review the supervisory role of boards of banks and financial institutions and to obtain feedback on the functioning of the Boards *vis-à-vis* compliance, transparency, disclosures, audit committees etc. and make recommendations for making the role of Board of Directors more effective and meaningful.

The Group submitted its recommendations in April 2002 after a comprehensive review of the existing framework as well as the current practices and benchmarked its recommendations with international best practices as enunciated by the Basel Committee for Banking Supervision (BCBS), as well as other committees and advisory bodies, to the extent applicable in the Indian context.

The major recommendations of the Consultative Group were the following:

- At the time of appointment of Directors in banks whether in public or private sector, due consideration should be given to their qualifications and technical expertise.
- Committee also recommended for the appointment of one more full time director on the boards of large-sized

nationalized banks.

- The appointment/nomination of independent/ non-executive directors to the Board of banks (both public sector and private sector) would be from a pool of professional and talented people to be prepared and maintained by RBI. Any deviation from this procedure by any bank should be with only the prior permission of RBI. Further, the Government while nominating directors on the Boards of Public Sector Banks should be guided by certain broad "fit and proper" norms for the Directors, based on the lines of those suggested by the Bank for International Settlements (BIS).
- It would be desirable to separate the office of Chairman and Managing Director in respect of large-sized PSBs. This functional separation will bring about more focus on strategy and vision as also the needed thrust in the operational functioning of the top management of the bank. The whole-time directors should have sufficient long tenure to enable them to leave a mark of their leadership and business acumen on the bank's performance.
- The Reserve Bank could arrange need- based training programmes\seminars\workshops\ to the directors at intervals to acquaint them, with emerging developments in and challenges facing the banking sector.
- The Reserve Bank may bring out an updated charter indicating clear-cut and specific guidelines on the role and the responsibilities expected from individual directors.
- In order to attract quality professionals, the level of remuneration payable to the directors should be commensurate with the time required to be devoted to the bank's work as well as to signal the appropriateness of remuneration to the quality of inputs expected from a member.
- It would be desirable to obtain an undertaking from every director to the effect that they have gone through the guidelines defining the role and responsibilities of directors, and understood what is expected of them and enter into a

covenant to discharge their responsibilities to the best of their abilities, individually and collectively.

- The information furnished to the Board should be wholesome, complete and adequate to take meaningful decisions. The Board's focus should be devoted more on strategy issues, risk profile, internal control systems, overall performance, etc. The procedure followed for recording of the minutes of the board meetings in banks and FIs should be uniform and formalized.
- It would be desirable if the exposures of a bank to stockbrokers and market makers as a group, as also exposures to other sensitive sectors, *viz.*, real estate etc. are reported to the Board regularly. The disclosures of progress made towards establishing progressive risk management system, the risk management policy, strategy, exposures to related entities, the asset classification of such lending's/investments etc. should be in conformity with corporate governance standards, etc.
- Finally, the banks could be asked to come up with a strategy and plan for implementation of the governance standards recommended and submit progress of implementation, for review after twelve months and thereafter half yearly or annually, as deemed appropriate.

Besides, the recommendations also focused on the role and responsibilities of independent/non-executive directors, their training and remuneration, commonality of directors of banks and NBFCs, information flows to/from the board, etc.

The draft policy is in consonance with treating banks as 'special' and setting upfront a roadmap in a transparent manner for existing and potential investors. The intention of the policy is to ensure adequate capital and consolidation in the banking industry with the regulator being aware of the intention of existing and potential shareholders.

In June 2002, the RBI requested banks (excluding foreign banks, RRBs and LABs) to place the Report as well as the list of recommendations before their respective Board of Directors.

During the year 2003 it was proposed to synchronize the approaches suggested by the Ganguly Committee and the SEBI Committee in regard to corporate governance by banks, and to extend such practices to NBFCs and other financial institutions.

The existing legal framework and significant current practices cover the following aspects:

- Composition of Boards of Directors;
- Guidelines on corporate governance;
- Guidelines for acknowledgement of transfer/allotment of shares in private sector banks issued as on February 3, 2004; and
- Foreign investment in the banking sector, which is governed by the Press Note of March 5, 2004 issued by the Ministry of Commerce and Industry, Government of India.

The ownership and governance of banks assume special significance. Legal prescriptions relating to ownership and governance laid down in the Banking Regulation Act, 1949 have, therefore, been supplemented by regulatory prescriptions issued by the Reserve Bank from time to time.

The Reserve Bank had put a draft comprehensive policy framework for ownership and governance in private sector banks emphasizing diversified ownership on July 2, 2004. Based on the feedback received on the draft policy, the Reserve Bank, in consultation with the Government of India, laid down a comprehensive policy framework on February 28, 2005. The broad principles underlying the framework ensure that:

- Well diversified ownership and control;
- Important shareholders are 'fit and proper'.
- Directors and CEO are 'fit and proper' and observe sound corporate governance principles.
- Private sector banks should maintain a minimum of Rs. 200 crore as capital. These banks have to increase its capital into Rs. 300 crore with in a period of three years. Its net worth should be equal to Rs, 300 crore at all times for optimal operations and for systemic stability and
- Fairness and transparency in the policies and processes.

The regulatory frame work in India focused its attention on ensuring good corporate governance through "fit and Proper" owners, directors, and senior managers of the banks. Transfer of shareholding of four per cent above requires acknowledgement form the RBI and such significant shareholders are put through a "fit and proper" test. Banks have also been asked to ensure that the nominated and elected directors are screened by a nomination committee to satisfy "fit and proper" criteria. Directors are also required to sign a covenant indicating their roles and responsibilities. The listed banks are also required to comply with governance principles laid sown by the Securities and Exchange Board of India (SEBI)

In order to attain a well-diversified ownership structure, it is to be ensured that no single entity or a group of related entities has shareholding or control, directly or indirectly, in excess of 10 per cent of the paid-up capital of a private sector bank. Where any existing shareholding by any individual entity/group of related entities is in excess of 10 per cent, the bank will be required to indicate a timetable for reduction of holding to the permissible level. Any bank having shareholding in excess of 5 per cent in any other bank in India will be required to indicate a time bound plan for reduction of such holding to the permissible limit of 5 per cent. The parent of any foreign bank having presence in India having shareholding directly or indirectly through any other entity in the banking group in excess of 5 per cent in any other bank in India will be similarly required to indicate a time bound plan for reduction of such holding to 5 per cent. In the case of restructuring of problem/weak banks or in the interest of consolidation in the banking sector, the Reserve Bank could permit a higher level of shareholding, including by a bank.

Apart from some changes in ownership structures with attendant consequences, another noteworthy aspect of enhancing corporate governance is the narrowing of gap between PSBs and other banks in terms of the policy, regulatory and operating environment. The PSBs as hundred per cent owned entities with no share value quoted in stock exchanges accounted for over three quarters of banking business seven years ago, while they now account for less than a quarter.

In this regard, it is noteworthy that recently, the functioning of bank boards in the private sector seems to have attracted significant adverse notice, both from market and from the supervisor. It is concluded that the representation of the Reserve Bank on the Boards is not desirable similarly, it is also conceded that the Reserve Bank has expressed its interest in divesting all its ownership functions in banks.

13

Local Area Banks

The Finance Minister in the budget speech in Parliament in 1996 highlighted the need for a local institutional set up for mobilizing the rural savings and make them available for investment in viable economic activities in their area of operation. The decision to establish Local Area Banks (LABs) was taken with the primary objective of bridging the gap in credit availability and to strengthen the institutional credit framework in the rural and semi-urban areas. They were initially operated as non-scheduled commercial banks. These banks were established in the private sector. Pursuant to the announcement of Local Area Banks by the Finance Minister in his budget speech, The Reserve Bank of India issued a set of guidelines regarding the setting up of Local Area Banks in our country. The RBI introduced the Local Area Bank Scheme on August 24, 1996.

13.1 Meaning of Local Area Bank

Local Area Banks (LABs) are local private commercial banks established in the rural and semi-urban areas with jurisdiction of over two or three adjacent districts. Their prime objective is to mobilize rural savings and make them available for investments for viable economic activities in their area of operation.

13.1.1 Area of Operation and Branch Licensing: The guidelines for setting up of Local Area Bank were announced by the Reserve Bank in august 1996. As per the guidelines, the area of operation of an LAB was restricted to a maximum of three geographically contiguous districts. LABs were allowed to open only one branch in an urban centre in a District and rest of the branches were allowed to be opened in the rural and semi urban centers subject to requisite clearance from the District Consultative Committee for the concerned district regarding rural branches.

13.1.2 Share Capital: As per the guidelines issued by RBI, individuals, corporate entities and societies in the private sector could promote local area banks. The minimum paid up capital required for setting up an LAB was fixed at Rs.5 crore. The promoter's contribution in minimum paid up capital was fixed at Rs. 2 crore. The promoters of these banks were required to bring the entire minimum share capital up-front. It was also decided that a family of a promoter group could hold equity not exceeding 40 per cent of the capital. The number of NRI promoters was not to exceed 20 per cent of the total number of promoters.

The NRI contributions to the equity capital of the bank were restricted to a maximum of 40 per cent of the paid-up capital. The entire initial share capital subscribed by the promoters (including their friends and relatives/associates) would have a lock in period of three years from the date of licensing of the bank. Further, the promoters' equity to the extent of 40 per cent of the initial paid-up capital was to be locked in for at least two years beyond the aforesaid period of three years subject to a review before expiry of five years from the date of licensing. Individual voting rights of a shareholder was restricted to a ceiling of 10 per cent of the total voting rights in terms of Section 12 (2) of the Banking Regulation Act of 1949.

13.1.3 Advancing of Loans: Local . 3anks were required to finance agriculture and allied activities, small-scale industries, agro-industrial activities, trading activities and non-farm sector. Priority sector advances by these banks were fixed at a minimum of 40 per cent of the net bank credit. Of the total priority sector advances, at least 25 per cent of the advances should be made to the weaker sections of the society i.e. small and marginal farmers, landless labourers, scheduled castes, scheduled tribes, beneficiaries of government-sponsored schemes etc. The advances to weaker sections should not be less than 10 per cent of the net bank credit.

13.1.4 Applicability of Statutes: The provisions of the Reserve Bank of India Act of 1934, the Banking Regulation Act of 1949, Regional Rural Banks Act of 1976 and Indian Companies Act of 1956, were to govern the Local Area Bank. With regard to the liquidity requirements and interest rates, the provisions applicable to the Regional Rural Banks (RRBs) Act, 1976, would govern Local Area Banks.

13.1.5 Jurisdiction of the Banks: A Local Area Bank can be established as a public limited company in the private sector under the Companies Act of 1956. These banks will be licensed under the Banking Regulation Act of 1949 and will be eligible for inclusion in the Second Schedule of the Reserve Bank of India Act of 1934 subject to the fulfillment of the eligibility criteria laid down in Section 42(6) of the said Act.

The regulatory responsibility over the Local Area Banks is vested in the Rural Planning and Credit Department (RPCD) of the RBI. The RPCD issues license for these banks as per provisions of Section 22 of the Banking Regulation Act of 1949 and grants permission for opening of branches at new places of business as per the provisions of Section 23 of the Act. The financial strength of the LABs is monitored through off-site returns and other statements required to be submitted by these banks to the RBI.

13.1.6 Appointment of CEO: The appointment of the Chief Executive Officer (CEO) and the Chairman of the Local Area Bank requires clearance of the RBI as per the provisions of Section 10B of the Banking Regulation Act of 1949. The fixing of remuneration of the CEO also requires prior approval of the RBI. The composition of the Board of these banks is to be in accordance with the provisions of Section 10A of the Banking Regulation Act of 1949. Because Local Area Banks are commercial banks in the private sector, banking policies as applicable to commercial banks are made applicable to them also except where those pertaining to areas of business, which they are not permitted to undertake.

13.1.7 Prudential Norms and Corporate Governance: LABs would be subject to prudential norms, corporate governance, accounting policies and other policies as laid down by RBI. From their inception these banks has to maintain capital adequacy at 8 per cent of risk weighted assets and comply with all the norms of income recognition, asset classification and provisioning with out any lapse.

13.1.8 Procedure of Licensing: Reserve Bank of India announced a set of guidelines on August 24, 1996 for the establishment of Local Area Banks (LABs) in the private sector. With the issuance of this notification, the Reserve Bank of India invited applications with supporting documents to fix eligibility of institutions for setting up of Local Area Banks. As per the procedure followed in such cases the RBI granted an 'in-principle' approval for setting up an LAB which laid down the terms and conditions to be fulfilled by the promoters before a license could be granted for commencement of banking business. The RBI could, at its discretion, call for any additional information required by it or withdraw/cancel the 'in–principle' approval in the event of non compliance with the conditions laid down in the 'in principle' approval.

13.2 Progress in Licensing of Local Area Banks

At the time of issuance of notification in August 1996 to the end June1999, the Reserve Bank of India received 215 applications from different states for the setting up of LABs. Of the applications received, 194 applications were rejected and disposed off. Almost all applications were disposed off due to the lack of fulfillment of the terms and conditions, which are stated in the notification. As on March 1999, only in the case of eight applicants "in- principle" approvals were given for the setting up local area banks. The 'in- principle' approvals for setting up of LAB were granted to, one each in the states of Maharashtra, Punjab, Andhra Pradesh, Tamil Nadu, Rajasthan and Gujarat and two in Karnataka. Of these, licenses were issued only to five Local Area Banks.

Till the end of March 2002, 227 applications were received by the RBI for the setting of LABs. Of these 227 applications received, 214 were rejected. 'In-principle' approvals for establishment of LABs were issued to 10 institutions .and 3 applications are pending examination. Of the 10 applicants who were granted 'in-principle' approvals, four of them were withdrawn, due to the inability of the promoters to fulfill the conditions stipulated in the 'in-principle' approvals. One application is pending for approval. Of these five banks were licensed under Section 22 of the Banking Regulation Act of 1949.

13.3 Commencement of Business by Local Area Banks

Following Local Area Banks commenced their operations in their allotted districts;

1. **Coastal Local Area Bank Ltd., Vijayawada:** The bank commenced its business on 27 December 1999, with its Head Office at Vijayawada. Their area operations was limited in the districts of West Godavari, Krishna and Guntur in Andhra Pradesh,
2. **Capital Local Area Bank Ltd., Phagwara:** The bank was established on January 14, 2000 with its Registered Office at Phagwara. Their area of operation was restricted to the districts of Kapurthala, Jalandhar and Hoshiarpur in the state of Punjab. Shri A.S. Samra and 25 individuals have promoted the bank.
3. **Krishna Bhima Samurdhi Local Area Bank Ltd., Mehboobnagar:** The bank was established on February 28, 2001 with its Head Office at Mahabubnagar. The area of operation of the bank was limited to three districts in two states. The bank will operate in the districts of Raichur and Gulbarga in Karnataka and Mehboobnagar in Andhra Pradesh.
4. **Vinayak Local Area Bank Ltd., Sikar:** It was established on 21 October 2000 in the state of Rajasthan. The bank was permitted to operate in the districts of Jhunjhunu, Sikar and Churu.
5. **South Gujarat Local Area Bank Ltd., Navsari:** Shri Kanaksinh M. Mangrola and nine others promoted the bank. The bank established on October 3, 2000 with its Head Office

at Navsari. The bank established in the state of Gujarat was operating in three neighboring districts viz. Surat, Navsari and Bharuch.

6. **The Subhadra Local Area Bank Ltd., Kolhapur:** The Subhadra Local Area Bank Ltd., Kolhapur, which was issued license on July 10, 2003. During the year 2002-03, RBI issued only one license for LAB. The bank commenced its business from September 30, 2003 in the districts of Kolhapur and Sangli in Maharashtra and Belgaum in Karnataka.

13.4 Failure\Merger of Local Area Banks

1. **Vinayak Local Area Bank Ltd.:** Out of the Five LABs, which have started, license in respect of one LAB viz., Vinayak Local Area Bank, Sikar established on October 21, 2000, was cancelled on January 16, 2002, because of major irregularities in its functioning.
2. **The South Gujarat Local Area Bank Ltd.:** South Gujarat Local Area Bank Ltd., Navsari opened six branches (1 urban, 2 semi urban, 3 rural) in its area of operation, and it incurred net losses consecutively for three years and it got merged with Bank of Baroda in 2004.

The affairs of the South Gujarat Local Area Bank were managed by a professional Board of Directors with broad based representation for different fields like agriculture, industry, banking etc. Board meetings are held at regular intervals. The Board has to set up six committees viz. Management Committee, Loan Committee, Investment Committee, Internal Inspection Committee, HRD Committee and Audit Committee. The bank has also an internal supervision and control system.

The South Gujarat Local Area Bank Ltd, which was set up on October 10, 2000, had suffered net losses for the three consecutive years. The financial position of the bank was steadily getting weakened and the banks capital and reserves got almost eroded and showed several significant adverse features. Because of the above situation, Reserve Bank of India made a recommendation to Government of India to place the bank under moratorium as per Section 45 (1) of Banking Regulations Act of 1949. Then the Government of India issued orders of moratorium in respect of the bank for a period of nine months from the close of business on November 13, 2003 to August 12, 2004. In the meantime, Reserve Bank prepared a draft scheme for the amalgamation of the South Gujarat Local Area Bank Ltd with Bank of Baroda and it was forwarded to the Government of India for its approval. Subsequently, Government of India sanctioned the Scheme of amalgamation of South Gujarat Local Area Bank Ltd. with Bank of Baroda. The Scheme of Amalgamation came into effect on June 25, 2004.

During the year ending March 31, 2005, only four LABs were functional in the country. They are the following;

- Coastal Local Area Bank Ltd, Vijayawada;
- Capital Local Area Bank Ltd., Phagwara,
- Krishna Bhima Samruddhi Local Area Bank Ltd., Mehboobnagar; and
- Subhadra Local Area Bank Ltd., Kolhapur.

Coastal Local Area Bank Ltd. Vijayawada opened nine branches (urban-3, semi-urban- 5, rural-1) in its area of operation.

A professional Board of Directors with broad representation for agriculture, industry, management, and banking areas manages the affairs of the bank. Board meets at regular intervals to discuss the affairs of the bank. The Board set up four committees viz. (i) Investment Committee, (ii) Audit Committee, (iii) Management Committee, (iv) Asset Liability Management Committee. The bank has placed in position the system of internal supervision and control.

Capital Local Area Bank Ltd., Phagwara opened eight branches (urban-1, semi-urban-3 and rural-4) in its area of operation.

The affairs of the bank were managed by a professional Board of Directors with broad based representation to different fields like agriculture and co-operation, industry, banking. The Board meets at regular intervals and set up several committee's viz. Credit sanctioning committee, Investment Committee, Audit

Committee, Management Committee, Asset Liability Management Committee. There is an internal audit department for audit of branches at half-yearly intervals.

Krishna Bhima Samruddhi Local Area Bank Ltd has opened three branches of which one was at an urban centre and the remaining two are rural branches.

A Professional Board of Directors with broad representation to agriculture, rural development, and micro finance manages the affairs of the bank. It also has set up an Audit Committee, Executive Committee and ALCO. The bank reportedly introduced an internal inspection system and periodic branch visit system.

Subhadra Local Area Bank Ltd., Kolhapur which commenced its operation in September 2003, suffered loss from the very first year of its operation. The deposits and gross advances of the bank increased significantly during the year 2004-05.

13.5 Working of Local Area Banks: Findings and Recommendations

The Reserve Bank of India appointed a three member Review Group under the Chairmanship of Shri G. Ramachandran, Former Finance Secretary, Government of India, in July 2002, to carry out a review of the operations of Local Area Banks functioning in the country and to make recommendations for revitalizing them. The terms of reference of the Group were 'to examine whether the Local Area Banks have fulfilled their objectives and purposes for which they were formed'. Review also included the question whether the scheme should be continued or not.

The Review Group evaluated the operations of all the four Local Area Banks in the country. The Group evaluated the following banks:

- The Coastal Local Area Bank Ltd. established on December 27, 1999,
- The Capital Local Area Bank Ltd. established on January 14, 2000,
- The South Gujarat Local Area Bank Ltd. established on October 3, 2000 and

- The Krishna Bhima Samrudhi Local Area Bank Ltd. established on February 28, 2001.

The Review Group finalized and submitted its report in September 2002. After wide discussions, the Group arrived at a conclusion that Local Area Banks established with high expectations had failed in achieving their desired objectives. However, in the preface of the report, the Group noted that Local Area Banks were in existence only for a short period and it would be difficult to draw a clear conclusion about their success or failure. They further observed that these banks would need a little more time to establish themselves firmly in the areas in which they are functioning and to win the confidence of both the investors and the borrowers.

The Group opined that Local Area Banks are tormented by a variety of problems such as poor mobilization of local resources, ineffective leadership, poor monitoring of end use of credit and mounting overdues. LABs have not made any impact on the local communities amongst whom they are functioning in terms of any of the relevant indicators such as 1) deposit mobilization 2) number of depositors 3) number of borrower accounts 4) amounts lent 5) number of rural branches and 6) number of poor people helped. A number of measures have to be initiated to strengthen them and new norms of capital and capital adequacy have to be laid down if the few banks, which have come into existence, are to survive and grow.

In order to draw the attention of the regulators, the Group identified the worrying features and fundamental issues in the functioning of LABs. The important issues identified in connection with the working of LABs and the proposed recommendations are given below:

1. Local Area Banks (LABs) are established with the objective of mobilizing the rural savings and making them available with investments for viable economic activities in their areas of operation. These banks were required to finance agriculture and allied activities, small-scale industries, agro-industrial activities, trading activities and in non-farm sector. Priority

sector advances to these banks were fixed at a minimum of 40 per cent of the net bank credit. Of the total priority sector advances at least 25 per cent of the advances should be made to the weaker sections of the society i.e. small, marginal farmers, landless labourers, scheduled castes, and scheduled tribes and beneficiaries under government sponsored schemes. The advances to weaker sections should not fall below 10 per cent of the net bank credit.

2. The group stated that since it is mandatory for LABs lend to these sectors the credit portfolio of an LAB will thus tend to be more risk prone than that of other banking institutions. In view of their size and location, they will not be able to diversify and to minimize the risks. Their inability to undertake other activities will also expose them to the concentration of risks. Further, since LABs depend on loan portfolio for their income and do not have diversified income stream, they have to necessarily expand their loan portfolio for generating income. This exposes them to the risk of adverse selection. Thus, there are inherent fundamental weaknesses in the business model of the LAB. These issues have to be addressed immediately.
3. Based on examination of the various aspects of the working of Local Area Banks the Group found that all LABs except one were trading heavily in securities. It was also observed that 67 per cent of the transactions in securities were routed through a single broker. Trading in securities is an inherently risky business. The Group contented that LABs located in rural areas with limited capital and meager financial resources were trading heavily in securities and are likely to become victims of the uncertainties of security market. After carefully considering the inherent risks, the Group recommended that LAB should be prohibited from trading in Government securities and other papers during a five-year period.
4. The Group found that Local Area Banks are achieving their business targets by heavily utilizing the services of intermediaries such as agents and quasi agents. They

cautioned about such strategies adopted and referred their defects in an institution like LAB. Therefore, the Group recommended that such strategies should be discouraged and should not be permitted to engage the services of agents and quasi agents for achieving their business targets.

5. It came to the notice of the Group that some of the Local Area Banks are not even maintaining an arms length relationship with their group companies and associates. The Group cautioned about the risks involved in such a type of lending. In view of the inherent weaknesses of these banks, great care has to be taken to ensure that no "Holding Out" is done by the sponsoring agency and the LABs with other group entities maintain an arms length relationship.
6. The study group opined that current net worth of Local Area Banks is not viable and not sufficient to meet the unexpected adverse trends and to overcome the threats like any panicky reaction from the part of its investors. The Group recommended for enhancing the capital base of Local Area Banks to at least Rs. 25 crore over a period of five years.
7. Since LABs are inherently of a high-risk portfolio and with out any possibility of reducing its risk in future, the Group advised them to maintain a minimum capital adequacy of 15 per cent.
8. They further recommended that in order to surmount unexpected adverse trends Local Area Banks are required to create an asset base of about Rs. 150 crore and to maintain a minimum capital adequacy of 15 per cent. The matrix as proposed by the Group was a net worth of Rs. 25 crore and a capital adequacy norm of 15 per cent would enable LABs to build an asset base of about Rs. 150 crore, a level at which their operations would become viable. Besides every one of the existing Local Area Banks should be required to submit a suitable road map for achieving the twin objectives of higher capital base and enhanced capital adequacy norm.
9. To facilitate the development of the existing Local Area Banks into viable commercial units the group suggested that it

would be appropriate to extend refinancing facility from NABARD and SIDBI. At present Local Area Banks are not eligible to draw refinance from NABARD and SIDBI because LABs are not scheduled commercial Banks. The Group therefore suggested that though a Local Area Bank may not be a scheduled commercial bank, it should not be denied access to refinance for its term lending from NABARD and SIDBI.

10. Even though Local Area Banks do not come under the category of scheduled commercial banks, they have to complete the entire procedural formalities similar to commercial banks when they open a new branch. The branch licensing procedure is very slow and is cumbersome. In this connection, they have to obtain permission from the District Consultative Committee and the Lead Bank of the District. The Group recommended that existing restrictions on branch licensing to LABs should be waived. They suggested that Local Area Banks should be treated on par with Cooperative Banks in the matter of opening new branches.
11. At present Local Area Banks are permitted to open only one urban branch in a district. In order to expand the business, to attain viability and to diversify their business and risk, the Group recommended that LABs should be permitted to open more branches in urban centres. A ratio of one urban branch to 10 rural/semi urban branches will perhaps be more appropriate.
12. Local Area Banks are new institutions and therefore they need to be regulated carefully and supervised closely in the initial stages. In the opinion of the Group, the regulation and supervision of LABs should be in the same wing of the RBI that regulates and supervises commercial banks. The Rural Planning and Credit Department (RPCD) should be relieved from its responsibility of regulating LABs.
13. The Group finally suggested that till the implementation of the proposed measures and the existing Local Area Banks became stable and sound, no new license should be granted.

13.5.1 Financial Performance of LABs: The financial performances of four Local Area Banks in the country for the last four years are given in Table 13.1.

Table 13.1: Financial Performances of Local Area Banks 2002-06 (Rs. crore)

Particulars	2002-03	2003-04	2004-05	2005-06
Interest Income	12.7	15.4 (21.2)	17.3 (12.3)	25.5 (47.3)
Interest Expenses	7.7	8.6 (11.7)	8.7 (1.2)	12.0 (38.0)
Operating Profit	2.7	2.9 (7.4)	3.4 (17.2)	5.4 (58.2)
Net Profit	0.2	0.1 (-50)	0.9 (800)	2.8 (211)
Deposits	113.4	157 (38.4)	200 (27.4)	290 (45)
Advances	76.8	103 (34.1)	130 (26.2)	197 (51.5)

Figures in bracket indicate percentage variation over the previous year.

Table 13.1 discloses that the total interest income of four Local Area Banks increased from Rs. 12.7 crore in the year 2002-03 to Rs. 25.5 crore in 2005-06. It recorded an increase of 47.3 per cent in 2005-06 compared to the previous year. However, the rate of growth in interest expenses during the year shows only an increase of 38 per cent over the previous year.

Total Deposits of Local Area Banks aggregating to Rs. 290 crore at the end of March 2006 represented a spectacular increase over that of Rs. 113.4 crore as on March 2005. This shows a compound annual growth rate of 26.5 per cent over a period of four years. The total Advances of LABs in the country also increased substantially and steadily from Rs. 76.8 crore in March 2003 to Rs. 197 crore in March 2006; registering a compound growth rate of 26.5 per cent per annum. The compound growth rate in respect of deposits and advances over a period of four years are the same viz. 26.5 per cent.

Local Area Banks bank began showing profits since their inception and posted a profit of Rs. 103.28 lakh for the year ending March 31, 2002. However, Subhadra Local Area Bank Ltd., Kolhapur, which commenced its operation in September 2003, suffered a loss in the first year of its operation.

The operating profit of Local Area Banks (Table 13.1) increased from Rs. 2.7 crore in 2002-03 to Rs. 5.4 crore during the year 2005-06. The operating profit increased by 58.2 per cent in the year 2005-06 compared to the previous year. The net profit of Local Area Banks also increased remarkably in the year 2005-06. It increased from Rs. 0.2 crore in 2002-03 to Rs. 2.8 crore in 2005-06. Total net profits of four Local Area Banks increased in the year 2005-06 by 211 per cent compared to the previous year.

14

Indian Commercial Banks in Foreign Countries

Banking institutions are indispensable part and parcel of a modern thriving economy. Today, no other developing country can boast of a banking system comparable to that of India in terms of its geographical coverage and range of services. Banks in India vary in their size and operations. Banking system in India consists of different classes of banks. Two broad categories of banks in India are Commercial Banks and Co-operative Banks. Commercial banks are further subdivided into Public, Private, Foreign and Regional Rural Banks. Public sector banks consist of nationalized banks plus State Bank of India and its Subsidiaries. In co-operative banks category, there are state co-operative banks, urban co-operative banks and primary co-operative banks. A number of Indian commercial banks both private and public operate in foreign countries either through their full-fledged branches or through representative offices.

14.1 Brief History of Commercial Banks Abroad

At the time of nationalization of banks in 1969, Indian banks had only minimal presence abroad. Even after nationalization, Indian banks did not succeed fully in extending their operations abroad. It was mainly because of lack of capital and resources of Indian banks to export. The banks in India are not well equipped to compete with foreign banks in respect of either technology or resources. Besides many restrictions were imposed by several foreign governments against expansion of Indian banks in their country.

The first foreign office of an Indian bank was established by Imperial bank of India in the nineteenth century by way of its opening branches in Colombo and Rangoon. Another branch of

Imperial bank of India was opened in London in the early 1920s. The Bank of India opened its branch in London in 1946. Subsequently the Indian Bank and the Indian Overseas Bank also established their offices in Singapore and Malaysia respectively. In the following decades, there was further expansion of branches in these countries and in London and Hong Kong by other banks namely United Commercial Bank, Central Bank of India and Bank of Baroda.

Bank of India and Bank of Baroda opened many branches in Kenya, Uganda, Nigeria, Guyana, Mauritius and Fiji. In 1950s, Indian banks also opened their branches in Tokyo and Osaka in Japan. At the time of nationalization of 14 major banks in 1969, there were 59 branches of Indian banks in 14 foreign countries.

Since nationalization, the expansion of Indian banks into foreign lands showed a negative trend due to several reasons. The development policy of some countries adversely affected the expansion and continuation of foreign branches in their countries. For instance, nationalization of banks in Eden in 1969 forced Indian banks to stop their operation there. Similarly, the operations of Indian banks in Nigeria and Uganda ended due to the amendment of the Ugandian Banking Regulations Act, which restricted the operation of foreign banks in their country. Meanwhile, the nationalization of Indian banks in 1969 led to discontinuance of the branches of nationalized banks in Malaysia and Thailand, where their law does not permit the functioning of any state owned or state controlled bank.

Amendment of banking regulations in Nigeria forced Bank of India (1962) to convert its offices into a subsidiary company of the bank known as "Bank of India (Nigeria) Ltd". In Uganda, branches of Bank of Baroda and Bank of India formed two subsidiaries to carry on the business of their foreign branches. Later these two subsidiaries got merged into one owned by the Bank of Baroda.

Legal requirement forced Indian Bank, Indian Overseas Bank and the United Commercial Bank to form a new banking company in Malaysia known as "United Asian Bank", Berhad

(1972). These three banks together contributed one third of the paid up capital of the new company and Malaysian Corporations and citizens contributed the balance. Eleven branches of these three banks were taken over by the newly formed banking company.

Contrary to the policy decisions, temporary permission was granted by the Government of Thailand for the continuance of the operations of the branches of nationalized banks in their country. The continuance of the operation of branches of Indian Overseas Bank in Bangkok was ensured through the creation of a new bank in the private sector known as Bharat Overseas Bank Ltd. in 1974. Bharat Overseas Bank Ltd. took over the business of the branches of Indian Overseas Bank. In 1974, Bharat Overseas Bank Ltd. was the only private sector bank in India with a foreign office. Consequent to these developments 19 foreign offices of various Indian banks closed their operations abroad between 1969 and 1973. During the Period, 1969-73 eleven new offices were opened by Indian banks. An important development in 1971 was the conversion of the representative office of State Bank of India in New York into a full-fledged branch with that status.

Since 1974, there were noticeable changes in the pace of overseas expansion of Indian banks. Twenty-three new foreign offices were opened during 1974-1975. Important developments during these periods were; opening of foreign branches by State Bank of India in Frankfurt, Maldives, Chicago, Dacca, Off –Shore branches in Bahamas, Toronto, Philippines, Iran and Bahrain etc. Bank of India's presence in Paris, Bank of Baroda's chain of branches in UAE, Brussels, Syndicate Bank and Punjab National Banks presence in London etc. were notable and commendable. At the end of 1976, ten Indian banks maintained a total of 90 branches and 6 representative offices in foreign countries.

14.2 Supervisory Initiatives Relating to Foreign Branches of Indian Banks

A Working Group was set up by the Reserve Bank of India in 1999 to study the entire gamut of management of overseas operations by Indian banks. Apart from officials from the Reserve

Bank of India, officials of major banks having overseas operations, were also given due representation in the Working Group. Important recommendations of the Working Group were the following:

1. Introduction of a new supervisory reporting system called the DSB-O returns to replace the existing RALOO (Returns on Assets and Liabilities of Overseas Offices) statements. The existing system to be rationalized with focus on market risks, which are not adequately captured under the present set up.
2. Introduction of comprehensive policies in respect of credit and investment management at the overseas branches taking into account the host country regulation/legislation. The objective was to improve the asset quality by taking advantage of the emerging opportunities in the overseas markets.
3. Formulation of appropriate risk management policies taking into account the scale and complexity of operations, risk philosophy and risk taking capacity of banks. Such policies should aim at identification of risks, their quantification, monitoring and control.
4. Banks have to introduce strong management information system that would provide comprehensive/valuable feed back to the top management on a timely basis to enable the top management to initiate appropriate action.
5. Periodicity of inspection of foreign branches to be decided by banks taking into account the instructions of the host country regulator in this regard, if any, and status of the branch. In addition, banks were to introduce a system of quick assessment/review of the larger foreign branches at intervals that are more frequent than before.
6. As regards supervision by the Reserve Bank, apart from the DSB-O returns, the quarterly DO letters from the Head Offices, copies of the head office inspection reports of the foreign branches and inspection reports of the host country regulator to be used as supplementary off-site tools. The Reserve Bank is required to undertake on-site supervision of

foreign branches, the frequency of which depends on its perception of supervisory concerns.

7. Banks have to initiate action on reviewing their personnel policies for smooth functioning of their overseas branches, viz. policy of placement, succession policy, retention policy etc.

In view of these recommendations, the Reserve Bank set up a new cell named 'Foreign Branches Cell' in the Department of Banking Supervision to oversee the implementation of these recommendations and also to provide sharper focus on the supervision of overseas operations. Further, the banks were advised to review their policies relating to credit, investment, risk management, etc. in the light of the Group's recommendations and furnish to the Reserve Bank the progress reports in this regard on a quarterly basis, which are being monitored in the Cell. The Cell began analyzing the portfolio appraisal reports of the overseas operations.

Reserve Bank held meetings with the individual banks .to discuss the performance of their foreign branches, problems faced by them and strategic plans for the immediate future. The Reserve Bank of India invited quarterly reports from the banks having overseas presence, detailing changes in the regulatory framework, pending issues relating to host country and home country supervision, business environment and perception of new opportunities, credit and control areas and compliance of audit/ inspection.

The supervisory action being undertaken includes discussion with the top management on the identified supervisory concerns and follow-up action on the assurances given by the bank. Other activities of the Cell include analysis of returns from overseas offices and undertaking country analysis on a periodical basis.

The most recent initiative undertaken by the Cell is the preparation of market intelligence reports on overseas markets. Such reports are being prepared and circulated in the department on a fortnightly basis. These reports are an important input for initiating supervisory action. The Reserve Bank has introduced

DSB-O quarterly reporting system consisting of seven returns in place of RALOO statements from the quarter ended June 2000. There was a noticeable change in the pace of overseas expansion of Indian banks since 1998.

14.3 Overseas Operations of Indian Banks during 1998-2006

Indian banks have been operating in several countries across the world by opening their own branches and subsidiary banks, joint ventures and representative offices. Representative offices have no operational responsibilities but play a valuable role in exploring and providing supporting services for their branches. Instead of opening a full-fledged branch, representative offices are particularly useful in those countries in which Indian banks venture for the first time.

Number of Indian commercial banks and their presence in foreign countries since 1998 are disclosed in Table 14.1

Table 14.1: Overseas Operations of Indian Banks from 1998-2006

Year	No. of Banks	No. of Branches	Subsidiary Companies	Joint Ventures	Repres-entative Offices
1997- 98	8	97	13	7	15
1998- 99	9	95	13	8	16
2000-01	9	94	15	5	14
2001-02	9	92	15	5	18
2002-03	9	92	15	5	18
2004-05	14	101	17	6	30
2005-06	18	112	18	6	35

Table 14.1 reveals that at the end of March 1998 eight Indian public sector banks had their branches abroad. The number of foreign branches of Indian banks declined from 98 to 97 during 1997-98. During the year, 1998 Bank of Baroda opened a branch at Durban in South Africa, while State Bank of India closed its branch at Panama. Two branches – Tanjong Pagar branch and

Singapore main branch – of UCO Bank got merged in to one.

During 1998-99 the number of foreign branches declined to 95 from 97 following the closure of their branches in London by the State Bank of India and the UCO Bank. The number of representative offices of Indian banks increased from 15 to 16 following the opening of two representative offices at Almaty in Kazakhstan by the Punjab National Bank and at Sydney in Australia by the State Bank of India and the closure of representative office by the Indian Bank in Jakarta. While there was no change in the number of wholly owned subsidiaries of Indian banks abroad, which remained at 13, the number of joint ventures abroad, increased to 8 following the opening of a joint venture – the 'Everest Nepal Bank' in Nepal by the Punjab National Bank.

At the end of September 2003, eight banks in the public sector and one bank in the private sector had their branches abroad. With the closure of State Bank of India's Flushing, New York branch in the USA, and the foreign currency-banking unit of Indian Overseas Bank in Colombo, the total number of overseas branches of the nine Indian banks got reduced to 92.

The number of representative offices of Indian banks abroad increased from 15 to 18 with the opening of representative offices in London and New York by ICICI Bank Limited, in Dubai by HDFC Bank Limited, in Shenzhen (China) and Ho Chi Minh City (Vietnam) by Bank of India, and in London by Punjab National Bank. The State Bank of India had earlier closed down its Representative offices in Ho Chi Minh City (Vietnam), Sao Paulo (Brazil) and Jakarta (Indonesia). Thus the number of joint ventures and subsidiaries abroad of Indian banks stood at 5 and 15, respectively.

As on October 20, 2005, fourteen Indian banks, nine from the public sector and five from the private sector had their overseas operations spread across 42 countries with a network of 101 branches (including 6 offshore units), 6 joint ventures, 17 subsidiaries and 30 representative offices. As on September 30, 2006, eighteen Indian banks had overseas operations spread over

47 countries with a network of 112 branches (including offshore units), 6 joint ventures, 18 subsidiaries and 35 representative offices.

Indian banks branch presence in foreign countries as on September 30, 2006 are given in Table 14.2

Table 14.2 discloses that Bank of Baroda has the highest overseas presence with 40 branches followed by State Bank of India (30 branches) and Bank of India (20 branches).

Bank of Baroda has the highest number of subsidiaries abroad (7) followed by State Bank of India with 5 subsidiaries and ICICI Bank 3.

State Bank of India is second in branch presence. It has 3 joint venture banks and 7 representative offices in 29 countries. Bank of Baroda had one joint venture bank and 3 representative offices in 20 countries, followed by Bank of India with one joint venture bank and four representative offices in 14 countries.

During the year 2006, Bank of India, the country's sixth-largest bank, signed an agreement to acquire 76 per cent stake in Indonesia's P T Bank Swadesi Tbk. ICICI Bank opened its representative offices in Thailand (Bangkok), Indonesia (Jakarta), and Malaysia (Kula Lumpur) thus extending its foreign presence to 17 countries. Canara Bank for the first time opened its full-fledged branch in Hong Kong in the year 2006. With the take over of "Bharat Overseas Bank Ltd." by the "Indian Overseas Bank" in March 2007, IOB regained its Bangkok branch in Thailand, thus increasing its overseas presence to six.

14.4 Branch Licensing Policy of Commercial Banks

Before the amendment of the provisions in the banking regulations act, for opening a new branch office, commercial banks were required to obtain from time to time an individual approval for each branch from RBI. Similarly, banks were not allowed to shift their place of business other than with in the same city, town or village with out the prior permission of RBI. The existing system of granting authorization for opening individual branches from time to time has been replaced by a system of

Table 14.2: Overseas Operations of Indian Banks (as on September 30, 2006)

Name of the Bank	No. of Branches	Subsidiary Companies	Representative Offices	Joint Ventures	Total
Punjab National Bank	1	-	4	1	6
State Bank of India	30	5	7	3	45
Bank of India	20	1	4	1	26
Bank of Baroda	40	7	3	1	51
Indian Bank	3	-	-	-	3
Indian Overseas Bank	5	1	2	-	8
UCO Bank	4	-	1	-	5
Canara Bank	1	1	1	-	3
Syndicate Bank	1	-	-	-	1
Bharat Overseas Bank	1	-	-	-	1
ICICI Bank Ltd.	4	3	7	-	14
IndusInd Bank Ltd.	-	-	2	-	2
Centurian Bank of Punjab Ltd.	-	1	-	1	2
UTI Bank Ltd.	1				1
Andhra Bank			1		1
Allahabad Bank			1		1
Total	112	18	35	6	171

giving aggregated approvals, on an annual basis, through a consultative and interactive process.

14.4.1 New Branch Licensing Policy: The Branch Authorization Policy was revised by the Reserve Bank of India in September 8, 2005. Branch licensing policy was rationalized and liberalized by giving reasonable leeway for the banks to open new branches in India.

As per the revised branch licensing policy, banks are required to submit a specific proposal relating to opening, closing, shifting of all categories of branches including off-site ATMs, conversion of branches and up gradation of extension counters in their annual plan. No separate permission was required for on-site ATMs that are opened within the branch office. The specific proposal for annual branch expansion of individual banks and their strategies and plans are discussed by the Reserve Bank with individual banks.

The branch authorization granted to banks is valid for one year from the date of issue of the consolidated letter of permission issued to banks by RBI. When bank is not in a position to open a particular branch because of any genuine reason, it can approach the Regional Office of the Reserve Bank for extension of time not exceeding three months. After opening branches, banks are required to communicate immediately the complete office address and date of opening of the branch to the regional office of the RBI. While submitting the proposal, banks are advised to follow certain procedures to comply with the requirements of Section 23 of the Banking Regulation Act of 1949.

RBI takes in to consideration several factors before sanctioning new branches to commercial banks. While considering the application for new offices, weightage is given to the nature and scope of banking facilities provided by a bank to common persons, particularly in unbanked and under banked areas. Due weightage is also given to a bank for their commitment to the basic banking activities viz. acceptance of deposits and provision of credit. Other factors which to be considered by RBI are given below:

- Priority sector advances of the bank.
- Pricing of products.
- Introduction of appropriate new products.
- Extent and use of technology for delivery of banking services.
- Quality of customer service as evidenced.
- Number of complaints received.
- Redressal mechanism in the bank.

RBI while licensing a new branch at a particular location also considers enhancement of healthy competition among banks in various localities. Regulatory comfort is also relevant in this context. This encompasses:

- Compliance with principles of regulation.
- The activities of the banking group and the nature of relationship of the bank with its subsidiaries, affiliates and associates.
- Quality of corporate governance, proper risk management systems and internal control mechanisms.

14.4.2 Branch Authorisation Policy for Foreign Banks: The branch authorization policy of Indian banks is also applicable to foreign banks, subject to the following conditions.

- Foreign banks are required to bringing an assigned capital of US$ 25 million upfront at the time of opening the first branch in India.
- Existing foreign banks having only one branch are expected to comply with the above requirement before their request for opening of second branch is entertained.
- Foreign banks are also required to submit their branch expansion plan on an annual basis.

In addition to the parameters laid down for Indian banks, the following additional parameters are considered for foreign banks:

- Track record of compliance and functioning in the global markets of the foreign bank.
- its group (reports from home country supervisors are sought, wherever necessary).
- Even distribution of home countries of foreign banks having

presence in India.

- Treatment given to Indian banks in the home country of the applicant foreign.
- Bilateral and diplomatic relations between India and the home country.
- India's commitments at WTO

ATMs are not included in the number of branches for such computation.

14.5 Off-Shore Banking

Off-Shore Banking or overseas banking unit refers to the setting up of banking units by foreign multinational banks in those countries, which offer facilities of off- shore banking services. These units obtain funds from international money markets and invest them in the country, where they set up the units or in various projects started by the said country elsewhere. Off – Shore Banking Units (OBUs) does not mobilize deposits from the country in which they are located and do not compete with the domestic banks. These units provide finance to those projects, which are of a capital-intensive nature and for importing costly capital equipments.

14.5.1 Revised Norms of RBI for Off- Shore Banking Units: Following the announcement in the EXIM Policy of 2002-07 by the Government of India, the Reserve Bank of India issued guidelines in November 2002 allowing banks operating in India to set up Off-Shore Banking Units (OBUs) in Special Economic Zones (SEZs) which would virtually be foreign branches of Indian banks located in India. Off-Shore Banking Units are exempted from the CRR and SLR requirements. They provide finance to SEZ units and SEZ developers at international rates.

The salient features of the scheme for setting up Off- Shore Banking Units in Special Economic Zones are:

- All commercial banks operating in India, authorised to deal in foreign exchange, are eligible to set up OBUs, with a preference for banks having overseas branches and experience of running OBUs.

- Banks would be required to obtain prior permission of the Reserve Bank for opening an OBU in a SEZ under Section 23(1) (a) of the Banking Regulation Act, 1949 (relating to opening of new place of business in India).
- Since Off-Shore Banking Units would be branches of Indian banks, no separate assigned capital for such branches would be required. However, with a view to enable them to start their own operations, the parent bank would be required to provide a minimum of US$ 10 million to its OBU.
- The Reserve Bank would grant exemption from CRR requirements to the parent bank in respect of its OBU branch.
- The sources of raising foreign currency funds would only be external.
- The OBUs would be required to follow scrupulously 'Know Your Customer' and other anti-money laundering instructions issued by the Reserve Bank.
- The OBUs would be required to maintain separate nostro accounts with correspondent banks, which would be distinct from nostro accounts maintained by other branches of the same bank.
- Deposits of Off Shore Banking Units will not be covered by deposit insurance.
- The loans and advances of OBUs would not be considered as net bank credit for computing priority sector lending obligations.

As per the guidelines issued in November 2002, allowing banks operating in India to set up Off-Shore Banking Units (OBUs) in Special Economic Zones (SEZs), Reserve Bank issued in principle approval to 10 banks for opening 14 such units. In the first phase, six banks were given in principle approval for opening nine such units. Such approved banks are as follows: 1) State Bank of India 2) Bank of Baroda 3) Union Bank of India 4) Oriental Bank of Commerce 5) Punjab National Bank and 6) ICICI Bank. Sanctioned units in SEZs are six in SEEPZ, Mumbai and one each in Kandla, Surat and Cochin.

Subsequently in the second phase, five banks (*viz.* Punjab

National Bank, Canara Bank, Bank of India, HDFC Bank and Vijaya Bank) were given permission to open five OBUs: two in Noida, UP and 3 in SEEPZ, Mumbai. Vijaya Bank, which was permitted to open an OBU in SEEPZ, Mumbai in 2003, did not renew its license.

Up to the end of September 30, 2006, Six Indian Commercial banks opened seven Off-Shore Banking Units in the country. These banks are:

- State Bank of India
- Bank of Baroda
- Union Bank of India
- Punjab National Bank
- ICICI Bank Ltd.
- Canara Bank

Of the seven functioning OBUs, five are located in SEEPZ, Mumbai and one each in SEEPZ, Noida (Canara Bank) and Kochi, Kerala (SBI).

15

Foreign Banks in India

15.1 Norms for Opening of Foreign Banks

Foreign banks were allowed to operate in India either through branches or their representative offices. To obtain license for a new branch in our country a foreign bank has to function in accordance with all the financial requirements and norms applicable to Indian commercial banks. Reserve Bank will grant permission to a foreign bank only after ascertaining the financial soundness of the bank, international and home country ranking, rating, international presence, and economic and political relations between the two countries etc. RBI should not in any way discriminate foreign banks against Indian banks. Foreign bank should be under the consolidated supervision of the home country regulator.

It has been stipulated that the minimum capital requirement for a foreign bank should be US$ 25 million, spread over 3 branches i.e. US$ 10 million each for the first branch and the second branch and US$ 5 million for the third branch. Additional branches will be permitted only after monitoring the performance of existing branches of the banks, their financial results, inspection findings etc. The number of licenses is fixed in conformity with India's commitment made to World Trade Organization, which is presently 12 licenses (both for new and expansion of existing banks) per year, excluding off-site ATMs, which also require licenses.

15.1.1 Revised Norms for Foreign Banks: As per RBI notification with effect from March 31, 2002, foreign banks were brought on par with Indian banks for computing the prudential credit exposure ceiling by broadening the concept of 'capital funds' as regulatory capital (*i.e.*, Tier I and Tier II capital) in India as defined under the capital adequacy standards. Consequent upon the adoption of the revised concept of capital funds, some foreign banks' exposures to individual/group borrowers exceeded the prudential exposure limits. Foreign banks are now not allowed to assume fresh exposure to single/group borrowers beyond the prudential credit exposure limits.

With a view to smoothening the transition to prudential exposure limits, relaxations were allowed in respect of the following matters:

- In case of merger/acquisition of different borrowing companies, foreign banks may continue with the excess group exposure till March 31, 2004 if their group exposure exceeds the prudential norm; and
- The existing fund and non-fund based facilities, such as, term loans, investments in bonds/debentures and performance guarantees, etc. exceeding the exposure ceilings, may continue until their expiry/maturity.

15.2 Foreign Direct Investment (FDI) in Banking

The Government of India raised foreign direct investment in banking companies from 49 per cent to 74 per cent. It was aimed at facilitating the setting up of subsidiaries by foreign banks and for attracting investments in private sector banks. Accordingly, the Reserve Bank proposed to the Government of India to lift the limit on voting rights. Even though comprehensive amendments to the Banking Regulation Act of 1949 are under active consideration of the Government and the Reserve Bank, an amendment to Section 12 of the Banking Regulation Act, 1949 (relating to voting rights of shareholders, among others) was suggested as an immediate measure to facilitate investment.

Foreign investment in banking is governed by the Foreign Direct Investment policy of Government of India. In the case of a nationalized bank, a ceiling of 20 per cent on all types of foreign direct investment in the paid up capital is stipulated as per the provisions of Banking Companies (Acquisition & Transfer of Undertakings) Acts of 1970-80.

In respect of investment by NRIs in the private sector banks, the policy restricted NRI investments to 40 per cent and FDI to 20 per cent, subject to the condition that the combination of NRI investment and FDI should also be within the overall prescribed ceiling of 40 per cent foreign equity in the sector. Foreign Institutional Investors (FIIs) were allowed to acquire 24 per cent in addition to the 40 per cent limit.

With the liberalization of Foreign Direct Investment regime in banking sector was brought under the automatic route. According to the Government of India announcement of May 21, 2001, FDI up to 49 per cent from all sources was permitted in private sector banks under the automatic route, provided it is in tune with the guidelines issued by the Reserve Bank from time to time.

The foreign investment includes, inter alia, shares issued in IPOs, private placements, American Depository Receipt (ADRs)/Global Depository Receipt (GDRs) and acquisition of shares of existing shareholders with the approval of Foreign Investment Promotion Board (FIPB). Issue of shares under automatic route will not be available to those foreign investors who have financial or technical collaboration in the same or allied field. However, such cases will require FIPB approval.

With a view to further liberalize foreign investment in the banking sector, in the Union Budget of 2003-04 the Finance Minister that the limit for foreign direct investment in banking companies would be raised from 49 per cent to 74 per cent. Accordingly in March 2004, the Government announced, an increase in the FDI limit in private sector banks from 49 per cent to 74 per cent under automatic route including investment by FIIs subject to guidelines issued by the Reserve Bank from time to time.

Foreign investment in private sector banks from all sources would be permissible up to a composite ceiling of 74 per cent of the paid-up capital of the bank. This would include FDI, investments under Portfolio Investment Scheme (PIS) by FIIs, NRIs and shares acquired prior to September 16, 2003 by OCBs, IPOs, private placements, GDRs/ADRs and acquisition of shares from existing shareholders. However, the FII investment limit cannot exceed 49 per cent, within the aggregate foreign investment ceiling of 74 per cent of the paid up capital and at all times, at least 26 per cent of the paid up capital should be held by residents.

15.3 Road Map for Presence of Foreign Banks in India

At present, foreign banks can operate in India through only one of the following three channels, viz.

- Branches
- A wholly owned subsidiary (WOS)
- A subsidiary with an aggregate foreign investment up to a maximum of 74 per cent in a private bank. With a view to delineate the direction and pace of reform process in this area and to operationalise the guidelines of March 4, 2004 in a phased manner, the Reserve Bank, on February 28, 2005, pronounced the programme for foreign banks presence in India. It is divided into the two following phases.

During the first phase, between March 2005 and March 2009, foreign banks which wish to establish their presence in India for the first time can choose to operate either through branches or set up a 100 per cent WOS, as per the one-mode presence criterion. For new and existing foreign banks, the proposal is to go beyond the existing WTO commitment of 12 branches in a year. Foreign banks already operating in India will be permitted to establish their presence by way of setting up a WOS or conversion of the existing branches into a WOS. For this purpose, criteria such as ownership pattern, financial soundness, supervisory rating and the international ranking will be considered. The WOS should have a minimum capital of Rs.300 crore and have to ensure sound corporate governance. The WOS will be treated on par with the existing branches of foreign banks for branch expansion with flexibility to go beyond the existing WTO commitments and preference for branch expansion in under-banked areas.

The Reserve Bank may also prescribe market access and national treatment limitation consistent with WTO as also other appropriate limitations to the operations of WOS, consistent with international practices and the country's requirements. During this phase, permission for acquisition of shareholding in Indian private sector banks by eligible foreign banks will be limited to banks identified by the Reserve Bank for restructuring. The Reserve Bank may permit such acquisition if it is satisfied that such investment by the foreign bank concerned will be in the long-term interest of all the stakeholders in the investee bank. When such acquisition is by a foreign bank with presence in India, a maximum period of six months will be given for conforming to the 'one form of presence' concept.

The second phase will commence in April 2009 after a review of the experience gained and after due consultation with all the stakeholders in the banking sector. In this phase, three interconnected issues are to be taken up;

- The removal of limitations on the operations of the WOS and treating them on par with domestic banks to the extent appropriate will be designed and implemented.
- The WOS of foreign banks, on completion of a minimum prescribed period of operation, will be allowed to list and dilute their stake so that, consistent with March 5, 2004 guidelines, at least 26 per cent of the paid-up capital of the subsidiary is held by resident Indians at all times. The dilution can be either by way of initial public offer or as a sale offer.
- During the third phase, foreign banks will be permitted to enter into merger and acquisition transactions with any private sector bank in India subject to the overall investment limit of 74 per cent.

The banking sector is set to open up in 2009 to foreign players in a far bigger way, making competition in the future an immutable fact.

15.4 Foreign Banks Branch Presence in India

A good number of foreign banks are operating in India by opening their branches in cities and metros. Foreign banks with their country of origin and number of branches in India at the end of September 2006 are given in Table 15.1.

Table 15.1: Foreign Banks and Their Branch Presence in India (March 2006)

Sl. No.	Name of Bank	Country of Incorporation	No. of Branches
1.	ABN-AMRO Bank N.V.	Netherlands	24
2.	Abu Dhabi Commercial Bank	UAE	2
3.	Arab Bangladesh Bank Ltd.	Bangladesh	1
4.	American Express Bank Ltd.	USA	7
5.	Antwerp Diamond Bank N.V.	Belgium	1
6.	Bank International Indonesia	Indonesia	1
7.	Bank of America	USA	5
8.	Bank of Bahrain & Kuwait	Bahrain	2
9.	Bank of Nova Scotia	Canada	5
10.	Bank of Tokyo	Japan	3
11.	BNP Paribas	France	8
12.	Bank of Ceylon	Sri Lanka	1
13.	Barclays Bank Plc	UK	1
14.	Calyon Bank	France	5
15.	Citi Bank N.A.	USA	39
16.	Shinhan Bank	South Korea	1
17.	Chinatrust Commercial Bank	Taiwan	1
18.	Deutsche Bank	Germany	8
19.	DBS Bank Ltd.	Singapore	2
20.	HSBC Ltd.	Hongkong	45
21.	JP Morgan Chase Bank N.A.	USA	1
22.	Krung Thai Bank Public Co.	Thailand	1
23.	Mizuho Corporate Bank Ltd.	Japan	2
24.	Mashreq Bank PSC	UAE	2
25.	Oman International Bank	Oman	2
26.	Standard Chartered Bank	UK	81
27.	Sonali Bank	Bangladesh	2
28.	Societe Generale	France	2
29.	State Bank of Mauritius	Mauritius	3
	Total		258

Table 15.1 shows that at the end of September 2006, in addition to domestic commercial banks, 29 foreign banks with 258 branches were operating in India. These banks originated from 19 foreign countries. On September 2005, the corresponding number of foreign banks and branches in India stood at 31 with 245 branches and they were from 19 countries. Foreign banks now operate mainly in metros and big trading centres to cater to the needs of big customers. The 258 branches of foreign banks are spread over 40 centres across 19 States/Union territories.

Of the foreign banks, operating in India Standard Chartered Bank has the highest number of branches, 81, followed by HSBC Ltd. with 45, Citi Bank N.A. with 39 and ABN-AMRO Bank N.V. with 24 branches. While four banks have 10 or more branches at the end of March 2006. Nine banks were operating only with one branch each. During July 2005 and June 2006, the existing foreign banks in India were granted approval to open 13 additional branches.

As on September 15, 2006, 29 banks from 14 countries have representative offices in India. Thus, overall, 58 foreign banks from 33 countries have presence in India either branches or their representative offices.

16

Commercial Banks: Challenges and Strategies

16.1 Prudential Norms

16.1.1 Capital Adequacy: The Governors of the Central Bank of Ten countries established Basel Committee in the year 1974. Member countries are represented by their central banks and also by the authority with formal responsibility for the prudential supervision of banking business where it is not the central bank. The Basel Committee meets regularly four times in a year. The committee has about twenty-five technical working groups and task forces, which meet regularly. The committee consists of members from different countries namely Belgium, Canada, France, Germany, Italy, Japan, Luxembourg, Netherlands, Spain, Sweden, Switzerland, United Kingdom and United States. The Basel Committee has now developed into a standard setting body on all aspects of banking supervision.

The RBI's association with the Basel Committee on Banking Supervision dates back to 1997 as India was among the 16 non-member countries that were consulted in the drafting of the Basel Core Principles. The Reserve Bank of India become a member of the Core Principles Liaison Group in 1998 and subsequently became a member of the Core Principles Working Group on Capital. With in the Working Group, the RBI has been actively participating in the deliberations on the New Basel Accord and had the privilege to lead a group of six major non G-10 supervisors, which put forward a proposal for a simplified approach for Basel –II to the Committee.

Basel I: The Basel Committee examined the causes for frequent bank failures in eight countries viz. Germany, Japan, Norway, Spain, Sweden, Switzerland, UK and USA. The committee studied and identified the causes for bank failures in these countries. They also examined the methods adopted for resolving the crisis and the regulatory changes implemented by these countries.

Basel I is an effort by international banking supervisors to arrest the erosion of banks' capital ratios. The wide spread concern on the declining profitability of banks, especially in the 'eighties' influenced the Basel for the implementation of capital adequacy norms. The concept of capital adequacy acquired further importance in the light of the massive defaults faced by the US, French and Italian bankers from their borrowers. Thus in 1988, the Committee decided to introduce a capital measurement system known as the Basel Capital Accord. The system provided for the implementation of a credit risk measurement framework with a minimum capital standard of 8 per cent by 1992. Since 1988, this framework has been progressively introduced not only in member countries but also in almost all other countries having banks with international operations. Minimum capital adequacy standard gained wide acceptance internationally and the countries are now moving towards the adoption of the new capital accord.

Basel II: All over the world, the banking structure and operations have undergone rapid changes in the late nineties. Financial liberalization and technical changes have created new and complex financial products and have increased their turnover in financial markets. The revolution in information technology and universal financial operations of banks increased competition both at national and international levels. Although the benefits of these developments have been substantial, they have also created more risks. The changed environment of operations of banks and banking crisis especially in Latin America and South-East Asia at the end of 90s called for the attention of Basel. They opined that baseline capital adequacy norm were not adequate (8 per cent) to avoid bank failures.

The Basle Capital Adequacy Accord was introduced in 1988 as a means for setting minimum capital asset ratios for international banks. Since banks in different countries encountered different degrees of risks, the rule of 'one-size-fits-all' aspect of the capital adequacy ratio of 1988 was therefore subject to intense debate in the post Basle I period. The speed and complexity of adjustment made it difficult for the supervisory authorities to effectively regulate financial entities in their countries. Besides, the original Accord emphasized only the credit risk aspect of banking operations, ignoring the other relatively important risk factors like interest rate risk, market risk and operational risk. Such criticism against the old accord seems to have led the Basle Committee on Banking Supervision to propose the new Consultative Paper on Capital Adequacy Framework, which aims at strengthening further the soundness of the financial system

Basel II is an effort by international banking supervisors to update the original international bank capital accord of Basel I, which has been in effect since 1998. United States as a member of Basel committee on Banking Supervision developed the Basel-II proposal. It aimed at improving the consistency of international capital regulations, to make regulatory capital more risk sensitive and promote enhanced risk-management practices among large, internationally active banking companies. In June 1999, the Committee issued a proposal for a revised Capital Adequacy Framework.

In response to the same, the Basel Committee on Banking Supervision (BCBS) came out with the new Consultative Paper on Capital Adequacy in June 1999 and invited suggestions from the policymakers, academicians and other institutions all over the world by March 2000. After taking into consideration the different suggestions of the various organizations, the second Consultative Paper on Capital Adequacy was released in January 2001. The new rules came into effect on 2005.

16.1.2 New Basel Capital Accord: The new capital Accord have both far-reaching and path breaking implications. The new Basel II accord is based on three-pillars, which are very significant.

1. Minimum Capital Requirement,
2. Supervisory Review Process and

3. Market Discipline

A. Minimum Capital Requirement: The first pillar set out is the minimum capital requirements. When the Accord was first established, it was primarily concerned with minimum capital standards to cover credit risk. The Basel II accord maintains both the existing current definition of capital and the minimum requirement of 8 per cent of capital to risk-weighted assets. The revised Accord will be extended on a consolidation basis to holding companies of banking groups. The Accord stressed on improvement in the measurement of risks. The credit risk measurement methods have been made more elaborate than those in the existing Accord. In view of the increasing internationalization of activities of banks, the Committee proposed to develop explicit risk weights for other risk categories such as operational risk, market risk and interest rate risk, which have assumed significant importance in the deregulated environment. For measuring credit risk, two options have been proposed viz. standardized approach and Internal Rating Based (IRB) approach.

Under the standardized approach, the existing approach for credit risk remains conceptually the same, but the risk-weights have been enlarged to encompass exposures to a broad category of borrowers with reference to the rating provided by rating agencies. For example, for corporates, the existing accord provides only a single uniform risk-weight of 100 per cent, but the new Accord provides four categories viz. 20 per cent, 50 per cent, 100 per cent and 150 per cent, which are based on the rating of the corporate.

Under the IRB approach, on the other hand, banks will be allowed to use its internal estimates of the borrower's credit worthiness to assess credit risk in the portfolio subject to strict methodological and disclosure standards.

B. Supervisory Review Process: The New Basel Accord redefines the regulatory approach to bank supervision and provides new incentives for banks to improve their risk-measurement procedures. The second pillar would seek to ensure that each bank has sound internal processes in place to assess the adequacy of capital based on a thorough evaluation of its risks. The new framework focuses on the importance of bank management in developing an internal capital assessment process and setting targets for capital that are commensurate with the banks particular risk profile and control environment. Supervisors would be responsible for evaluating how well the banks are assessing the capital adequacy needs relative to their risks. The internal processes would then be subjected to supervisory review and interference at appropriate stages. In effect, the existing supervisory review process comprising on-site inspection, off-site surveillance and external auditing is being supplanted through the review of the internal capital adequacy assessments of banks. The new Accord therefore places significant emphasis on the supervisory authorities for identifying, reviewing and evaluating a bank's internal capital adequacy assessment as well as its compliance with regulatory capital ratios, failing which supervisors are supposed to intervene to ensure that banks are able to withstand normal business shocks.

C. Market Discipline: The third pillar of market discipline extends strong incentives to banks to conduct their business in a safe, sound and efficient manner. It is aimed at strengthening market discipline through enhanced disclosure by banks. It also takes cognizance of the fact that technology and market practices have altered substantially than the days of the old accord and consequently envisages a change in the monitoring function of the regulatory authorities.

Effective disclosure is essential to ensure that market participants can better understand banks risk profile and the adequacy of their capital position. The new framework sets out disclosure requirements in several areas, including the way in which banks calculate their capital adequacy and their risk assessment methods. The ever-increasing awareness of banks on credit risk and the higher reliance on advanced risk management techniques could lead to further consolidation of banks through mergers and acquisitions. It is essential in the case of emerging economies, which still encounter the several structural issues, and where banks remain the dominant financial intermediaries. First, the New Accord is quite complex in view of its sophistication and could, over the next couple of years, shift scarce supervisory resources away from direct supervision towards implementation of these specific proposals. Secondly, as a corollary to the earlier point, this complexity of the New Accord would demand enormous skill, which domestic banks may find hard to obtain. Thirdly, because of the increased flow of resources to capital regulation, banks capital may be seen as a panacea for the prevention of bank failure and supervisory oversight in respect of other bank-specific parameters might become common, more so in the belief that adequate capital would keep banks insulated from failure. As observed in the second Consultative Paper, increased capital ratios should not be viewed as the only option for addressing increased risks confronting the bank. Fourthly, increased reliance on external rating agencies could lead banks to loosen their own credit rating models and place explicit responsibility on supervisors to take such agencies into their regulatory fold.

An important rationale behind the pillar of market discipline is to provide sufficient information to enable the user to assess whether the available capital is sufficient to meet credit, market and other risk requirements. To the extent that such disclosures are comprehensive and objective, it is expected to help market participants to judge how a bank's management of its capital adequacy relates to its other risk management processes and how well it is able to withstand future volatility.

16.1.3 Risks Encountered by Banks: Risks are inherent in banking business, which are very high in derivatives trading, securities underwriting, corporate advisory businesses, improvements in information technology and on-line electronic banking. Management of risk also gained prominence. The major financial risks, which banking institutions faces are;

- Credit risk
- Interest rate risk

- Foreign exchange risk and
- Liquidity risk

A. Credit Risk: Credit risk remains predominant for banking institutions. It depends on both internal and external factors. External factors include the state of the economy, commodity and equity prices, exchange rates and interest rates. The internal factors reflect deficiencies in loan policies and administration of loan portfolio, weaknesses in prudential credit concentration limits, appraisal of borrowers' financial position, excessive dependence on collateral and inadequate risk pricing, absence of loan review mechanism and post sanction surveillance. Such risks may extend beyond the conventional credit products such as loans and letters of credit and appear in more complicated, less conventional forms, such as credit derivatives.

B. Interest Rate Risk: Interest rate risk arises because banks fix and refix interest rates on their resources and on the assets in which they are deployed at different times. Changes in interest rates significantly influence the net interest income, depending on the extent of mismatch between the times when the interest rates on asset and liability are reset. Any such mismatches in cash flows (fixed assets or liabilities) or reprising dates (floating assets or liabilities) expose banks' net interest margins to variations.

C. Foreign Exchange Risk: The foreign exchange risk, in turn, is the risk inherent in running open forex positions and has become more pronounced in recent years owing to the wide variation in exchange rates. Such risks arise owing to adverse exchange rate movements, which may affect a bank's open position, either spot or forward, or a combination of the two, in a specific foreign currency.

D. Liquidity Risk: Finally, the liquidity risk arises from funding of long-term assets by short-term liabilities, making liabilities subject to rollover or refinancing risk. Banks that fund domestic assets with foreign currency deposits are susceptible to such risk, especially when sharp fluctuations in exchange rates and market turbulence makes it difficult to retain sources of financing.

Besides these financial risks, banks are exposed to other risks *viz.*, operating risks, legal risks, etc. Irrespective of the nature of risk, the best way for banks to protect themselves from risks is to identify the risks, accurately measure and price it, and maintain appropriate levels of reserves and capital. The development of a holistic approach to assessing and managing the many facets of risks still remains a challenging task for the financial sector and this raises the issue of how to identify the optimal strategies to curtail these risks.

Keeping this in view, as early as October 1999, the RBI has issued guidelines for risk management systems in banks. This has placed the primary responsibility of laying down risk parameters and establishing the risk management and control system on the Board of Directors of the bank. However, the implementation of the integrated risk management could be assigned to a risk management committee or alternately, a committee of top executives that reports to the Board. Banks are required to constitute a high level credit policy committee to deal with the issues pertaining to credit sanction, disbursement and follow-up procedures and to manage and control credit risk. Banks were further advised to concurrently set up an independent credit risk management department to enforce and monitor compliance of risk parameters/prudential limits set by the Board/Credit Policy Committee. The present set of guidelines are purported to serve as a benchmark to banks

16.1.4 Implementation of Basel II in India: The RBI in May 2004 had announced its annual policy statement in which it stated that banks in India should examine in depth the options available under Basel II and advised banks should draw a road map by December end 2004 for migration to Basel II. They were also advised to review the progress made at quarterly intervals. Banks have also been advised to formulate and operationalise the Capital Adequacy Assessment Process (CAAP) with in the banks as required under Pillar II of the New Framework. However, taking into account the state of preparedness of the banking system, it was decided in October 2006 to provide banks some more time to put in place appropriate systems to ensure full compliance with Basel II.

According to the new schedule, foreign banks operating in India and Indian banks having presence outside India are to migrate to the standardized approach for credit risk and the basic indicator approach for operational risk under Basel II with effect from March 31, 2008. All other scheduled commercial banks are encouraged to migrate to these approaches under Basel II in alignment with them but in any case not later than March 31, 2009.

Commercial banks in India started implementing Basel II with effect from March 31, 2007. Initially banks will adopt the Standardized Approach for credit risk and Basic Indicator Approach for operational risk. After adequate skills are developed, both at the banks and at supervisory levels, some banks may be allowed to migrate to the Internal Rating Based (IRB) Approach.

16.1.5 Measures Adopted by RBI for Implementation of Basel II: For the introduction of Basel II accord by Indian banks, RBI initiated several measures. First, RBI advised the banks to undertake a self-assessment of the various risk management systems with specific reference to the three major risks covered under the Base II. They were also directed to take necessary remedial measures to update the systems to match up to the minimum standards prescribed in Basel II.

RBI advised banks to formulate and operationalise the Capital Adequacy Assessment Process (CAAP) as required under Pillar II of the new framework. Other initiatives are viz. Implementation of Risk Based Supervision (RBS) in 23 banks on a pilot basis. Banks are encouraged to formalize their Capital Adequacy Assessment Process (CAAP) in alignment with their business plan and performance budgeting system. In order to have greater transparency in the financial position and risk profile of banks RBI expanded the area of disclosures.

With a view to enable banks to migrate Basel II, the RBI adopted a participatory and consultative approach. A Steering

Committee comprising senior officials from 14 banks (inclusive of private, public and foreign) and representatives from the Indian Banks Association and the RBI was set up. The committee formed sub-groups to address specific issues. Based on the recommendations of the Steering Committee, draft guidelines were issued to the banks for the implementation of the new Capital Adequacy Framework.

16.1.6 Capital Adequacy Ratio: Capital adequacy has been the cornerstone of prudential regulatory framework in India. It is an important indicator of the financial health of a banking institution. It helps to improve and maintain the confidence of the customers and acts as a shock absorber to absorb unforeseen losses. The capital adequacy norms for Indian banks are based on the Capital Accord of the Basel Committee. The Committee has prescribed risk- weighted approach for assets with weights, being assigned to both on-and off-balance sheet exposure of a bank. It encouraged banks to be more risk sensitive against both on-and off-balance sheet exposures.

Capital adequacy ratio is defined as the ratio between a bank's total capital and its risk-weighted assets. The capital adequacy ratio of Indian banks prior to the implementation of banking sector reforms was very weak. It accounted for only 1.5 per cent of the risk- weighted assets of the banks. Narasimham Committee observed that erosion of profitability was the major cause for the low accumulation to reserves. The RBI therefore recommended that the commercial banks were achieve the capital adequacy of 8 per cent by the year 1996.

The Committee on Banking Sector Reform (Chairman: Shri M. Narasimham) was constituted on December 26, 1997 to review the progress of implementation of financial sector reforms recommended by the Committee on Financial Systems (CFS) (1991), and to suggest remedial measures for strengthening the banking system, covering areas of banking policy, institutional structure, supervisory system, legislative and technological changes. The recommendations of the Committee, submitted in April 1998, were considered in consultation with the Government of India and some of the decisions were announced on October 30, 1998.

As a part of the follow-up of the recommendations of the Narasimham Committee II, it was decided in October 1998 to raise the stipulated minimum capital to risk-weighted assets ratio (CRAR) of scheduled commercial banks by one percentage point to 9 per cent from the year ended March 2000. Taking into consideration the substantial off-balance sheet exposures of banks, the Narasimham Committee (1998) recommended the enhancement of capital adequacy ratio to 10 per cent by 2002. In support of this decision, the Union Budget, 1998-99 had announced raising of the minimum capital adequacy ratio to 9 per cent by March 31, 2000 and to 10 per cent thereafter at the earliest.

In October 1999, banks were advised to assign a risk-weight of 2.5 per cent to cover market risk in respect of investments in securities outside the SLR by the year ending March 31, 2001 (over and above the existing 100 per cent credit risk-weight). A market risk-weight of 2.5 per cent had been prescribed for Government and other approved securities from March 31, 2000. Further, banks were advised in April 2000 to assign a risk-weight of 100 per cent only on those State Government guaranteed securities issued by defaulting entities and not on all the securities issued or guaranteed by the concerned State Government. With regard to provisioning for standard assets, it was clarified that the general provision of 0.25 per cent on standard assets should be made on global portfolio basis and not on domestic advances alone. It was also announced that the general provision on standard assets would be included in Tier II capital, together with other 'general provisions/loss reserves', up to a maximum of 1.25 per cent of the total risk weighted assets.

Recognizing that the nationalized banks need to augment their capital base to cope up with the changing operational environment, the Government has permitted banks to access capital market, both at home and abroad. However, the amount of capital, which can be raised by the nationalized banks from the capital market, has been constrained by the minimum shareholding of 51 per cent by the Central Government. This was facilitated through amendments in the relevant Acts, which permitted PSBs to raise equity from the market up to a threshold limit of 49 per cent. The Government had contributed an aggregate amount of Rs. 20,446.12 crore towards recapitalization of nationalized banks by end-March 1999. The Government did not provide any amount on this account in 1999-2000 and 2000-01.

In January 2006, RBI allowed Indian banks to augment their capital funds by issue of innovative perpetual debt instruments eligible for inclusion as Tier I capital; debt capital instruments eligible for inclusion as Upper Tier II capital; perpetual non-cumulative preference shares eligible for inclusion as Tier I capital and redeemable cumulative preference shares eligible for inclusion as Tier II capital. A number of banks have issued these instruments both in India and overseas to shore up capital

Capital Adequacy Ratio of Indian commercial banks (Bank Group-wise) from March 1998 to 2006 is depicted in Table 16.1.

Table 16.1 reveals that the overall CRAR for all commercial banks increased from 11.5 per cent at the end of March 1998 to 12.3 per cent at the end of March 2006. Compared to the year 2005, CRAR of commercial banks shows a slight decline in the year 2006. However, the ratio continued to be significantly above the stipulated minimum of 9 per cent. The table shows that at the end of March 2006, CRAR of only new private sector banks got improved, while those of all other banks groups declined. The CRAR of foreign banks was 13 per cent at the end of March 2006, which was higher than all other bank groups.

16.2 Non-performing Assets in Commercial Banks

Non-Performing Assets (NPAs) have become a nuisance and headache for the Indian banking sector for the past several years. One of the major issues challenging the performance of commercial banks in the late 90s adversely affecting was the accumulation of huge non-performing assets (NPAs). The quality

Table 16.1: Capital Adequacy Ratio: Bank Group-wise (per cent)

Bank Group	March 1998	March 1999	March 2000	March 2001	March 2002	March 2003	March 2004	March 2005	March 2006
Nationalized Banks	10.3	10.6	10.1	10.2	10.9	12.2	13.1	13.2	12.3
State Bank Group	14.0	12.3	11.6	12.7	13.3	13.4	13.4	12.4	11.9
Old Private Sector Banks	12.3	12.1	12.4	11.9	12.5	12.8	13.7	12.5	11.7
New Private Sector Banks	13.2	11.8	13.4	11.5	12.3	11.3	10.2	12.1	12.6
Foreign Banks	10.3	10.8	11.9	12.6	12.9	15.2	15.0	14.0	13.0
Scheduled Commercial Banks (Total)	11.5	11.3	11.1	11.4	12.0	12.7	12.9	12.8	12.3

of loan portfolio is very crucial for the health and existence of the banks. High level of NPAs has many implications on profitability, productivity, liquidity, solvency, capital adequacy and image of the bank.

16.2.1 Meaning of NPA: NPAs are those loans given by a bank where the borrower defaults or delays repayment of interest or principle. An asset, which ceases to generate income for the bank, is called non-performing asset. Where assets are non-performing, a provision is required to be maintained for such assets. High level of NPAs calls for high provisioning and it will adversely affect the profitability and viability of the bank.

The Narasimham Committee defined "NPA as an advance where on the date of the balance sheet an amount to be paid to the bank (interest and or installment of principal) is past due for a period of 180 days".

16.2.2 Classification of Advances: Loans and advances given by banks are classified into four categories, which ranges between "standard to loss assets".

i) Standard assets ii) Sub- standard assets iii) Doubtful assets and iv) Loss assets

'Standard assets' generate income to the bank. These assets are performing assets. Such assets do not create any problem for the banks. When it fails to generate income, it becomes non-performing assets (NPA). The risk on standard assets is only minimal and limited. No provision is required for standard assets.

'Sub- standard assets' have been classified as NPA for a period not exceeding two years. When installments of the loan are overdue for a period exceeding one year they are to be treated as sub-standard assets. These assets require a provision of 10 per cent of outstanding balances.

'Doubtful assets' are assets, which remain non-performing assets for a period exceeding two years. In term loans, where the installments of the principal remain overdue for a period exceeding two years they are treated as doubtful. Doubtful assets require a provision of 100 per cent of unsecured portion of advances. 'Loss asset' is an asset when the bank or internal auditor or the inspector of RBI identifies the loss, but the amount is not written off wholly or partially.

16.2.3 Reasons for NPA: At the beginning of 1990s, most of the banks in the public sector were unprofitable. Weak credit appraisal, compulsion to lend for priority sectors and Government sponsored schemes, political interference, faulty lending policy, defective credit recovery mechanism, ineffective monitoring over the use of funds, unscientific repayment schedule, absence of strong legal recovery system, inadequate risk management practices and many other factors were responsible for the mounting level of overdues in banks.

With the commencement of reforms of the economy in 1991, commercial banks were advised to follow Basel Capital Accord. Consequently, Reserve Bank of India issued the first set of comprehensive guidelines for Income Recognition and Asset Classification (IRAC) in commercial banks in April 1992. The RBI, in a cautious move, adopted time bound provisioning method, and averted a near crisis by not imposing write off of the entire loan asset impairment amount based on present value of realizable cash flow upon recognition of NPA. The Narasimham committee-II on financial sector reforms set a target of bringing the gross NPA level of banks to an international level of 5 per cent by year 2000 and 3 per cent by year 2002.

16.2.4 Magnitude of NPAs: The quality and performance of advances have direct bearing on the profitability and viability of banks. Several steps have been initiated by the Reserve Bank in conjunction with the Government of India to control the NPAs of banks. Since the initiation of income recognition and asset classification norms, NPAs of scheduled commercial banks have come down rapidly.

The gross and net non-performing assets as a percentage of advances are the critical indicators of the quality of a bank's loan portfolio. Net NPA is derived from Gross NPA by excluding (i) balance in interest suspense account, (ii) DICGC\ECGE claims received and kept in suspense account pending final settlement, (iii) part payment received and kept in suspense account, and

(iv) total provisions held. Net NPAs to the total advances is more relevant and internationally recognized than the gross NPA concept.

Table 16.2 indicates the gross and net NPAs of scheduled commercial banks as a per cent to advances and total assets from 1995-96 to 2005-06. Reflecting the success of financial sector reforms, particularly in the regulatory and supervisory process, banks made substantial progress in clearing up the non-performing assets from their balance sheets.

Table 16.2: Gross and Net NPAs of Scheduled Commercial Banks

Year Ending March	Gross NPA % to advances	Gross NPA % to Total Assets	Net NPA % to Advances	Net NPA % to Total Assets
1996	18.0	8.2	8.9	3.6
1998	14.4	6.4	7.3	3.0
2000	12.8	5.5	6.8	2.7
2002	10.4	4.6	5.5	2.3
2004	7.2	3.3	2.8	1.2
2006	3.3	1.9	1.2	0.7

The gross NPAs (Table 16.2) as a percentage of advances of scheduled commercial banks declined from 18.0 per cent in 1995-96 to 3.3 per cent in 2005-06. Gross NPA as per cent to total assets also dwindled to 1.9 per cent in 2005-06 from that of 8.2 per cent in 1995-96.

Net NPAs as a percentage of total advances is considered as one of the best indicator to assess the overall financial health of banking institutions. Net NPAs as per cent to advances (Table 16.2) declined from 8.9 in 1995-96 to 1.2 per cent in 2005-06. Net NPAs to total assets also declined from 3.6 per cent in 1995-96 to 0.7 per cent in 2005-06. Although the net NPAs of the commercial banks in India have witnessed a decline over the past several years, they are still high when compared to developed countries.

The gross NPAs as Percentage to gross advances of different bank groups are exhibited in Table 16.3.

Table 16.3: Gross NPAs as Percentage to Gross Advances of Different Bank Groups

Year ending March	Public Sector Banks	Old Private Sector Banks	New Private Sector Banks	Foreign Banks	All Commercial Banks
1998	16.0	10.9	3.5	6.3	14.4
2000	14.0	11.3	4.2	7.0	12.8
2002	11.1	11.0	8.9	5.4	10.4
2004	7.8	7.6	5.0	4.6	7.2
2006	3.7	4.3	1.7	1.9	3.3

The bank group wise gross NPAs as percentage to advances shown in Table 16.3 reveals that NPAs declined across bank group's since1997-98. In the year 2005-06, also all bank groups witnessed a decline in the ratio of NPAs to gross advances compared to the previous year. On March 31, 2006, among bank groups, the old private sector banks had the highest gross NPA ratio at 4.3 per cent followed by public sector banks with 3.7 per cent, foreign banks with 1.9 per cent and new generation private sector banks with 1.7 per cent.

At the end of March 2006, the ratio of net NPAs to net advances of public sector banks and old private sector banks was less than 2 per cent at the bank group level. Net NPA ratio of new private banks and foreign banks were 0.8 per cent. As at the end of March 2006, 66 banks (as against 51 last year) out of 84 (as against 88 last year) had net NPAs to net advances ratio at less than 2 per cent.

16.2.5 Regulatory Measures by RBI to Reduce NPAs: Reserve Bank and the Government of India took several measures to expedite the recovery of NPAs by banks. For this purpose, several channels of recovery measures have been designed of which the following are the most important.

A. One-Time Settlement/Compromise Scheme: The RBI in consultation with the Government of India issued guidelines for recovery of loan dues owned to commercial banks up to Rs.10 lakh. The time limit for processing of applications received under the revised guidelines for compromise settlement of chronic NPAs of public sector banks, was extended up to December 31, 2003. Based on the requests received for further extension of the time limit for operation of the guidelines and in consultation with Government of India, the time limit for receiving applications was further extended up to July 31, 2004 by the government.

For improving flow of credit to Small and Medium Enterprises (SME), the Union Finance Minister issued detailed guidelines on debt restructuring mechanism for units in the SME sector. These guidelines were issued in September 2005, to all scheduled commercial banks to ensure that they restructure debt of all eligible SMEs. The one-time settlement scheme for recovery of NPAs below Rs.10 crore provides for a simplified, non-discretionary and non-discriminatory mechanism for one-time settlement of chronic NPAs in the SME sector. The scheme covers all NPAs in the SME sector, which have become doubtful or loss as on March 31, 2004 with outstanding balance of Rs.10 crore and below on the date on which the account was classified as doubtful. The last date for receipt of applications from borrowers was March 31, 2006. The processing under the revised guidelines was required to be completed by June 30, 2006.

B. Lok Adalats: Lok Adalats were granted judicious status with the enactment of the Legal Service Authority Act of 1987. It is a convenient method for settlement of disputes between banks and small borrowers. Consequently, RBI issued necessary guidelines to banks and other financial institutions advising them to resort mechanism of Lok Adalats for the recovery of debts. The Government revised the monetary ceiling of cases to be referred to Lok Adalats organized by Civil Courts from Rs.5 lakh to Rs.20 lakh. The number of cases settled by commercial banks with Lok Adalats stood at 8,16,068 involving an amount of Rs.4,263 crore at the end of March 2006. The number of cases decided was 3,07,189 involving an amount of Rs. 1,574 crore. The recoveries effected in 2,40,819 cases stood at Rs. 649 crore as on March 31, 2006.

C. Debt Recovery Tribunals: The Recovery of Debts Due to Banks and Financial Institutions Act was enacted in 1993 to provide for the establishment of tribunals for expeditious adjudication and recovery of debts due to banks and FIs and for matters connected therewith and incidental thereto. The amendments made in 2000 and 2003 to the above Act and the rules framed there under have strengthened the functioning of Debt Recovery Tribunals (DRTs). Based on the recommendations of the Reserve Bank, for improving the functioning of Debt Recovery Tribunals, Government of India set up a working group. The Additional Secretary, Government of India, chaired the working group. As on March 2006 out of 71,399 cases (involving Rs. 1,11,293 crore) filed with DRTs by the banks, 36,803 cases (involving Rs.42,792 crore) have been adjudicated by them. The amount recovered so far through the adjudicated cases is placed at Rs. 14,992 crore.

D. Corporate Debt Restructuring: The Scheme of Corporate Debt Restructuring (CDR) was started in 2001 with a view to put in place a mechanism for timely and transparent restructuring of corporate debts of viable entities which face problems, outside the purview of Board for Industrial and Financial Reconstruction (BIFR), DRT and other legal proceedings. RBI constituted a special group for reviewing the Corporate Debt Restructuring system on September 2004. Smt. Shyamala Gopinath, Deputy Governor, Reserve Bank of India headed the group. Based on the recommendations of the special group, RBI issued draft guidelines to commercial banks and financial institutions for their comments and implications. Based of the feed back received from the draft guidelines, final guidelines on Corporate Debt Restructuring system were issued to all commercial banks, financial institutions and RRBs on November 2005.

The number of cases and value of assets restructured under the CDR mechanism stood at 94 and Rs.64,017 crore, respectively, as on June 30, 2004. The major beneficiaries were iron & steel, refinery, fertilizers and telecommunication industries, accounting for more than two-third share of value of assets restructured.

E. Securitization and Reconstruction of Financial Assets and Enforcement of Security Interest Act, 2002 (SARFAESI): The Act provides, inter alia for enforcement of security interest for realization of dues without the intervention of courts or tribunals. The Security Interest (Enforcement) Rules, 2002 has also been notified by Government to enable secured creditors to authorize their officials to enforce the securities and recover the dues from the borrowers. The Supreme Court in its judgment dated April, 2004 in M/s. Mardia Chemicals has upheld the constitutional validity of the Act and its provisions except that a sub section 2 of Section 17 by the secured creditor, in case the borrower wants to appeal against the secured creditor's notice under Section 13 (4) of the Act. It has declared Section 17 (2) as unconstitutional and violative of Article 14 of the Constitution of India. In the wake of this judgment, many banks have pointed out practical difficulties, which are likely to arise in speeding up the recovery of NPAs. The suggestion of banks, IBA and other organizations in this regard are being examined to carry out necessary amendments in the Act. In the Union Budget 2004-05, the Government proposed to amend the relevant provisions of the Act to address appropriately the Supreme Court's concerns over a fair deal to borrowers while, at the same time, ensuring that the recovery process is not delayed or dilated.

As on March, 2006, commercial banks issued 1,33,665 notices involving an outstanding amount of Rs. 41,053 crore. Of this, banks have recovered an amount of Rs. 7,296 crore in respect of 72,178 cases. Further more, an amount of Rs. 4,410 crore has been received through 35,090 compromise proposals.

F. Asset Reconstruction Companies (ARCs): To address the problem of accumulated NPAs, the first Narasimham Committee, suggested the setting up of an Asset Reconstruction Fund, but this suggestion could not be implemented. Reiterating this arrangement, the second Narasimham Committee and Varma Committee suggested the setting up of an Asset Reconstruction Company (ARC). The ARC, which would take over all loan assets in the doubtful and loss categories, would issue to the banks NPA Swap Bonds representing the realizable value of the assets transferred, provided the stamp duties are not excessive.

Securitization and Reconstruction of Financial Assets and Enforcement of Security Interest Act, 2002 was enacted to pave the way for setting up of Asset Reconstruction Companies (ARCs) in India. To solve the problem of bad loans, several institutions have initiated steps towards establishment of ARCs, which takeover non-performing loans of banks and FIs at a discounted rate, and manage and dispose such assets. Under the Act, it is envisaged that ARCs shall be registered with RBI and RBI would issue necessary guidelines to ARCs for conducting business. RBI issued the guidelines on April 2003. However the Act was, challenged by a group of companies led by M/s. Mardia Chemicals and Industries Ltd.

The first ARC was granted registration in August 2003. The Reserve Bank has so far granted certificate of registration (CoR) to four Asset Reconstruction Companies out of which Asset Reconstruction Company (India) Limited (ARCIL) has already started its operations. During 2005-06 ARCIL acquired 559 cases of NPAs from banks\FI with total dues amounting to Rs. 21,126 crore from 31 banks and Financial institutions. The portfolio of assets acquired by ARCIL was diversified across major industry segments, which were generally performing well in the stock market.

In order to have a sound capital base of Asset Reconstruction Companies and a stake in the management of the NPAs acquired, the requirement of owned funds for commencement of business has been stipulated as not less than 15 per cent of the assets acquired or Rs. 100 crore, whichever is less.

Supply of Information on Defaulters by Credit Information Bureau, deregulation of interest rates, freedom to charge lending rates, prudential norms in line with international standards etc, were the other measures initiated by RBI to reduce NPAs in banks.

16.3 Banking Sector Reforms in India: An Overview

The Narasimham Committee on financial sector reforms paved the way for far reaching reforms in the banking sector in India and they ushered as the "second banking revolution". It recommended sweeping changes in the financial sector as per international norms to cater to the needs of the sector and to strengthen it. To transform Indian banks from largely domestic ones to truly international ones, and to tackle their internal deficiencies, the Narasimham Committee I & II put forward several recommendations.

The Government and the RBI accepted and implemented all the major recommendations of the Narasimham Committee. The banking development underwent radical transformation in the wake of these reforms process. Since reforms, the Indian banks moved away from the traditional means and social banking to modern mixed and viable banking. A comprehensive picture of the decisions initiated by the RBI and the Government of India consequent to the banking sector reforms were given below:

16.3.1 Contours of Banking Sector Reforms: The primary objective of financial sector reforms was to ensure financial stability and maintain confidence in the financial system by enhancing its soundness and efficiency. First phase of financial sector reforms commenced in the early 1990s was aimed at creating efficient, productive and profitable service industries especially the banking sector. The second phase of reforms, beginning from the second half of 1990s, was aimed at strengthening of the financial system and introduction of structural improvements.

Prudential norms and supervisory strengthening were

introduced in the first phase of reform cycle, followed by interest rate deregulation and gradually lowering of statutory preemptions. The introduction of prudential norms relating to income recognition, asset classification and 100 per cent provisioning for all non-performing assets was a turning point in the reform process. The prudential norms introduced during 1992-93 were continuously monitored and refined to bring them on par with international best standards.

An important milestone in the process of banking sector reforms in India was the deregulation of interest rates. The interest on deposits and advances was deregulated barring certain specific classes such as savings deposits accounts, non-resident Indian (NRI) deposits, small loans up to Rs. 2 lakh and export credit. Commercial banks have now the freedom to set interest rates on their deposits subject to minimum floor rates and maximum ceiling rates. Deregulation of interest rates creates healthy competition among the banks. However, administered interest rates still prevail in small savings schemes of the government.

The reforms process also envisaged major changes in the banking sector by way of reduction in cash reserve ratio and statutory liquidity ratio requirements, abolition of mass recruitment by Banking Service Recruitment Board (BSRB) and implementation of Voluntary Retirement Scheme (VRS).

Narasimham Committee recommended new private sector banks in order to enhance the efficiency, productivity and competition in the banking sector. RBI decided to set up new banks in the private sector and necessary guidelines were issued in this connection on January 1993. Since 1993, eleven new private sector banks and one public sector bank were set up. All new private sector banks were listed and there is considerable foreign investment (both FDI and FII) in these banks. In five of the existing eight private sector banks, foreign shareholding had crossed 50 per cent.

One of the major objectives of banking sector reforms was to enhance efficiency and productivity through increased competition. Foreign banks were allowed to operate in India in a more liberal environment since 1993. The Government of India raised foreign direct investment in banking companies from 49 per cent to 74 per cent.

A unique feature of the reform of public sector banks, which dominated the Indian banking sector, was the process of financial restructuring. As part of the reforms programme, there was infusion of capital by the Government in the public sector banks, which was followed by expanding the capital base with equity participation by the private investors. The Government ownership in nationalized and State Bank of India was brought down by allowing them to raise capital from the equity market up to a threshold limit of 49 per cent. The Government holding in public sector banks range from 51 per cent (Oriental Bank of Commerce and Dena bank) to 76 per cent (Bank of Maharashtra). All public sector banks, which issued shares to private shareholders, were listed on the stock exchanges and are subject to the same disclosure and market discipline standards as other listed entities. Public Sector Banks were encouraged to raise their Tier II capital.

Consolidation of the banking sector was another important development of the reforms process. The process of consolidation has been taking place in India since 1990. The Narasimham Committee recommended merger of strong banks, in the public and private sectors between themselves and in some cases even with development financial institutions and non-banking financing companies. The Reserve Bank of India issued broad guidelines for merger of banks on May 2005, containing merger proposals between two banking companies or between a banking company and a non-banking financial company, which were applicable to both private and public sector banks. Merger and amalgamation of weak banks with strong banks, as a policy measure for strengthening the structure of the banking system, resulted in the merger of 23 banks with in a seven-year period.

A significant development in the process of banking sector reforms was the setting up of Board for Financial Supervision (BFS) in 1994. It consisted of select members of the RBI Board with a variety of professional experts to give direction on a continuing basis on regulatory policies and supervisory practices. The BFS has been focusing on the supervisory strategy in respect of off-site surveillance for banks, all-India financial institutions and NBFCs, on-site inspection, restructuring the system of bank inspections in terms of focus, process, reporting and follow-up, strengthening internal control and management information systems. The BFS ensures an integrated approach for supervision of commercial banks, development of financial institutions, non-banking finance companies, urban co-operatives banks and primary dealers.

Another impressive milestone in the reforms programme has been in relation to commencement of Banking Ombudsman Scheme in June 1995. It facilitated satisfactory disposal of customer complaints in a time-bound manner through methods of conciliation, mediation and arbitration. To enlarge the extent and scope of the authority and functions of Banking Ombudsman, the RBI partially modified both the Banking Ombudsman Schemes of 1995 and 2002 in the year 2005.

The RBI introduced the Local Area Bank scheme in August 1996. It was established with the primary objective of bridging the gap in credit availability and to strengthen the institutional credit framework in the rural and semi-urban areas.

Guidelines on asset-liability management (ALM) were issued in February 1999 for implementation by banks from April 1, 1999. The internationalization of commercial banking operations are subject to significant mismatch between assets and liabilities. Banks have to face several types of risks, which are likely to arise such as, the interest rate risk, liquidity risk and foreign exchange risk. Asset-Liability Management Committees (ALCOs) has been set up in all banks and are headed by Chairman and Managing Director/Executive Director to manage various risks from risk-return perspective.

Incentives for technological changes were an integral part of the reform process. An impressive measure in banking sector reforms was in relation to the implementation of modern, efficient and global electronic payment and settlement systems. RBI constituted a National Payments Council (NPC) in May 1999 with the objective of providing perspectives and recommendations regarding broad policy issues to help design, develop and maintain an integrated and robust payment and settlement system for the country.

Recognizing the greater impetus ascribed towards payment and settlement systems, a clearing corporation known as Clearing Corporation of India Ltd. (CCIL) was established in April 2001 for clearing and settlement of government securities and foreign exchange transactions.

The Electronic Fund Transfer (EFT) system is in operation since February 1996 and Special Electronic Fund Transfer (SEFT) System from April 2003. The operationalisation of the NEFT in November 2005 was a major step in the direction of setting up and operating a national level payment system. The beginning of Electronic Credit Clearing Services in April 1995 and Electronic Debit Clearing facility in August 1994 was another noteworthy achievement.

Reserve Bank of India also introduced Real Time Gross Settlement (RTGS) System in March 2004 with a view to enhance the efficiency of the cheque clearing system. The implementation of Cheque Truncation System (CTS) in December 2006 was yet another measure from the side of RBI for improving the efficiency of paper-based clearing systems.

For giving grater importance to the payment and settlement system, Reserve Bank of India constituted an apex body called Board for Regulation and Supervision of Payment and Settlement Systems (BPSS) in March 2005. BPSS were entrusted with the task of giving policy directions in the area of payment and settlement systems.

IRDA Act was passed in 1999, which allows private equity in insurance sector. Amendments to the Banking Companies Acquisition and Transfer of Undertakings Act allow banks to enter in to insurance business. Reserve Bank issued detailed guidelines for banks' entry into insurance business in August 2000.

Based on the recommendations of the "Working Group for Harmonizing the Role and Operations of Development Financial Institutions" RBI ended the reverse-merger of a large DFI with its commercial banking subsidiary, which is a major initiative towards universal banking. The salient operational and regulatory issues to be addressed by the financial institutions for conversion into a universal bank were also communicated by RBI through a circular in April 2001.

Banks were allowed to diversify into various financial services and are now offering a whole range of financial products like universal banks. Commercial banks made promising operations in mutual funds, lease financing, factoring, merchant banking and other related activities.

An important landmark in the process of banking sector reforms was the development of an institutional mechanism (Credit Information Bureau India Ltd.) for sharing and dissemination of credit information about borrowers/ potential borrowers. With a view to strengthen the legal mechanism and facilitate credit information bureaus to collect, process and share credit information about borrowers of banks/FIs, the Credit Information Act was passed by both the houses of Parliament in May 2005. The RBI is now framing detailed guidelines on the basis of which it would consider applications from Credit Information companies. This will facilitate setting up of a few more credit information companies in India.

The Reserve Bank, in consultation with the Government of India, laid down a comprehensive policy framework for corporate governance in banks in February 2005. The regulatory framework focused on ensuring good corporate governance through 'well diversified ownership and control'. It also focused on 'fit and proper' owners, directors and senior managers. Transfer of shareholding of four per cent and above requires acknowledgement from the RBI and such significant shareholders and are put through a "fit and proper" test. Banks have also been asked to ensure that a nomination committee to satisfy "fit and proper" criteria screens the nominated and elected directors.

Directors are also required to sign a covenant indicating their roles and responsibilities. The listed banks are also required to comply with governance principles laid sown by the Securities and Exchange Board of India (SEBI).

Accounting standards and disclosure norms were also strengthened with a view to improve governance and bringing them in alignment with the international norms.

Minimum capital to risk weighted assets ratio has been kept at nine per cent, i.e. one per cent above the international norm. Banks are required to maintain a separate Investment Fluctuation Reserve (IFR) out of profits, towards interest rate risk, at five per cent of their investment portfolio under the categories 'held for trading' and 'available for sale'. In January 2002, the RBI advised banks to build up an IFR of a minimum of 5.0 per cent of their investment portfolio within a period of 5 years. Banks were given the freedom to build up IFR to a maximum of 10.0 per cent of the portfolio depending on the size and composition of their portfolio with the approval of their Boards.

Based on the EXIM Policy of 2002-07, the Reserve Bank of India issued guidelines in November 2002 allowing banks operating in India to set up Off-Shore Banking Units (OBUs) in Special Economic Zones (SEZs) which would be virtually foreign branches of Indian banks located in India.

Branch licensing policy was rationalized and liberalized by giving reasonable freedom for the commercial banks to open new branches in India. The Branch Authorization Policy was revised by the Reserve Bank of India in September 2005.

Banks were instructed in November 1994 not to engage brokers either for inter-bank securities transactions or for transactions with non-bank clients except through members of NSE where the transactions are transparent. Banks have since been permitted to undertake securities transactions through members of the Over The Counter Exchange of India (OTCEI), which undertakes fully automated, nation-wide trading operations in equity and debt segments.

Impressive institutional and legal reforms were undertaken in the banking sector to facilitate quicker recovery of loan arrears. Recovery Tribunals were established consequent to the passing of Recovery of Debts Due to Banks and Financial Institutions Act, 1993. Eight special recovery tribunals were set up at Kolkata, New Delhi, Jaipur, Guwahati, Ahmedabad, Patna, Bangalore and Chennai with an Appellate Tribunal at Mumbai and Jabalpur for expeditious adjudication and recovery of debts.

Another important landmark in the history of reforms process was the enactment of the Securitization and Reconstruction of Financial Assets and Enforcement of Security Interest Act (SARFAESI) of 2002, which paved the way for setting up of Asset Reconstruction Companies (ARCs) in India. Reserve Bank of India issued draft guidelines on securitization of standard assets in April 2005. The guidelines on Corporate Debt Restructuring system were issued to all commercial banks, financial institutions and RRBs in November 2005.

The reform process, which initially focused on commercial banks, aimed at their transformation into sound institutions, was later extended to other institutions such as Regional Rural Banks (RRBs), cooperative banks (both urban and rural), All-India Financial Institutions (AIFIs) and Non-Banking Financial Companies (NBFCs). To improve the operational viability of RRBs the route of merger/amalgamation was implemented by RBI in 2005. It brought down the total number of RRBs in the country to 102 from that of 196.

As part of the reforms process, with to view to attract vast sections of the unbanked population, Reserve Bank of India advised commercial banks to review their existing practices on opening of accounts. Consequently all banks were advised in November 2005 to make available a basic banking 'no-frills' account either with 'nil' or very low minimum balances as well as charges that would make such accounts accessible to vast sections of population. With a view to encourage financial inclusion the Know Your Customer (KYC) procedure for opening small accounts were simplified.

In order to provide hassle- free credit to bank customers in rural areas with out the insistence of security, RBI issued guidelines on December 27, 2005 regarding the issue of General Credit Card (GCC) scheme. In order to calibrate bank credit to the changing needs of the society, the scope and definition of priority sector was widened by including more and more new items and by enhancing credit limit of the constituent sub-sectors. Accordingly, RBI issued revised guidelines in the year 2004-05.

Setting up of specialized branches viz. corporate branch banking, NRI branch, personal banking branch, commercial branch, twelve hours branch banking, overseas branch, offshore branch, Hi-Tech agricultural branch etc are the other steps initiated by Reserve Bank for improving the efficiency, viability and profitability of commercial banks.

16.3.2 Impact of Banking Sector Reforms: The reforms measures have had a profound impact on the financial landscape in recent years. The changes staring in the face of bankers relate to the fundamental ways of banking, which is undergoing a rapid transformation in the world of today in response to the forces of competition, productivity, reduced operating margins, better asset/liability management and risk management, anytime and anywhere banking. Globalization, financial deregulation, development of technology, especially computerization of operations of branches with Core Banking Solutions intensified competition and improved customer service and operational efficiency. Many Indian commercial banks are now competent enough to face the challenges with in the country and from foreign banks. Consequent to reforms, the financial sector became intensely competitive with several new competitors like new private sector banks, foreign banks, non-banking financial companies, merchant bankers mutual fund and insurance companies.

The development of new sophisticated technology in banking sector resulted in financial engineering through product innovation and business strategies. Consequent to reforms, Indian banks are offering up to date products and services to their customers, which are similar to services, offered by banks in developed countries. Customers are fast moving away from the traditional branch-banking system to the convenience and comfort of remote electronic banking services or virtual banking.

A change, which is taking place slowly but in a steady pace, is the use of alternatives to cash by most of the constituents of banks. The large-scale use of credit, debit and new smart cards for settlement of financial transactions, proves beyond doubt that cash is slowly losing its prominence of yesteryears.

Various measures initiated over the last decade-and-a half have significantly strengthened the commercial banking sector in terms of profitability, asset quality and capital position. Capital and asset quality are the two crucial parameters reflecting the soundness of a banking institution. There was a marked and steady improvement in the asset quality of commercial banks over the past one decade. The percentage of gross non-performing assets to gross advances got reduced considerably to 3.3 per cent in 2005-06 from that of 24.8 per cent in 1993-94. The present capital adequacy of Indian banks is comparable to those at international standards. Banks in India are prepared to migrate to the Basel II capital accord with effect from March 31, 2007.

The reforms measures have also resulted in an improvement in the profitability of banks. The operating profit to assets ratio of scheduled commercial banks, which was 1.69 in 1995-96, increased to 2.03 in 2005-06. Net profit to assets of scheduled commercial banks remained in the range of 0.47 to 1.13 during the period 1995-96 to 2005-06. There was a compositional shift in favour of non-interest income reflecting the increasing importance of non-fund based activities of the banking sector.

Bibliography

Bibliography

Aggarwal, P.C. (1987), 'Frauds in Banks – An Analytical study', The Chartered Accountant, Vol. XXIX, No. 6 (Dec.).

Aggarwal, B.P. (1981), Commercial Banking in India (New Delhi: Classical Publishing Company).

Aggarwal, H.N. (1979), A Portrait of Nationalized Banks - A Study With Reference to Their Social Obligations (New Delhi: Inter-India Publications).

Allen, F. (1988), 'The Determinants of Bank Interest Rate Margins', Journal of Financial and Quantitative Analysis Vol. XXIX, No. 6 (Dec.).

Bajaj, M.K. (2000), 'Customer Relations Management' IBA Bulletin, (Sept.).

Bakshi, S. (2001), 'Banks Foray into Insurance - Prospects and Problems', Bank Quest, The Journal of The Indian Institute of Bankers. Vol.72. No.4 (Oct – Dec.).

Bank for International Settlements, *Supervision of Financial Conglomerates: A Report by the Tripartite Group of Bank, Securities and Insurance Regulators*, July 1995.

—*Electronic Banking Group Initiatives and White Papers*, Basel Committee on Banking Supervision, October 2000.

—*Management and Supervision of Cross-Border Electronic Banking Activities*, Basel Committee on Banking Supervision, July 2003.

—*Risk Management Principles for Electronic Banking*, Basel Committee on Banking Supervision, July 2003.

—*International Convergence of Capital Measurement and Capital Standards: A Revised Framework,* Basel Committee on Banking Supervision, June 2004.

—*Basel II: International Convergence of Capital Measurement and Capital Standards - A Revised Framework,* Basel Committee Publications No. 107, July 2004.

Banking Soundness, Monetary Policy and Macro-economic Management: Random Thoughts, *RBI Bulletin*, February 1998.

Bhasin, T.M. (2001), 'E-Commerce in Indian Banking', IBA Bulletin, Vol. XXIII, Nos. 4 & 5 (April – May).

Bhatt, P.R. (1999), 'Profitability of Commercial Banks in India', Indian Journal of Economics (March).

Chopra, K. (1987), Managing Profitability and Productivity in Public Sector Banking (Jalandhar: ABS Publications).

Consolidation and Universal Banking. by Saunders, Anthony. *Journal of Banking* & Finance, Feb. 99, Vol. 23 Issue 2-4.

Corrocher, N., "Does Internet banking substitute traditional banking? Empirical Evidence from Italy," Working Paper, *CESPRI, No. 134,* November 2002.

Das, A. (2002), 'Risk and Productivity Change of Public Sector Banks', Economic and Political Weekly, Vol. XXXVII, No. 5 (Feb. 2).

De Kock, M. 1974. *Central Banking*. St. Martin's Press. New York.

Desai, V. (1980), Indian Banking – Nature and Problems (Bombay: Himalaya Publishing House).

Diniz, E, "Web Banking In USA," Journal of Internet Banking and Commerce, Vol.3, No. 2, June 1998.

Eapen, P.G. (2000), 'Automated Teller Machines- Security Issues', IBA Bulletin , Vol. XXII, No. 9 (Sept.).

—*Economic Survey,* Ministry of Finance, Government of India (various issues).

Egland, Kori L., Karen Furst, Daniel E. Nolle, Douglas Robertson, "E-banking over the Internet", Quarterly Journal, Vol. 17, No. 4, Office of Comptroller of the Currency, December 1998.

EPW Research Foundation, Increasing Concentration of Banking Operations, *Economic & Political Weekly*, Vol. XLI, No.11, 2006.

Expansion of Commercial Banking Powers ... or, Universal Banking is the Cart, not the Horse. by: Boyd, John H. *Journal of Banking* & Finance, Feb. 99, Vol. 23 Issue 2-4.

Experts Split on Safety of Universal Banks. by: Seiberg, Jaret. American Banker, 11/14/97, Vol. 162 Issue 220.

Furst, K; Lang, W., William and Nolle, E., Daniel, "Internet Banking: Developments and Prospects," Working Paper, Center for Information Policy Research, Harvard University, April 2002.

Ganesh. K. (1979), 'Monitoring Profitability in Banks', The Commerce (July).

Ghosh, D. N. (1988), 'Commercial Banking: Lessons From Indian Experience', SBI Monthly Review, (Nov.).

Goiporia, M. N. (1987), 'Emerging Banking Challenges', The Journal of The Indian Institute of Bankers (July-Sep).

Government of India. 1972. *Banking Committee Report.*

Honohan, P (2001), 'Recapitalising Banking Systems: Implications for Incentives and Fiscal and Monetary Policy', Policy Research Working Paper No. 2540.

Kohli, S.S. (2001), 'Indian Banking Industry: Emerging Challenge', IBA Bulletin, Vol. XXIII, No. 3 (March).

Malhotra, R.N. 1990. The Evolution of Financial System, The Nineteenth Frank Moraes Memorial Lecture.

Metzer, S.R. (2000), 'Strategic Planning for Future Bank Growth', The Banker's Magazine (July- Aug.).

Mohan, Rakesh. 2003. "Transforming Indian Banking: In Search of a Better Tomorrow." *RBI Bulletin*,

——2004. "Agricultural Credit in India: Status, Issues and Future Agenda." *RBI Bulletin.*

——2004, "Indian Banking and e-Security." *RBI Bulletin*, November.

——2004, "Ownership and Governance in Private Sector Banks in India." *RBI Bulletin.*

— Financial Sector Reforms in India: Policies and Performance Analysis, *RBI Bulletin*, October 2004.

N. Vittal. (2001), 'The Emerging Challenges: strategies and solutions for Indian Banking', IBA Bulletin, Vol. XXIII, No. 3 (March).

Nachane, D.M. (1999), 'Capital Adequacy Ratios: An Agnostic Viewpoint', Economic and Political Weekly, Special Nos. 3 & 4.

Naha, P.K. (1990), 'Two Year Action Plans in Banks – A Review', PNB Monthly Review, (Nov.).

Nair, S.N. (2000), 'E-Commerce and the Emergence of E-Banking', IBA Bulletin, Vol. XXII, No. 10 (October).

Ojha, J. (1997), 'Productivity and Profitability of Public Sector Banks in India: An International Comparison', SBI Monthly Review (July).

Panandikar, S.G. (1975), Banking in India (Bombay: Orient Longman).

Pathrose, P.P. (2001), 'Hi-Tech. Banking Prospects and Problems', IBA Bulletin , Vol. XXIII, No. 7. (July).

Ram, T.T . (2002), 'Deregulation and Performance of Public Sector Banks', EPW, Vol. XXXVII, No. 5.

Ramaswamy, M. (1977), 'Bank Deposits and Interest Rate Reduction', The Journal of The Indian Institute of Bankers (July-Sept)

Rangarajan, C. (2000), 'Banking in The Hi -Tech. Environment', The Journal of The Indian Institute of Bankers. (Jan-March).

Rao, N.V. (2000), 'Changing Indian Banking Scenario: a Paradigm shift' IBA Bulletin , Vol. XXIV No. 1.

Rao, P. (1978), 'Profits in a Bind', Business India (Nov.).

Rao, P.K. (1999), 'IT in Financial Services Industry: Innovations and Implications', Chartered Secretary , (Sept.).

Reserve Bank of India, Annual Report, Various Issues.
——1970, The History of the Reserve Bank of India: 1935-5.
——1985, Reserve Bank of India: Fifty Years (1935-85).
——1997, Report of the Committee on Capital Account Convertibility (Chairman: Shri S.S. Tarapore)."
——1998, Committee on Banking Sector Reforms (Chairman: M. Narasimham)
——1998, Payment Systems in India.
——2000, Report of the Advisory Group on Transparency in Monetary and Financial Policies.
——2001, Report on Internet Banking.
——2002, Report of the Working Group on Electronic Money.
——2003, Risk-Based Supervision Manual.
——2004, Financial Sector Reforms in India: Policies and Performance Analysis." RBI Bulletin, October.
——2006, Report on Trend and Progress of Banking in India.

Sabnani, P. (2000), 'Universal Banking', IBA Bulletin, Vol. XXII No.7 (July).

Satya, (1984), 'Banks: Improving Productivity and Profitability' The Journal of India Institute of Bankers, (Sept.).

Satyamurty, B. (1994), 'A Study on Interests Spread Management in Commercial Banks in India', NIBM, Working Paper.

Senapati, M. (1999), 'Financial Services in the Internet Era', ICFAI Reader, (Nov.).

Shah, S.G (1979), 'Bank Profitability: The Real Issues', The Journal of India Institute of Bankers, (July- Sept.).

Shah, V. D. (1986), 'Empirical Relationship between Size & Cost at Branch Level', Prajnan Vol. XV, No. 318, (Jan.- March).

Sham, L. (1978), 'Performance of Commercial Banks Since Nationalization of Major Banks: Promise and Reality', EPW, (Aug.).

Shastri, R.V (2001), 'Technology for Banks in India-Challenges', IBA Bulletin , Vol. XXIII, No. 3 (March).

Shrives, Dhal (1992), 'The Relationship between Risk and Capital in Commercial Banks'. Journal of Banking and Finance.

Shurethy, S. (1999), E-Business with Net. Commerce. (Singapore: Addison Wesley Longman).

Shyam, R. (1988), Workshop on Profit Planning (Bombay: Bankers Training College, RBI).

Singh, S. (1989), 'Profitability in Commercial Banks in India', PNB Monthly Review (Oct.).

Subrahmanyam, G. 'Some Conceptual Issues in Productivity 1984), Measurement', Prajnan (April-June).

Sushila, S. (1987), Banks and Customers: A Behavioural Analysis. (New Delhi: Shri Ram Center for Industrial Relations and Human Resources).

Swamy, B.N.A. (2001), 'New Competition, Deregulation and Emerging Changes in Indian Banking: An Analysis of the Comparative Performance of Different Bank- Groups', Bank Quest, The Journal of India Institute of Bankers, Vol. 72 No.3 (July- Sept.).

The Central Banking Enquiry Committee, 1931 (Chairman: Sir Bhupendra Nath Mitra).

Vageesh, N.S (2000), 'New Private Banks; New Kids on the Block', Business Line, (March).

Varde, 1988), 'Effectiveness, Efficiency and Customer Services in Banks', RBI Bulletin , (April).

Varde, S. (1983), Profitability of Commercial Bank (Bombay: NIBM)

Verghese, S.K (1983), 'Profits and Profitability of Indian Commercial Banks in the Seventies', EPW, (Nov.).

Verghese, S.K. (1983), Profits and Profitability of Indian Commercial Banks in the Seventies (Bombay: NIBM).

Verma, D. (2000), 'Banking on Change', ICFAI Reader, (May).

Index

Index

A

A.S. Ganguly, 251
Advisory Committee on Flow of Credit to Agriculture, 30
Advisory Group on Corporate Governance, 247, 251
Advisory Group on Insurance Regulation, 180
American Depository Receipt (ADRs), 287
Andrew Sheng (1996), 167
Annual Action Plans (AAPs), 27
Annualized Percentage Rates (APR), 77
Arbitration and Conciliation Act of 1996, 199
Asset Management Corporations (AMCs), 168
Asset Reconstruction Companies (ARCs), 312, 320
Asset-Liability Management Committees (ALCOs), 316
Associated Chambers of Commerce and Industry of India (ASSOCHAM), 242
Automated Teller Machines (ATMs), 64

B

B.R. Act, 1949, 150
Bank for International Settlements (BIS), 252
Bank of Credit and Commerce International, (Overseas) Ltd. Bombay (BCCI), 157
Banking Companies Act, 41
Banking Codes and Standards Board of India (BCSBI), 220
Banking Companies (Acquisition & Transfer of Undertakings) Acts of 1970-80, 286
Banking Companies Act of 1980, 21
Banking Companies Act, 1949, 7
Banking Industry: Vision 2010, 151
Banking Laws (Amendment) Act 1969, 14
Banking Laws (Amendment) Act 1985, 16
Banking Ombudsman Scheme 2002, 207
Banking Regulation Act of 1949, 224, 259

Banking Service Recruitment Board (BSRB), 314
Basel Committee for Banking Supervision (BCBS), 247, 294
Basle Capital Adequacy Accord, 293
Basle Committee on Banking Supervision, 294
Board for Financial Supervision (BFS) in 1994, 315
Board for Industrial and Financial Reconstruction (BIFR), 310
Board for Regulation and Supervision of Payment and Settlement Systems (BPSS), 129, 317
Branch Authorization Policy, 280

C
Capital Adequacy Assessment Process (CAAP), 299, 300
Capital Adequacy Ratio of Development Credit, 235
Capital Adequacy Ratio of New Private Sector Banks, 235
Capital to Risk Weighted Assets Ratio (CRAR), 164, 182
Central Counter Party (CCP), 133
Central Vigilance Commission (CVC), 85
Centralized Funds Management System (CFMS), 110
Cheque Processing Centres (CPCs), 124
Cheque Truncation Based Clearing, 129
Cheque Truncation System (CTS), 110, 112, 127, 128, 317
Clearing Corporation of India Limited (CCIL), 132
Committee of Directors' of the "All India Rural Credit Survey", 8
Committee on Financial Systems (CFS) (1991), 301
Companies Act of 1956, 143, 223
Confederation of Indian Industries (CII), 242
Co-operative Credit System, 181
Core Banking Solutions (CBS), 85
Corporate Debt Restructuring mechanism, 36
Corporate Debt

Restructuring system, 310
Credit Information Bureau (CIB), 134, 142
Credit Information Bureau of Sri Lanka Act, 137
Credit Information Scheme, 139
Customer Facilitation Centre (CFC), 112
Customer Service Department (CSD), 220

D

D.D. Gadgil, 23
DDoS (Distributed Denial of Service), 99
Debt Recovery Tribunals (DRTs), 160, 310
Deferred Net Settlement Systems, (DNS), 130, 132
Department of Information Technology, 90
Department of Telecommunications (DoT), 114
Development and Research in Banking Technology (IDRBT), 98
Development Financial Institutions (DFIs), 177
Differential Interest Rate Scheme (DIR), 31
District Credit Plans (DCPs), 27
District Level Review Committee, 27
Do Not Call Registry (DNCR), 78
DoS (Denial of Service) attacks, 99
Dun and Bradstreet' (D&B), 135

E

Electronic Clearing Service (ECS), 115, 121
Electronic Credit Clearing Service, 122
Electronic Fund Transfer (EFT) system, 317
Enactment of Banking Laws (Amendment) Act 1969, 14
ERMA (Electronic Record Method of Accounting), 110
EXIM Policy of 2002-07, 282, 319

F

F.K.F Nariman, 24
Financial Executives Institute, 137
Financial Restructuring Authority (FRA), 160
Foreign Branches Cell, 275
Foreign Direct Investment (FDI) in Banking, 286

G
G. Ramachandran, 264
Ganguly Committee, 254
General Agreement on Trade in Services (GATS), 175
General Credit Card (GCC) Scheme, 36, 50
General Insurance Business (Nationalization) Act of 1972, 178
General Insurance Business (Nationalization) Amendment Act of 2002, 173
General Insurance Corporation of India (GIC), 173
Global Depository Receipt (GDRs), 287
Growth of Joint Stock Commercial Banks, 6

H
High Power Committee on Lead Bank Scheme, 27
High-Level Advisory Committee, 228
History of Commercial Banking in India, 2
Housing and Development Finance Corporation (HDFC), 226

I
I.G. Patel, 228
Imperial Bank of India Act of 1920, 6
Income Recognition and Asset Classification (IRAC), 306
Indian Banks Association (IBA), 66, 84, 149
Indian Commercial Banking system, 41
Indian Companies Act of 1956, 8, 259
Indian Financial Network (INFINET), 110
Indian Money Market, 40
Indira Gandhi, 51
Indonesia Bank Restructuring Agency (IBRA), 168
Industrial Development Bank of India (IDBI), 229
Institute of Chartered Accountants of India (ICAI), 241
Insurance Act of 1938, 172, 178
Insurance Advisory Committee (IAC), 179
Insurance Regulatory and Development Authority (IRDA) Act, 1999, 178
Interactive Voice Response Service (IVRS), 106
Internal Rating Based (IRB), 295
Internal Working Group on

RRBs, 56
Investment Research and Information Services Ltd., (IRIS), 139

J

Joint Parliamentary Committee (2002), 165
Joint Stock Companies Act, 1850, 5

K

Know Your Customer (KYC), 75

L

Lead Bank Scheme (LBS), 27
Legal Service Authority Act of 1987, 309
Life Insurance Corporation Act of 1956, 178
Local Area Banks (LABs), 257
London Stock Exchange, 238

M

M. Narashimham, 51
M.N. Goiporia, 62
M.S. Varma, 158, 249
M.V.S. Chalapathi Rao, 55
Magnetic Ink Character Recognition (MICR), 124, 127
Magnetic Media Based Clearing System (MMBCS), 110, 127
Man Mohan Singh, 61
MICR (Magnetic Ink Character Recognition), 110
MICR Cheque Clearing System, 110
Minimum Standards of Operational Efficiency, 127
Monetary and Credit Policy of April 2000, 145
Monetary and Credit Policy, 181
Monopolies Enquiry Commission, 11

N

N.H. Siddiqui, 141
Narasimham Committee (1998), 302
National Bank for Agriculture and Rural Development (NABARD), 35
National Clearing Centres (NCC), 110
National Credit Council (NCC), 13, 23
National Economic Policy, 62
National Electronic Fund Transfer (NEFT), 121
National Payments Council (NPC), 129, 317

National Securities Depositories Ltd., (NSDL), 83
Nationalization Act (22 of 1969), 16
Nation-Wide Funds Transfer System (NEFT), 115
New Economic Policy, 222
Non-Banking Finance Company (NBFC), 166, 183
Non-Performing Assets (NPAs), 134
Non-Scheduled Commercial Banks, 41

O

On-Line Reject Repair (OLRR), 127
Organizational Framework for the Implementation of Social Objectives, 23
Oudh Commercial Bank, 5
Over The Counter Exchange of India (OTCEI), 319

P

P Chidambaram, 56, 188
Paper Currency Act in 1860, 4
Personal Identification Number (PIN), 68
Portfolio Investment Scheme (PIS), 287
Priority Sector Advances, 33
Public Key Infrastructure (PKI), 115
Punjab National Bank, 5
Purveyors of Credit, 21

R

R.B. Barman, 128
R. Gandhi, 74
R.K. Hazari, 32
R.N. Malhotra, 179
RALOO (Returns on Assets and Liabilities of Overseas Offices), 274
Rangarajan Committee on Computerization, 62
Real Time Gross Settlement (RTGS) System, 317
Regional Rural Banks (RRBs) Act, 1976, 259
Regional Rural Banks, 41
Reserve Bank (Transfer of Public Ownership) Act 1948, 15
Reserve Bank of India Act 1934, 6, 138, 146, 223
Retail Electronic Funds Transfer, 130
Risk Management and Control System, 299
RRB Act 1976, 55, 58
Rural Automated Teller Machines (Rural ATMs), 69
Rural Banking Enquiry Committee' (1950), 8
Rural Credit Survey

Committee, in 1951-52, 12
Rural Infrastructure Development Fund (RIDF), 35
Rural Planning and Credit Department (RPCD), 259

S
S.P. Talwar, 129
S.R. Mittal, 90
Saraf Committee (1994) on technology issues, 62
SBI Act of 1959, 9
Scheduled Commercial Banks (SCBs), 40, 124
Securities and Exchange Board of India (SEBI), 83, 166
Securitization and Reconstruction of Financial Assets and Enforcement of Security Interest Act, 2002 (SARFAESI), 311, 320
Security Interest (Enforcement) Rules, 2002, 311
Service Area Approach (SAA) scheme, 31
Setting up of the Banking Commission, 14
Shared Payment Network System (SPNS), 67
Short Messaging Service (SMS) technology, 103
Small and Medium Enterprises (SME), 36, 309
Small Industries Development Bank of India (SIDBI), 36, 149
Small-Scale Industries (SSI), 34
SMART Rupees System (SMARS), 79
Social Control over Commercial Banks in 1967, 23
Special Act (XLVII of 1920), 6
Special Agricultural Credit Plans (SACP), 34
Special Economic Zones (SEZs), 282, 319
Special Electronic Fund Transfer (SEFT), 110, 115, 317
Standing Committee on Customer Service, 77
Standing Committee on International Financial Standards, 180
Standing Conference of Public Enterprises (1996), 242
State Electricity Boards (SEBs), 37
State Level Bankers Committee (SLBC), 36
Structured Financial

Messaging Solution (SFMS), 116
Swadeshi Movement: A Momentum for New Banks, 5

T
The Bank of Bengal, 3
The Bank of Calcutta, 3
The Banking Companies Act, 7
The Presidency Bank Act, 4
Travancore Banking Enquiry Committee, 155

U
United Commercial Bank, 16

V
V.S. Vyas, 57
Vasudevan Committee on Technology Upgradation, 114
Vision Document, 111

W
Wide Area Network (WAN), 110, 144
Working Group for Harmonizing the Role and Operations of Development Financial Institutions, 176

Y
Y.B. Chavan, 32